WANDERING IN STRANGE LANDS

ALSO BY MORGAN JERKINS

This Will Be My Undoing

WANDERING IN STRANGE LANDS

A DAUGHTER OF
THE GREAT MIGRATION
RECLAIMS HER ROOTS

Morgan Jerkins

HARPER

An Imprint of HarperCollinsPublishers

HarperCollins books may be purchased for educational, business, or sales promotional use. For information, please e-mail the Special Markets Department at SPsales@harpercollins.com.

FIRST EDITION

Library of Congress Cataloging-in-Publication Data has been applied for.

ISBN 978-0-06-287304-0

20 21 22 23 24   LSC   10 9 8 7 6 5 4 3 2 1

CONTENTS

WANDERING IN STRANGE LANDS

PROLOGUE

The Milkman's Baby

I WAS SEVEN years old when I learned that I wasn't my father's only daughter. He pulled me to his side and said he had something to show me. I assumed that it was a gift. He would regularly visit me at my mother's home, bringing niceties along with his charisma and swagger. Instead, he pulled out his wallet and showed me photos of three girls before saying, "These are your sisters." The oldest was eleven years my senior, the middle child was eight years my senior, and the last was just fifteen months my senior. I don't remember saying anything in response. I didn't have the words to express what I felt. Later, I learned that my father not only had three other daughters, but a wife and a dog, as well. They were, from all appearances, the picture-perfect family. I felt like an outsider among my blood, a feeling that would stay with me until I was an adult.

My original birth certificate indicates that my story is half missing. I was born Morgan Simone Regis Jerkins; the Simone and Regis were officially my middle names. My mother's name is Sybil Yvonne Jerkins, but there was a blank spot where my father's name should've been. My parents weren't married. In fact, when I was conceived, their relationship had already run its course. The details as to what happened are debatable, but nevertheless there was an omission. On paper, half of my lineage is unknown, although I've known my father my entire life. When I came into this world, almost a month early, my dad took one look at me and jokingly said, "That's the milkman's baby," because I was so light. I was the lightest person in my church congregation and people would often make jokes about my skin to my mother. They'd assume that my father was white because I burned in the sun, or they'd say whatever melanin I had would be lost in the winter. I took all the jokes in stride because I knew that I was loved nevertheless. But on the inside, I was in immense pain because I knew that in many ways my maternal and paternal families were different with regards to their own histories.

My father was born and raised in Fayetteville, North Carolina, and migrated to the North to start his own medical business. Almost forty years and thirty offices later, he's one of the most prominent doctors in South Jersey. The resemblance between my father and me allows for locals to be able to connect the dots. There were moments in Macy's or at a doctor's office when someone would regard my face and know that I was my father's daughter. The connection would momentarily reaffirm my existence, but that feeling wouldn't last very long. I was more commonly known as Morgan Jerkins in schools and among friends. It was easier to be known this way because I was already living primarily with my mother. Throughout most of my childhood, I felt more like a Jerkins because my dad and his family were an enigma to me.

For one thing, my father's name, Jon, is spelled like a Frenchman's. His surname, Regis, is French as well. Unlike all the Baptists and Pentecostals I grew up with, he was raised Catholic. And most significant, he carried with him a kind of Southern respectability that, from my point of view, was very distinctive. My father was a first-generation migrant, while my mother was second-generation, and this difference was crucial. He was rooted, and she was flighty, never staying in one place for too long. Forgetfulness even of her family's past was not necessarily a bad thing for my mother. But for my dad, the past was everything. My father frequently travels to a home in North Carolina that's been in his family for over sixty years. When he speaks of Fayetteville, he tips his nose to the sky and grins. Although my father has been in the North since the early eighties, he knows there is nothing like that soil "down there," and that attachment to the land is something black Northerners, including my mother, just do not have.

There's been a certain air about him for as long as I can remember. Whenever he walked into a room, he projected authority. And whenever I visited my father's home, my mother would devote painstaking effort to making sure that I looked the part. I had to wear jewelry as a sign of sophistication, my clothes had to be ironed, and my posture had to be straight; I had to show that I was just as well adjusted as my three sisters, whom I envied tremendously. They visited my father's family more often than I did, and they'd met my paternal grandfather and had more memories of my paternal grandmother than I will ever have. When I first visited my father's family in the South, people would incorrectly guess whose daughter I was, or they'd plainly state that they didn't know who I was. My father's family was always still mindful of the South, whereas my mother's family seemed to have always been in southern New Jersey.

Only recently have I learned where my maternal grandparents were born. They once lived in Atlantic City and eventually moved to a quieter and whiter suburb in Atlantic County to give my mother and her three siblings a better life. But no home has been in our family name for longer than twenty-three years. My mother moved more than ten times in the earlier part of her life. These vicissitudes might signal an erratic nature to an outside observer, but my family was simply conditioned to believe that movement meant advancement. Every home had to be better than the last. Being too grounded might lead to stagnation. We weren't rooted like my father's family. The Regises' oral histories were abundant, whereas those of the Jerkinses were vaguer and incomplete.

Much of my conversation with my mother's side of the family is characterized by whispers and silences. My maternal grandfather would place a fake mouse outside the door of his children's bedroom whenever grown folks were about to talk, so that my mother and aunt would not eavesdrop. My mother was never that severe in her approach, but I knew that I might be scolded if I stepped outside of my bedroom when adults were conversing. This was one way in which knowledge of who I am and where I came from was kept from me. Even when I was given the space to speak with an adult, like my mother, the conversations were full of dead ends. As a child, if I ever inquired about why we sang a particular song at a family dinner or why we held certain superstitions, I was never satisfied with the answer. "That's just what we do" or "That's just what black people do" was never good enough for me. As an adult, I've realized that my family simply didn't know how to draw connections with how they think, act, and navigate their lives in a way that forges a community of relatives. They might've been satisfied in the unknown, but I wasn't.

No one spoke about the past—the goal was to move forward and never look back. Neither my mother nor I has taken a trip to the South to visit family. We don't talk about the soil like my father and his people. We can talk about the make and model of cars with more accuracy than about the flora and fauna of our homeland. While my father prides himself on origins, my mother prides herself on originality. She believes that you can create your own identity as long as you keep moving.

I moved to New York in 2015 as a way to not get stuck, forging an identity as an author and editor in the hub of the publishing world. When people would ask me where I was from, my throat would dry up. "New Jersey," I'd reply. If pressed, I'd specify, "southern New Jersey." And if their curiosity hadn't cooled by then, I'd say "Atlantic City"—the most famous locale in the state's southern region. This response would leave me feeling ashamed for two reasons: (1) southern New Jersey doesn't seem so fashionable, and (2) I knew that wasn't the full story. I knew that my Jerkins line had to be as storied as my father's, but I didn't know those stories. How did both families arrive in the same county? How did this Southern man and this Northern woman meet in a hospital, fall in love, and create me? I felt I was midway between two poles, constantly in flux as to who I was and where I came from. My body, like my lineage, was a mystery. Because I didn't have a full narrative from either of my two families, I was not confident in my identity and culture. A sense of loss defined both components. My half-baked statements about my heritage stemmed from a particularly insular Northern upbringing.

Yet my story is not uncommon. From 1916 to 1970, six million African Americans made a grand exodus from the South to the Northeast, Midwest, and West Coast in search of a better life. This exodus is most commonly known as the Great Migration. Some had families waiting for them at the other end, while others just took a chance to start anew in a place where no one knew their names. Many families allowed their memories to evaporate along with the steam of the locomotives on which they arrived. Many didn't want to talk about their traumatic experiences in the South. Folks like me are the result of these omissions. I've spoken to people whose families are generations deep in the North, to investigate this pestering suspicion that we are still intuitively linked to the South. Often, at the start of these conversations, I'd hear an apology. The people I spoke with didn't know where their families migrated from, and if they did, they never visited. Or they knew where their families migrated from, but didn't know why their ancestors left or if any family remained on ancestral land. Their grandparents and great-grandparents didn't talk about the past, so they didn't know how much help they would be to my project. I'd assure them that

I knew what it was like to carry blank spaces and missing pieces. We held no confidence in our origins as African Americans. We resided at terminal points in history, unable to look back.

According to historian and University of North Carolina–Chapel Hill professor W. Fitzhugh Brundage, "Much about the transmission of African American memory, for example, remains terra incognita. Historians have been silent about how deep structural changes in African American communities since the mid-twentieth century have affected the dissemination of African American memory."[1] Much of the information lost during major internal migrations of African Americans has yet to be accounted for. Documentation takes precedence over oral history—a Eurocentric outlook that prioritizes the written word over our own voices. If we were to take my life as an example, documentation initially "proved" that half of my parentage was lost, even though I knew who my father was. I carried Regis as a middle name even while my father's name was absent from my birth certificate. What of the countless families whose lives have been documented, yet whose realities offer an opposing narrative?

Because ruptures in cultural memory characterized much of my life and the lives of others in my community, I decided to consider these gaps an opportunity rather than an impasse. I was weary with my conception of self, of the diaspora, as one of loss. I was frustrated by how much had been lost from our arrival to the colonies during the transatlantic slave trade to the post-emancipation period, when we scattered across the country in massive waves. But the glimmering moment emerged when I wondered, if both of my families had been in this country for several generations, then could it be that a significant recovery of my family's history could be made right here on this American landscape? The only way to find out was to make a journey in reverse and create symbolic bridges between those families who fled and those who remained on the lands of their people.

For this book, I traveled to the Georgia Lowcountry, to South Carolina, and to Louisiana to speak to some of the oldest micro-ethnic groups of African Americans before traveling west of the Mississippi to further detail the effects of migration on memory and black identity in Oklahoma and California. I followed the migratory routes of yesteryear and discovered surprising similarities among African Americans of these particular regions regarding what they feel is at stake in their communities and who they are as a people. Each section is devoted to a particular region. In each chapter, I've included the scraps, rubble, and frayed threads of my personal history alongside those of descendants of migrants to illuminate how cultural conditioning via religion and spirituality, connection with nature, or understanding of black identity has been altered through both systemic and personal forces. The undertaking has a dual purpose: to excavate the connective tissue that complicates but unites us as a people, and to piece together the story of how I came to be by going back and looking beyond myself—a liberating and healing pilgrimage.

Despite all the differences I encountered, I ultimately came away from my journey feeling that all is not lost. Much of our cultural history that has not been retained can be found in people you have yet to encounter and places where you have not yet traveled.

I know because I've met them, and they've been waiting to meet you, too.

PART I

Lowcountry, Georgia, and South Carolina

I

IF I WERE to travel through the migratory routes, like the Southeast to the North in reverse, I first had to nail down the purpose. I had the desire to reconnect with what I felt had been lost, once my families moved away from the South. But I shifted from asking myself, "What has been lost?" to rather, "What has not been fully explained but maintained whenever my family came together?" What were some of the traditions, anxieties, and sayings that were worth investigating? I had never been where my families came from in America, and arguably neither had my parents and their siblings, so these cultural aspects—albeit persistent—were full of gaps. I hoped that by returning to the South I could recover some of the reasons underlying why we black people do what we do that may had been lost or altered with the movement up North.

One of the most fascinating parts of my upbringing was how cautious my family could be about certain things. We stayed away from the water, and I knew that there had to be a deeper reason than that it would "damage" my hair. The contradictions tied to such cautions were intriguing. My elders despised rootwork and magic and yet believed they worked. Could there be a place where I could find people still connected to their ancestors enough to help me fill in the pieces as to how water and magic functioned in my ancestors' lives?

I wanted to begin with my mother's side, because her family's story had fewer details than my father's. Her father, my maternal grandfather, was born in Georgia, and that's all I knew before I started planning my trip to the South. During the Great Migration, African Americans moved from all the states of the South but mainly from Alabama, Mississippi, Louisiana, Texas, and Georgia. Between 1910 and 1930, Georgia was the state with the largest emigration of black people—over 195,000.[1] Comparing 1950 and 1920, Georgia was the only state of the top five sendoff states aforementioned to have a net decrease in its African American population—over 140,000.[2] There was also a geographical pattern to the migration. If your family was from Mississippi, chances are they wound up in Chicago. If your family was from Georgia, chances are your ancestors wound up in Philadelphia, as mine did at first.[3]

Georgia was where I wanted to begin my journey. I wanted to know about people who chose to stay connected to the land and all its abundance. I wanted to find out more about water, magic, and kinship networks before we distanced ourselves from our ancestral lands. But, before I could discover the unknown, I decided to start with what I did know—the only cultural component that did not change, from my experience, no matter which black home I visited in America: food. And it was through food that I was led not to all of Georgia but to a particular region, not to black people as a whole but to a specific ethnic group to which all African Americans are undoubtedly indebted.

When I sit down to eat with my family, I call the food we eat soul food, but that name in and of itself indicates movement. As Adrian E. Miller, author of *Soul Food: The Surprising Story of an American Cuisine*, puts it, "'soul food' . . . [is] . . . the food of that area [interior South] that has been transported across the United States by African-American migrants who left during the Great Migration. . . . As people left the South, they did what any other immigrant group does: They tried to re-create home." The word *soul* began to mean "emotional fervor" in the 1940s when black jazz artists, disillusioned because their white counterparts were getting better-paying gigs, infused their music with black church styles from the rural South to make their music something the whites couldn't imitate.[4] With the advent of the Black Arts Movement in the 1960s and '70s, black Americans, especially those who were products of the Great Migration, pushed for more autonomy and group similarities through music, literature, and food. There was an outpouring of creativity. This period produced such literary luminaries as Audre Lorde and Nikki Giovanni and music greats like Marvin Gaye and Curtis Mayfield. As for food, the famed Sylvia's Restaurant in Harlem and Roscoe's House of Chicken and Waffles in Los Angeles were established in the 1960s and '70s, respectively.

I've come across some black people who won't touch any soul food unless the cook has been vetted by an old auntie or other well-respected relative. Potato salad, for example, is one of the biggest responsibilities for many black barbecues, and it's an honor not to be taken lightly. Aside from potato salad, there are many other popular soul food dishes that one might see on a Sunday or holiday table, such as macaroni and cheese, collard greens, chitlins, yams, sweet potato pie, or peach cobbler. These dishes originated down South, and Northerners continued to prepare them after the Great Migration. I'd never learned how to properly cook any of these foods, because I didn't think it was that important. I thought that standing over a hot stove for hours to feed a whole family, then cleaning up afterward was directly opposed to my burgeoning feminist ideals. Because the women in my family coaxed me to cook and fix people's plates more than they did my male cousins, all I wanted to do was set the table or watch TV like the rest of the guys as an act of defiance. I had to humble myself once I moved farther north to Manhattan and was living on my own.

I had finally been living in an actual apartment by myself after three years of rooming with two men from 2015 to 2016 and then squeezing into a cramped studio from 2016 to 2018. New Year's Eve was approaching, and I had a full kitchen all to myself. I always eschewed the Sunday dinner tradition due to having no family and not many friends in Harlem, but there was one ritual that I wanted to perpetuate in my home as a kind of christening: New Year's Eve dinner.

Every New Year's Eve, I could feel the heat surging in my mother's house. We'd go to a watchnight service* at church and return home. Hours later, I would be sequestered in my room upstairs, but the smell of something heavenly would slip through the cracks in the door. I closed my eyes and envisioned the boiling yams or the black-eyed peas marinating in a large, black Crock-Pot on the counter. The black-eyed peas require the most attention for this meal. They have to soak in a pot of water overnight. A quick hot-water rinse will not do. Then the peas are drained in a colander before being placed in the Crock-Pot with bacon or smoked turkey legs, where they would soften for hours.

Unlike girls in my mother's generation, I was not forced to stand in the kitchen beside the women and watch them cook so that I'd be able to feed a family someday. The kitchen was the biggest indication of the generational divide. While my mother cracked eggs, grated cheese, and peeled potatoes, I was upstairs filling out scholarship applications, studying for exams, writing. I wanted to prioritize academic and professional success rather than the culinary arts. Food would have to wait. Until I finally did achieve that success and made a home and realized I had no idea how to nourish myself.

On New Year's Eve, I stood in my kitchen and knew that something was amiss. I knew what I had to do to begin this year right:

*The watchnight service is a New Year's Eve tradition for many Christian denominations, such as Methodists, Anglicans, and Pentecostals. In African American communities, it is said that enslaved blacks gathered in churches on New Year's Eve in 1862 to wait for the Emancipation Proclamation to go into effect on that January 1, 1863. This tradition is still carried on to this day.

I had to cook the collard greens for money and the black-eyed peas for good luck. I had to make the rice in chicken stock and bake the corn bread just right. I needed the butter, the sugar, the salt, and the pepper. I needed to use my hands for more than writing. My mother was delighted when I told her what I set out to do. She and I hopped on a six-a.m. phone call to talk measurements, textures, and tastes for when things went as planned or had gone awry. Toward the end of the call, I asked my mother why we ate these foods for superstitious reasons. Collard greens were green like money and black eyed peas with their dots did look like dice. She paused. "It's just something that we done. It's something black people do."

I knew that my mother wasn't aware of the origins, but that was enough motivation for me. If soul food, like my ancestors, came from the South, then perhaps that's where my journey had to begin. Eating collard greens and black-eyed peas on New Year's Day connects black people from the North and South. As African Americans migrated north, they had to decide whether to keep eating their Southern food culture, such as hog or hominy, or assimilate to a middle-class, "respectable" menu, beef and wheat replacing pork and corn?[5] Soul food is much richer in flavor and seasoning than middle-class white food, but it's also saltier and extremely high in fat. Because of soul food's health risks, criticism was rampant.

In 1920, Dr. A. Wilberforce Williams, a physician and the health editor of the *Chicago Defender*, wrote a column in which he criticized Southern food for its liver- and digestive-system-damaging condiments, such as hot sauce, "heavy meats," and "excessive carbohydrates." Because the *Chicago Defender* was the most influential newspaper among African Americans at that time (more than two-thirds of its readership was outside of Chicago[6]), Dr. Williams's words had an impact and bolstered stereotypes that new migrants were dirty, stuck in the past, and in need of refinement.[7] These migrants' loyalties to class and region were at odds with each other, and food was at the nexus of these struggles. If they were striving for a better life, did their plates have to change too?

In a place like Chicago, locals prided themselves on the integration of restaurants, but when migrants arrived with their out-of-place behavior, the city's elite establishments began to ban black people, new and local alike. In my personal life, I have both seen and passed judgment on certain foods for being too Southern or reminiscent of slavery, like the way bacon is exalted but pig's feet causes one's face to contort, how ham is desirable but chitlins, or pig intestines, are seen as evidence of backwardness. Growing up, it was not uncommon for me to hear a joke that watermelon was "slave food." These tensions illustrate the divide between black people of a particular class in the North, those who are the descendants of migrants, versus those who live in the South. As black people moved north, certain foods were forsaken so that we could adopt a modern and progressive identity. Foods themselves don't have meaning, but we impose meaning on them. The various kinds of meanings and associations that we have with foods all come from our conditioning, that being our background and social standing. Nevertheless, food symbolizes much of who we are as African Americans.

Much of the food that has sustained us for centuries came from West Africa through the plantations. Cured pork was one of the biggest staples on a plantation. The American sweet potato is reminiscent of, though not identical to, the African yam. Other foods that were imported from Africa and grown on American soil include peanuts, okra, and of course, watermelon. The fusion of African and Anglo-American cultures brought new foods to our cuisine: fried chicken, fish, collard greens, corn bread, corn fritters, grits, beans, and rice, to name a few. The community or family cohesion fostered by eating soul food at a particular time or day isn't something we "just do." All my life I thought that Sunday dinners had become a tradition because Sunday was a day of rest, the last few hours of freedom before the workweek began again. Then I learned that slaves would eat a large breakfast, remnants of it for lunch, and a one-pot meal for dinner. On larger plantations, a staff prepared the meals for the day. On Sundays and holidays, however, slaves would gather for a communal meal. The need for communal eating persisted throughout the centuries due to enslavement and then the economic constraints of segregation. Sharecroppers often came up short because of the boll weevil or soil exhaustion growing tobacco and cotton without crop rotation. Compounding these stressors, white landlords refused to allow black tenants to farm their portions of the land for food. No free man or woman of color wanted to buy a single product and risk careening the family further into debt. Communal eating benefited all, and black people maintained this connection with one another and with their ancestors.[8]

Despite all the research I did, I could not figure out why the superstition was attached to these foods. Why did collard greens and black-eyed peas have to be eaten on New Year's Day and why for money or good luck specifically? Where did that come from?

The answer to my persistent questions should have been a no-brainer. Once when I opened a bag of black-eyed peas—Goya, the brand my mother told me to buy—I noticed on the back a recipe for something called hoppin' John. Hoppin' John called for black-eyed peas, bacon, celery, bay leaves, thyme, scallions, bell peppers, onions, and a few other ingredients. I wondered if the name was a nod to Southern dialect or some element of black Southern cuisine. As it turns out, the answer was the latter. Hoppin' John and its associated superstitions originated from the Georgia and South Carolina Lowcountry and its people known as the Gullah, Geechee, or Gullah Geechee. The origins of the names are undetermined. Some say that Gullah derived from Angola or the Gola people, who live in parts of Liberia and Sierra Leone. As for Geechee, the origin could be the Ogeechee River, which flows for close to three hundred miles through the state of Georgia, or the Kissi people, who reside in Guinea, Sierra Leone, and Liberia.

Hoppin' John for good luck and collard greens for prosperity is a tradition found in the Gullah Geechee culture. Every time African Americans adhere to this custom on New Years' Day, their plates link those at the table with over three hundred years of African American history. The Lowcountry is a two-hundred-mile stretch of land that spans the Georgia and South Carolina coasts, along with the Sea Islands.[9] It is believed that over half of the 388,000 Africans brought to the lands that became the United States first arrived in the Lowcountry.[10] According to the International African American Museum, 80 percent of African Americans can trace an ancestor who set foot onto a Charleston dock first.[11] Despite this rich history, I had heard of Gullah people only twice in my life—on Nickelodeon's 1990s children's television show *Gullah Gullah Island* and from a close friend whose late grandmother was Gullah. The Gullah Geechee people are the oldest sub-ethnic group of African Americans.

Three crucial elements explain how the Gullah Geechee people were able to retain so much of their African-ness, including their cooking: the landscape, their immunity to diseases, and the conditions of slave labor on plantations. The Lowcountry was distinguished not only by its formidable heat, ubiquitous palmetto trees, and Spanish moss, but also by the crops that could be grown there. In the eighteenth century, tobacco ruled the Chesapeake region, and cotton dominated the South, but for the Lowcountry, nothing compared to the rice cultivation.[12] White settlers knew how to profit from rice but not necessarily how to cultivate it and that's why Africans from the aforementioned countries were captured and used as labor. In 1839, Georgia harvested 12.2 million pounds of rice,[13] but South Carolina was the foremost producer, averaging sixty-six million pounds a year before the Revolutionary War and becoming one of the richest colonies.[14] Africans enslaved in the Lowcountry retained not only their farming methods, but also their West African foods, such as watermelon, peas, okra, rice, collard greens, and sweet potatoes. In addition, their nearness to water added plentiful seafood to their diet.[15]

The wetland environment is a hotbed for diseases, but enslaved Africans were more resistant to them than white people, so whites were vastly outnumbered in the Lowcountry. Unlike other plantations, where slaves were not done working on their particular duties until the entire crew was finished, on rice plantations, if slaves were done early, they could assist others, till their own plots of land, or engage in cultural activities. Therefore enslaved Africans were able to foster community within a rather isolated region, and anthropologists and historians have argued that these preconditions have made Gullah Geechees a distinct people who were able to keep West African traditions alive in spite of their oppression.[16]

If the Gullah Geechee people had been able to protect unadulterated customs from the motherland, then I would go to them. I would start in Georgia and then move on to South Carolina, where I would conduct research in the Sea Islands of both states. But I couldn't venture into either territory blindly. I made sure to make contact with someone from each of the places I planned to visit ahead of my trip. Although I'm black like my liaisons, I'm not from the area, and I thought it best to tread carefully.

My instinct served me well when I reached out to one local historian from Georgia via e-mail. Instead of responding through the same medium, she called me early in the morning to get a sense of who I was as a person. Her name was Tiffany Young, and she was born and raised in Gainesville, Georgia, before moving around in the state from Darien to Savannah. She calls herself the Gullah Geechee griot, and she's been doing genealogical and historical research independently for over thirteen years. I just wanted to get the logistics down about where I was going to and how to best prepare in terms of apparel and budgeting, but Young was more focused on how Gullah Geechee people were losing their ways due to governmental interference and people moving to the mainland.

She wanted to talk about Sapelo Island, a barrier island that can be accessed only by ferry, a place where she said the remaining Gullah Geechee people were being taxed 500 percent more than in previous years. I wish she'd been exaggerating. On the contrary, she was understating the figure. In 2012, McIntosh County, Georgia, of which Sapelo Island is a part, wanted 540 percent more than the previous year.[17] For some parcels of land on the island, taxes increased as much as 1,000 percent from those prior to 2012. She recalls a time when Gullah Geechee people would sew fishnets and grow tomatoes, onions, bananas, blueberries, collard greens, and yams. But their numbers are dwindling: "So many people want to move to the cities or surrounding cities where they get more. The job market that they're interested in isn't prevalent here. From the language to the food—even the healing remedies are dying out. People are just getting more dependent on going to the doctor." Young was excited that I would be coming down and confirmed that I was doing the right thing by reaching out ahead of time because her people were so vulnerable. But she warned me: what I was about to see was like nothing that I ever had seen before. The spiritual force of the Lowcountry would be more easily felt and the threat of racial intimidation more widespread than elsewhere. I should trust in my calling and be aware.

In April 2018, I traveled to Darien, which is about an hour outside of Savannah. While New York City was struggling to climb out of the mid-60s in temperature, Darien was swirling between the mid-70s and high 80s. I could smack my lips and taste the salt from the marshes. The scenery reminded me less of an American coastline than the mangroves of Liberia or the swamps of Sierra Leone. The heat made the sweat cover my skin thickly like a pomade, and the mosquitoes were relentless. The cheap insect repellent that I wore was no match for the gnats' hunger for flesh, either. There was no Lyft service; I'd assumed there would be and so hadn't rented a car. There were no restaurants within walking distance of my hotel; I had to settle for Burger King. There was no nightlife. Large cypress trees were all I could see from my hotel window. As night fell, I began to regret not staying in Savannah, renting a car, and making the daily trip back and forth.

As a visitor, I thought Darien to be stuck in the past, an assessment shared by the locals. There is a story in Darien. The son of a conjure woman was said to have robbed a bank. No evidence had been uncovered to prove that this man had done it, but in those days black skin was enough proof. The story goes that he fled the town before the mob could get to him, so they lynched his mother instead. Before the mother's neck snapped, she declared that the city shall never prosper, and it seems her words outlasted her life. According to Tiffany, every time people bid on properties or buy them outright to bring stores and therefore capital to the community, they are never successful. In 2016, Darien had a poverty rate twice as high as Georgia's average.[18] There is a strip mall in the center of town, eerily vacant. People say the mall was built where a plantation house once stood. Before that, it was Indian sacred ground. Some people claim to have seen an indigenous person on horseback silently passing through to observe the defilement that had taken place. The bodies of enslaved children are said to be buried underneath Highway 17. Whether or not one believes in the effectiveness of the mother's curse, the message is quite clear: life is infused with death within these town limits, and there is something spiritually aberrant about this place.

The night before my adventures began, I watched *Daughters of the Dust*, the best-known depiction of Gullah Geechee culture in American cinema. Coincidentally, at the beginning of my first book, on black womanhood, I used a long quote from this movie to explain complexity, without realizing that soon I'd be here in the Lowcountry where the movie is based: "I am the first and the last / I am the honored one and the scorned one." The words were spoken by Nana Peazant, the matriarch of the Peazant family. The family's cohesion is on the brink of disappearing because some relatives will stay on Saint Simons Island in Georgia and others will cross the water and depart to the mainland. Their children and their children's children will scatter all over the United States. The knowledge of the island will grow dimmer with each generation that passes. My first interpretation of Nana's words were that of contradiction. Nana Peazant is both all and nothing at all. But as I sat in my hotel room only a boat ride away from one of the most famous Sea Islands, the words took on a different form. I am the first and the last. I interpreted this statement as Nana saying that she has started her legacy and even when she dies, she'll be around to see it through to the end. That, to me, was hopeful.

In one of my favorite scenes in the movie, the Peazant family is having a picnic on the beach. While the women are preparing the food, the man of the family is out looking beyond the shore. I drew parallels to my family life, how the women convened together to cook and the men were preoccupying themselves with other affairs. The camera pans toward the large helpings of okra, shrimp, onions, potatoes, and corn. One woman is plucking a chicken, and another is boiling water, a bucket of live crabs next to her. I could identify all the foods on their plates and taste them in my mouth too. Viola Peazant, Nana's daughter, is returning home for a final meal with her family. She reads a prayer from *Prayers for Dark People*, by W.E.B. DuBois. She says, "The earth about us, O Lord, is swelling with fruitage and may remind us that this is the seedtime of life."[19] Her words, interposed with her relatives' cooking, are most appropriate because it's at this dinner that Nana will stress the importance of cultural preservation. For black Americans, food and cultural memory cannot be divorced. When we eat soul food, we are sated with nutrients and endowed with a mindfulness of the past.

When I chose not to cook with my mother and grandmother, I was missing out on more than learning a vital skill. I was losing a connection with them and the mothers who came before them. As I looked down at my Whopper Jr. with cheese and medium fries, I envisioned a plate of seafood and vegetables that I hoped to devour sometime during my trip. I wanted to compensate for all those years of removing myself from cooking by learning all that I could about this place and its riches. I tried to push past the shame of all that I didn't know, because I was there now. And if Young believed that it was my calling to be there, I had to lean into that belief.

She said to me, "All of you people that are from up north, your grandparents or your great grandparents came from the South, right? There's no running from it or getting around it." At some point, one has to reckon with the past. The past was always within my home, and I consumed that past every time I ate a meal cooked by an older family member. But soon I would have to enlarge my field of view to see the connections between the "up north" folks like me and the Southern folks like Tiffany, to understand the differences and what else was at stake. Food was the entry point, and now I had to walk through that portal. Like the African Americans of yesteryear, I would have to understand the waterways.

2

I REMEMBER THE accident as if it happened yesterday.

My uncle Rodney had a home with a large swimming pool in an isolated area within a town called Galloway in South Jersey. Backyard games had been set up. Hamburgers and hot dogs were on the grill. Gospel music was playing. Everyone was cheerful. Until a scream tore through the atmosphere like a machete piercing skin. If I focus hard enough, I can still hear it. I didn't know where to look until I saw three men from my church, running faster than I'd ever seen them go, dive into the water to pull out a small, visibly shaken child. He almost drowned. But the party didn't stop. Instead, the adults wrapped a towel around the boy and sat him in a corner, where he preoccupied himself with sucking his thumb for the rest of the day. I don't even remember the boy's name. But what I do know is that I never forgot him, and I was bewildered at how everyone resumed their activities as though the near-drowning wasn't some major traumatic event—almost as if it were routine for a black child to be teetering on the verge of death if water was anywhere nearby.

I'm not sure that I ever got over that scene, because my relationship with water is just as traumatic. At one point in my life, I was that little boy, and so was my mother. We both had accidents in which we almost drowned. My mother never learned how to swim. Her parents never taught her, and that didn't make sense to me. My mother and her siblings grew up in Atlantic City, a five-mile barrier island called Absecon Island that is located along the Jersey Shore of the Atlantic Ocean. Surely if they were living that close to the water, they would've learned to swim in it, right? There were many blacks who lived in Atlantic City just like my family. I wondered if my mother's peers didn't swim either.

At one point, Atlantic City's black population surpassed that of Harlem. This was due in large part to the Great Migration intersecting with the hotel boom. After Atlantic City was incorporated in 1854, African Americans from the South migrated to the Jersey Shore in search of better-paying jobs. Ninety-five percent of African Americans there worked as laborers or in the service industry at white-owned hotels.

My grandfather, Fred II, whom I affectionately call Pop-Pop, was one of them. He washed dishes in a hotel whose name he cannot recall, and from there he went on to construction. Fred II was born in June 1943, and he worked in Atlantic City from the late 1950s to early 1960s, when Jim Crow was still in effect. Segregation in public spaces was maintained to appease white tourists from the South, who did not want to integrate with black people.[1] One of these segregated spots was Chicken Bone Beach, a beach exclusively for African Americans. My grandfather never swam there. Neither did my grandmother, Sylvia, whom he married in the mid-1960s. Sylvia gave birth to four children, and despite their proximity to the water, none learned to swim.

When I ask my mother why, she always tells me that it had to do with our hair. We never learned to swim because of our hair. But many black men we knew who kept their hair short didn't swim either. She was at a loss for words. She's never considered that. Not swimming is so ingrained in our culture that growing up, she'd often hear both black and white people joking about it. She concluded that this was something we "just didn't do," at least not often, and those inside and outside the community knew it.

I was privileged enough to take a swimming class. I was the only black child in it, so I wondered if not swimming was also about access. I got emotional. How could we joke about not knowing how to swim when there were those, like that boy I saw at my uncle's party, who could've died? What about the ones who had? Was this comedy a coping mechanism for our pain? How have I and the rest of my community learned to fear an element that's necessary to our lives?

My relationship to water is characterized by many ironies and contradictions. I'm putting language to a hostility that has been in my family for generations, though never parsed. My hesitation in articulating this fear is almost equal to the fear of water itself. But it's not just fear. It may not even be just hostility. We don't sneer at its waves, the sound that it makes, or its depth. We fear its uncertainty, the unknown beyond its surface. Maybe a better word is *intimidation*.

I was born in Somers Point, the oldest settlement in Atlantic County. A fourth of its area is water. My own name means "of the sea." I've traversed the four-mile-long Atlantic City boardwalk many times, replete with saltwater taffy, but I can count on one hand the number of times I've swum in the Atlantic Ocean. My family and I had our bathing suits. We might have even dipped our toes in when the waves rushed against the shore. Maybe. But the idea of submerging ourselves entirely in the water was met with such obvious dismissal from one another that the beach itself seemed like nothing more than a pretty picture. We were there but never really a part of it. It was as if there were borders and restrictions that no one could see but us.

There were black people I knew who swam, but there was always an albatross of precaution awaiting us at the entrance of a swimming pool or the mouth of a large body of water. My mother or some other female relative would be sure to give us a warning.

"Don't put your head underneath the water, or else the chlorine will mess up all that pretty hair."

"Don't go off into the deep end."

"Be where I can see you."

"Don't horseplay too much."

"Don't swim when there's no adult around."

Or simply, "Don't you get in that pool."

When I ask my mother why she never learned to swim while growing up on an island, she says after a pause, "I don't know. I guess they [her parents] never taught us because they didn't want to lose us." I found her answer quite intriguing. If my mother and her siblings learned how to swim, then logically they would be able to return to shore. But maybe their knowledge of swimming wasn't what her parents feared most. Maybe it was a fear of who might kidnap them from the lake or river. It is estimated that 80 percent of enslaved Africans knew how to swim, but when the transatlantic slave trade was ongoing, some Africans forbade their children from swimming for fear of them being lost to them forever.[2] The circumstances were different than they were four hundred years before, but irrespective of time and space, my grandparents still felt an almost instinctive fear that their children might be taken away in the water.

This intergenerational fear is one that could be explained through epigenetics, the study of how we inherit certain mechanisms without there being a change in our DNA sequences. Dr. Rachel Yehuda, professor of psychiatry at Icahn School of Medicine at Mount Sinai, conducted a study to gauge how trauma is passed down from Holocaust survivors and found that, years later, their children inherited this PTSD because of how overactive their amygdala was. The amygdala is the site in the brain that is responsible for processing our emotions, retaining memory, and tapping into our survival instincts. Through the research, Dr. Yehuda concluded that when people experience trauma, their genes are affected, and now those influenced genes will pass on to their offspring. Sociologist Dr. Joy DeGruy added to the conversation about trauma transmission when she coined the phrase *post-traumatic slave disorder* to publicize the effects of trauma on the descendants of the enslaved.[3]

Carl Zimmer of the *New York Times* wrote in his Matter column that the history of African Americans is shaped by two journeys: the transatlantic slave trade and the Great Migration.[4] Both journeys involved one or many bodies of water. The Atlantic Ocean is one of the most traumatic sites in all of African American experience. One-third of all captured Africans died before their feet were ever planted on any dock in the Western Hemisphere. In the four centuries of the triangular trade, ten to eleven million people were brought to the New World. This figure does not include those who died aboard the ships due to suicide or dehydration, nor those who were tossed overboard when sick from one of the rampant illnesses. The Atlantic Ocean is the unofficial burial ground for uncounted captured Africans, a sunken graveyard.[5]

Zimmer also reported that a team of geneticists found that genetically related African Americans are usually found along the routes taken when their ancestors left the South. In light of this research, the aversion to water becomes explainable as an ingrained fear shared among many African Americans throughout this country. This commonality is often discussed in media:

"Everybody knows black people can't swim. If we could, we wouldn't be here."—Marsha Warfield, Chicago

"I can't really swim. Today I took my first swim lesson since I was five. My dad learned in his sixties, so I feel like I'm ahead of schedule."—John Legend, Ohio native

"My dad almost killed me one time. When I was younger, I couldn't swim . . . nobody ever taught me how to swim. My dad picked me up, grabbed me, and threw me in seven feet. As soon as I hit the water, I almost died immediately."—Kevin Hart, Philadelphia

"So, we have to spend our Saturday with people that we don't
like so that you can prove to someone whose opinion you don't
care about that you can swim? Which, might I remind you, you
cannot."—Dr. Rainbow to Dre, *Black-ish*, Los Angeles

"Because this water drown my family, this water mixed my
blood . . ."—Frank Ocean, New Orleans by way of Long Beach, CA

I had recognized that the problems of African Americans with
water was not specific to my own family through jokes, lyrics, and
script writing—through comedy. What we felt about water wasn't
funny and yet I laughed. I knew that comedy often comes from
pain, and I wanted to know more about this pain. How and where
and how many times was it inflicted? Could the South provide me
with any answers?

I made the mistake of painting with a broad stroke when talking
with Tiffany about the water. Instead of saying, "The black people
I know . . . ," I said, "Black people don't swim." Tiffany cut me off.
"Oh no, no, that's not true! That's not true."

Where Tiffany lives, in the Lowcountry, the water is an invalu-
able resource that holds much black history and is thus revered.
Marquetta Goodwine, also known as Queen Quet and chieftess of
Gullah Geechee nation, says, "We literally live on the water, and
I often say to people, the waterways are our bloodline. . . ." There
are two things that are crucial to the sustainability of a Gullah
community: traditional burial grounds and community access to
water.[6] Land and water have to be both spiritually and physically
in alignment with each other. Part of the reason why the water is
the bloodline for Gullah people is because it is one of their main
sources of food. The waters allow them to harvest fish and shell-
fish.[7] From just below Georgetown, South Carolina, to the Florida
border, a thousand islands comprise the South Carolina and Georgia Lowcountry. Some islands, like Absecon Island, border the
Atlantic Ocean; others might be as far as twenty miles from the

mainland. It wasn't until the end of World War I that bridges were constructed to close the gap between these rural communities and the more industrialized regions on the mainland. In fact, in the 1930s, those who traveled to the Sea Islands found residents who had never even *visited* the mainland.[8] The ocean, lakes, marshes, and rivers encircle the lives of Gullah people. Not only does the water provide the food they need to stay alive, but it is a portal between the living and the dead.

One of the first places that I visited on the Georgia Sea Islands was Saint Simons Island, which was the day to Darien's night, so to speak. Miraculously, I was able to secure a Lyft to take me across the F. J. Torras Causeway, which connects Brunswick, near Darien, to Saint Simons. When I told my driver where I was going, he groaned because the people "over there" were different. As he lamented the multimillion-dollar estates and golf courses that we were about to see, I searched among the waters to find the site of Igbo Landing.

John Couper and Thomas Spalding, two slave merchants, purchased captured Nigerians for $100 apiece and put them on a slave ship called the *Wanderer* in 1803. From it, the captives were unloaded and then loaded onto another ship, called the *York*, to take them to Saint Simons, where several sprawling plantations awaited them. The story goes that seventy-five slaves rebelled and drowned their captors. Once the ship reached Dunbar Creek, the Africans were singing as they marched ashore and, following their chief's command, entered the marshy waters and drowned themselves. Some say that the Africans' souls flew back to Africa. The Igbo Landing has been so influential in African American folklore that it's been popularized by Alex Haley and Toni Morrison,[9] among others. But you wouldn't know that upon visiting, because there's no official historical marker.

Some of Tiffany Young's ancestors worked on Saint Simons Island. If you looked into her family history, you'd say that the water nurtured her family line in the Lowcountry. The earliest ancestors that she could find were part of an event now infamously known as the Weeping Time, the largest slave auction in history. In March 1857, nine hundred slaves were gathered on a racetrack in Savannah, Georgia, and within two days, families were separated and divided in order to settle the massive debt accrued by their original owner, Pierce Butler. The slaves' crying and wailing combined with the sound of the torrential downpour to suggest the name, the Weeping Time.[10] Tiffany's ancestors were sent to both Butler Island, which I'll get to later, and Hampton Point Plantation, which is now an exclusive neighborhood and an eighteen-hole championship golf course on Saint Simons Island.

Over the years, Young has positioned herself as a noninstitutional cultural historian, meaning that she makes pilgrimages both by herself and with groups and speaks in an undiluted and touristy way. One of the biggest events that she organized was a homecoming for a group of Igbo women from Nigeria to Dunbar Creek. The homes and lots for sale on Dunbar Creek go from $349,000 to $1.6 million. You cannot freely access it. Nevertheless, Tiffany was able to get close enough to the site with her group to embellish the "Flying Africans" tale. But upon arrival, they were met with angry white people and their raging dogs, forcing them to leave. Though the story of Igbo Landing is taught in schools around coastal Georgia, there is no public acknowledgment, such as a memorial that commemorates the event.[11] The lack of public acknowledgment spans many decades. In the 1940s, a sewage disposal plant was built beside the site, much to the chagrin of local African Americans.[12] Our fear of the water was learned all along the Mississippi River, on the Atlantic Ocean, in the bayous and swamps of the Deep South, and in swimming pools in the North.

Black people's ambivalence toward water has been engineered for decades even in the North. Before the influx of African Americans, working-class and middle-class white people swam in separate municipal pools. Due to the Great Migration, middle- and working-class whites formed a common identity in order to "other" black people. As a result, middle- and working-class whites began to share the same municipal pools, where black people were prohibited.[13]

In some cities, like Pittsburgh, police and city officials encouraged whites to assault black people if they saw blacks using their pools.[14] Such discrimination was common. One of the most famous photographs of this kind of violence is a 1964 photograph of a white motel manager named James Brock, who poured muriatic acid, which is used to clean pools, in the water when he saw blacks swimming in a Florida pool with whites. Although muriatic acid should be used with caution, its concentration was small enough that one swimmer drank some of the water to calm others' fears.[15] Nevertheless, racial terrorism became closely associated with leisure swimming. It's not surprising that black people would avoid the water altogether, for fear of what might happen. That fear is passed along to children, who may never learn how to swim. Unfortunately, because of this hostility, black children are dying in record numbers.

According to the Centers for Disease Control and Prevention (CDC), African American children are three times as likely to die from drowning as white children.[16] In 2010, the USA Swimming Foundation published a study that found that 70 percent of African American children do not swim, as opposed to 40 percent of white children.[17]

Despite all these reasons to fear water, there are places in America, particularly in the Lowcountry, where African Americans are in harmony with land *and* water—but barely. One such place is Sapelo Island. Among the fifteen barrier islands along Georgia's coastline, Sapelo is the fourth largest. Georgia and South Carolina are responsible for 80 percent of the East Coast's salt marshes, and Sapelo has some of the most unified of them. The island was first settled by Native Americans ten to twenty thousand years ago.

In the mid-1500s, the Spanish took control of it, then the English in the late 1600s. As the French and English dominated it in the 1700s, West Africans were enslaved to work the land.[18] Most Gullah Geechee descendants can trace their earliest ancestor to Bilali Muhammad, who was first a slave in the Bahamas before being taken to Sapelo. Thomas Spalding, one of the antebellum planters on the island, had hundreds of slaves, including Bilali. Other planters derided Spalding's supposedly too kind treatment of his slaves, so among them Sapelo Island was called Nigger Heaven.[19]

The descendants of Bilali Muhammad have surnames that refer to the types of labor that their ancestors were assigned. The Grovners tended the groves, the Handys built things, the Gardners cultivated gardens, the Hoggs took care of the hogs, the Walkers walked livestock, and the Baileys baled tobacco. Cornelia Bailey is arguably Sapelo Island's most famous resident. Born and raised on the island, Cornelia immortalized the stories of her people in her book *God, Dr. Buzzard, and the Bolito Man: A Saltwater Geechee Talks About Life on Sapelo Island,* written with Christena Bledsoe. Bailey also started the Red Bean Project to commercialize Sapelo red peas. She passed away at the age of seventy-two in 2017.[20] In the book, Bailey recalls the time when hundreds of Gullah Geechee people lived on the island. At present, there are around fifty.

I was scheduled to visit Sapelo Island the morning after I arrived in Darien. The ferry to the island was scheduled to leave a dock in nearby Meridian at 8:30 a.m. My taxi driver was parked outside of my hotel before the sun started its transit from the east. We passed Confederate flags in front of homes on large lots of land. The Spanish moss hung like canopies over the road, a common sight in the Lowcountry. I was a black woman alone being driven in the dark by a stranger to a destination unknown to me in one of the harshest of the old slave states, but I had to put these thoughts aside and trust the driver. I was relieved at least that, like myself, the driver was black. We turned on Blount Crossing Road where the signs for Sapelo Island at last appeared. Doboy Sound, which separates Sapelo Island from the mainland, stretched farther than my eyes could see. I was so overcome by the beauty of the pink-and-blue skies that I made the mistake of getting out of the car to take pictures before I applied insect repellent. A large black cloud of gnats immediately surrounded me. Even after I rubbed the repellent into my skin, they clung to me and expired on my arms. It had been quite some time since I had been near the water, and I had forgotten how relentless the bugs could be in the mugginess they love.

One by one, cars began to pull up to the dock, some with PROUD SALTWATER GEECHEE tags on the back. I noticed that Geechee people may identify themselves with respect to the water. If you're a Saltwater Geechee, you live on one of the Sea Islands, such as Sapelo. If you're a Freshwater Geechee, you live on the mainland. Several white children in SAPELO ISLAND SPRING BREAK T-shirts jumped out one by one from a chrome minivan. The ferry coming from Sapelo Island pulled up alongside the dock to allow those who stayed overnight to depart. From the surface-level optics, Sapelo did not seem as disastrous as Tiffany portrayed it to be, especially if there were people willing to vacation on the island. But I hadn't actually gone there yet.

To board the ferry, I had to pay five dollars in cash for a round-trip ticket. Before I boarded, a coordinator asked me whom I was going to see. The coordinator I spoke with was a white woman, which felt . . . strange. If I was going on a tour given by a Gullah Geechee guide, shouldn't the mainland coordinator also be a Gullah Geechee? The unevenness peeved me.

This was one of my first subtle clues as to who was and was not in power.

I was going to see JR Grovner, one of the only tour guides on the island. The state owns the ferry, which makes three runs between Sapelo Island and Meridian Dock each day, two on Sunday, and none on holidays.

The tension between the mainland and island is exacerbated by the limited service, as many Sapelo Island residents find it hard to run errands on the mainland, maintain employment, or have easy access to other family members. Despite the skyrocketing real estate taxes, there is no school, fire department, hospital, or police force.[21] Children who live on the island and participate in extracurricular activities at their mainland schools often have to stay with family or friends because the ferry will not accommodate their schedules. Those with disabilities find both the ferry and dock dangerous. The parking area is covered with gravel, which makes it difficult for those who use a cane or wheelchair to traverse. When the tides are low, the ramps leading to the ferry are steep and often slippery and wet. Those using a cane or wheelchair must be carried by someone. For anyone experiencing chest pains or diabetic shock outside of ferry hours with no other help available, the only hope is prayer.

There are no hospitals or medical services on the island. In case of injury, medical personnel have to be called in, or the injured person has to be transported off the island. The state, specifically the Department of Natural Resources, limits boat traffic between the island and mainland. There are eleven major sea islands off the coast of Georgia. Three are connected by bridges (St. Simon's, Tybee, and Jekyll) and five can only be reached by a private boat or charter (Wassaw, Blackbeard, Wolf, Ossabaw, and St. Catherine's.) Sapelo is included with two other islands, Little St. Simon's and Cumberland, that provide ferries to and from the mainland, but it is the only one under this subgroup whose ferry service is controlled by the state.[22]

When the ferry pulled away from the dock and moved to where the Duplin River empties into Doboy Sound, I stood on the deck and took in the fresh air, captivated by the long stretches of marshland. Several birds that I had mistaken for seagulls followed behind the boat. They were actually black skimmers, who get their name from their habit of skimming the surface of tidal sloughs. The ecology of this area is why many travel from all over the world to study the salt marshes and diversity of animals. Resident scientists of the University of Georgia Marine Institute live on Sapelo year-round to conduct their research. After thirty minutes, we arrived at the Sapelo Island dock. As soon as I descended from the ferry, I was taken aback by the trees. They were tall and expansive—sentries, as I liked to call them. They seemed to have stories embedded in their leaves and trunks.

JR Grovner, my tour guide, is a dark-skinned man in his late thirties. JR has been doing tours on the island since he was ten years old. I was the first one at his van, and I soon realized that I was the only black person on his tour. I chose the front seat. He stopped my hand as I reached for my seat belt. "You don't need to do that here," he said. I was confused. What if we hit someone else on the road? What if he made too sharp a turn and my face smashed into the windshield? As if I knew the land better than he did. There were no other cars on the roads. For one, Hurricane Matthew had scattered large trees that blocked off certain paths. There were no traffic lights, no stop signs, no median lines. This was a place where you don't need to have an actual driver's license. I saw a twelve-year-old maneuver a car into a parking lot better than I could—and she was carrying two smaller passengers in the back seat.

The first stop of the tour coincidentally aligned with one of the questions that had been brewing since my first call with Tiffany: What is our truest relationship to water? If water is no longer to be feared, what circumstances and systems continue to instill that fear?

Water held memories of ancestors' deaths, but it also could promise a life beyond this one. In Behavior Cemetery, where Cornelia Bailey is buried, most of the grave markers and epitaphs are written on wooden boards nailed to surrounding trees, along with some of their loved ones' favorite things. There is a belief that that particular favorite item will be with the person in the afterlife. The graves face east. In the Bible, particularly in the Books of Malachi and Matthew, the arrival of God's kingdom will come from the east. For the Gullah people, there are two possible reasons for this tradition: (1) They want to be ready for when the archangel Gabriel blows his trumpet from the east signifying the return of Christ, though Gabriel is only specified as the trumpeter in negro spirituals and not scripture, or (2) they want the bodies to face Africa so that the souls can return there in the afterlife.

A song moved to the forefront of my mind—"Take Me to the Water." Any time a baptism was about to be performed in a black church, this song would be sung. It was sung at my baptism and at the many baptisms that my mother attended. "Take me to the water / To be baptized . . . / I'm going back home, going back home." It's one of those songs that you've heard so many times that you can sing it absent-mindedly. I never thought of its meaning other than the obvious: someone (re)dedicating his or her life to Christ. The water, one's forehead is sprinkled with it or one's entire body is submerged in it, symbolically washes away one's sins so one can begin anew. But that's not all. No. Not for African Americans. I thought about other water-based hymns, such as "Get Away, Jordan," in which we ask to cross over to see the Lord, or "Wade in the Water," in which the singer encourages the listener to believe that God will calm the water en route to freedom. If, for the Gullah people, water could lead to freedom and heaven was an idealized Africa, then when I was baptized, "going back home" meant that water was not my guide and my inheritance. I would belong to God, and the water would take me to Him. As I looked at the many graves, I thought about the bodies underneath, their spirits elsewhere.

There was a fence around the cemetery, and I asked JR why this was so. He told the group that people had been vandalizing the graves and stealing food and valuables left for the dead. He was noticeably cryptic. Before the rest of the group returned to the vehicle, I asked JR what was one thing he was afraid to tell people on these tours. He said he never wanted to tell them if anything was for sale. I inferred that the more of them who buy the land, the less of a connection the remaining Sapelo Island Geechees have to that land and its waters. This disruption further diminishes their culture and community.

In 2015, fifty-seven Sapelo Island property owners and residents and two local groups, the Help Organization Incorporated and the Raccoon Hogg Community Development Corporation, filed a federal racial discrimination lawsuit against McIntosh County. Besides their grievances over the ferry schedules and lack of basic services on the island, the plaintiffs noted that there is no water department on the island. The water pressure for the fire hydrants is too weak to quell any flames. Though the Department of Natural Resources does provide water services, the plaintiffs claimed that the water is "rust-colored, cloudy . . . has a foul taste and odor . . . at times . . . foamy and has particles floating in it." A recent report confirmed that the water tested high for polychlorinated biphenyl, or PCB, which is carcinogenic and can cause immunological and neurological damage to children. In 2017, the Department of Natural Resources tested a water sample and found that it also had double the allowable amount of lead. I made an immediate parallel to Flint, Michigan, a city with a predominantly black population that has not had clean water for more than five years. Because of this lack, Sapelo Island locals cannot drink the water that surrounds them; they must get their water from the mainland. They have no access to a sanitary sewer system but only septic tanks that are emptied infrequently, causing them to overload and overflow. It appeared to me that the water, once crucial for Sapelo Island locals to survive, was now a dangerous threat.

In the complaint, some black Sapelo Island residents who lived on Hog Hammock asserted that they had been forced to sell their homes because they could not handle the tax inflation. Many white people vacation on the island, and white developers encroach on the land in zones that McIntosh County specifically delineated in order to protect the Gullah community. After the Civil War, many Gullah people were able to earn money for their labor, which they then used to buy their own land. In 1912, Howard Coffin, one of the founders of Hudson Motor Car Company, bought the entire island except for those black communities. One of the most iconic sites on the island was formerly known as Spalding Mansion or Spalding Plantation Manor, named after Thomas Spalding. During the Great Depression, tobacco heir and environmentalist R. J. Reynolds purchased the mansion—now known as Reynolds Mansion—as well as the vast majority of the island. Reynolds's goal was to consolidate all the black communities from their various waterfront properties throughout the island into one—Hog Hammock—and make the rest of the island a wildlife preserve. The Gullah people got a deed of land in Hog Hammock but could not get land back on the north end because they could not prove their ownership.[23] To this day, Gullah people cannot reclaim land for which they still pay property taxes. Many roads on the island are still undeveloped, and yet the Department of Natural Resources provided a culvert for a driveway for one particular white couple who occasionally vacation on Sapelo.

On an island where there once resided five thriving communities of West African residents—Hog Hammock, Shell Hammock, Lumber Landing, Belle Marsh, and Raccoon Bluff[24]—only the first on the list remains, and 97 percent of the island is now owned by the state of Georgia. R. J. Reynolds's wife sold the land to the state after his death.[25] As Tiffany lamented, "People don't be listening. That's what brings me to tears, chile. People do not listen, they don't care. They leave us here to perish, and they want our legacy to die so that there's no argument. We look like a fool trying to argue with them—no, no, no."

After JR showed us the Native American shell rings, Hog Hammock, and the Reynolds mansion, he let us relax on the beach, where I learned a little bit more about him. He had a particular disdain for the Department of Natural Resources—with good reason. In 2016, he filed a lawsuit against them on the grounds of employment discrimination. Back in 2012, there were open captain positions, and JR applied for one, and in 2013 he applied for a mate position. Both jobs would have given JR some management authority over the waters that his ancestors used. He was already working as a boat captain for a construction business, as well as being a tour guide. He had the qualifications, and yet a white person was chosen over him for both jobs. A Washington, DC, civil rights firm, Relman, Dane & Colfax, which also represented the fifty-seven Sapelo Islanders in the previous case, filed a lawsuit on Grovner's behalf. While that case was pending, Grovner applied for another position, but the Georgia Department of Natural Resources disregarded the application because of the ongoing litigation. Another lawsuit was filed in retaliation. A judge dismissed the initial case on the grounds that there wasn't enough evidence to prove racial discrimination. But the second case continued forward, and it was settled for an undisclosed amount.

As for the future of Sapelo, JR is pessimistic. To him, Sapelo is not developing. Black people are leaving the island for the mainland, and those who remain aren't banding together to retain their properties. Gullah and Geechee are still used as a pejorative term indicating an uneducated, lazy, unrefined person, so some younger descendants reject the label. Worst of all, he thinks other black people don't give a damn about what's happening to those on the island. I was the only black visitor on my tour. Grovner laments that more do not come. "Black people like to shop—city lights." Once we got back into the car and drove farther, one white woman asked if there was any land for sale there.

I don't remember what JR said. I know that he didn't say yes or no outright. When she asked the question, I was too gobsmacked to remember what happened afterward. I bet he'd been asked this question many times before. I sensed the dissatisfaction in his brow, an expression that I'd misinterpreted as manly steeliness at the beginning of the trip. He was tired. The home that he knew was shrinking before his very eyes. Many of the people who tilled the land were either dead and disrespected or neglectful and modernized from moving inland. I now understood why he didn't specify just which kind of tourists were stealing from Behavior Cemetery and why he was afraid of telling any tourists that anything was for sale. He was being cryptic because white tourists were providing him with a sustainable income. Circumlocution was his safety net, and given all the problems faced by the island's black locals, Grovner knows his presence here is important.

As for me, the outsider who happened to find Sapelo and meet JR, I was the minority by my presence but the threatening majority in my thoughts. When he spoke of blacks drawn to the city lights, he was talking about me. That's what I idolized since I was young. I had no other option. After all, my grandfather was drawn to the city lights too, hence his move to the Jersey Shore. That's all I knew. I moved to New York City because I imagined it was the place where my publishing dreams could come true.

By this movement, however, we had forgotten those who came before us and how much they had flourished where they were. This separation of ourselves from home, wherever that may have been, and from yesteryear's synergistic relationship among us, the land, and the water, had as much to do with capitalistic development as with our forgetfulness about what was once ours. The Jerkins family grew up on an island yet never learned how to swim. Sapelo Island families, such as the Grovners, may have learned to swim, but now their travel on the water surrounding them was restricted to the ferry services. We are united along these two poles of experience, access or lack thereof. We are mindful that the water is treacherous. It's roiled by the forces of white supremacy and inter-generational disconnect.

Tiffany and her fiancé joined me in the latter half of the tour as we headed back to Darien. She had to tell me about her discovery. As I mentioned, there's a rumor that the bodies of enslaved children are somewhere underneath Highway 17, which spans the entire Lowcountry, as well as parts of Virginia and Florida. In McIntosh County, the rumor has circulated for years among local politicians, journalists, and others. Over lunch, Tiffany said to me, "If you're native to McIntosh, more than likely you were enslaved between Sapelo and Butler."

Butler Island is located just one mile outside of Darien via Highway 17 and across the Butler River Bridge. I felt unsettled even before Tiffany began speaking as a part of her private tour, because I had never been on a plantation before. I couldn't help but imagine the unspeakable things that happened there. Palmetto trees flanked the main house on both sides. A seventy-five-foot chimney of the rice mill demonstrates the significance of this particular plantation. Before electricity, water would flow in through a tidal gate to power the machinery. The delta of the Altamaha River and the surrounding marshlands were perfect for rice cultivation.[26] Tiffany estimates that there were up to forty plantations in and around this small county because of the water and the rice. As a test, Tiffany drove me to Butler Island, where we stood on a bridge among the rice fields. She asked me if I could see the alligator. The seconds felt like hours. I squinted behind my glasses and found nothing but the tall weeds. When Tiffany and her fiancé finally pointed out the alligator, I joked that I would've been dead if I'd had to create dikes and levees to cultivate rice. But many did die. The enslaved Africans were brought to this area mainly because of their previous knowledge of how to cultivate rice. They developed the irrigation systems, levees, ditches, culverts, floodgates, and drains. The danger of these jobs came not only from the master's brutality, but from nature itself.[27]

In the 1950s and '60s, alligators were hunted almost to extinction. Alligator skins were also very valuable during slavery, but of course the risks were great. One could lose an arm or one's life. So white hunters used slave babies as bait to trap alligators, a legend much disputed until it was unfortunately confirmed to be true.[28] Hunting wildlife is still popular in and around Butler Island Plantation, especially for waterfowl and shorebirds. The Altamaha River, famous for its ducks, attracts hunters throughout the year. Tiffany expresses much disdain for the hunting game here, believing that the state of Georgia prioritizes the wildlife over commemoration of the enslaved who worked this land. Tiffany, who carried around a large binder with maps, coordinates, and historical documents, is not affiliated with the state whatsoever.

Our first stop was in front of the plantation historical marker, which reads:

Famous rice plantation of the 19th century, owned by Pierce Butler of Philadelphia. A system of dikes and canals for the cultivation of rice, installed by engineers from Holland, is still in evidence in the old fields, and has been used as a pattern for similar operations in recent years.

During a visit here with her husband in 1839–40, Pierce Butler's wife, the brilliant English actress, Fanny Kemble, wrote her "Journal of a Residence On A Georgia Plantation," which is said to have influenced England against the Confederacy.[29]

"This is the only Georgia historical marker," Tiffany says. "You know these are about three or four thousand dollars apiece. I've been trying to get one, but they won't help me. They pick three for the state each quarter, and generally it's a competition for them to give you one, but my agenda has not succeeded in six years."

Upon later research, I found out that the costs are a bit higher. A Georgia historical marker costs $5,000, and there are restrictions, as laid out in the Georgia Historical Society guidelines: "Historical markers are not monuments. Overly adulatory language that departs in any way from an objective and dispassionate recounting of the historically documented facts will not be approved. Further, marker texts with lists of names (such as *in memoriam* tributes) are discouraged."[30]

"What do you wanna put on yours?" I asked Tiffany.

"Basically who we are. Our family names and how we were enslaved here. There's nothing talking about us. This is about the authors. All the books that they write are about slavery here, but they don't talk to you about that." The historical marker for Butler Island Plantation did not adhere to these guidelines, for calling a British actress "brilliant" is neither objective nor dispassionate but adulatory. Why was this part of history approved while Tiffany's was not?

What *they* don't talk to you about are the unspeakable atrocities that have happened on Butler Island. At one time, five hundred slaves worked in the fields. Summer brought upon malarial fevers. The mortality rate on rice plantations was second only to that on Caribbean sugarcane plantations. Half of the children born and raised on Butler Island died before their sixth birthday; 60 percent died before the age of sixteen.[31] According to Barbara J. Little's *Text-Aided Archaeology*, infants and children comprised 50 percent or more of the annual deaths on Butler Island. For example, in 1820 there were 416 slaves working on Butler Island. Among them, there were 16 deaths, and 9 of those were infants and children. In 1830, the slave population dropped to 395. There were 25 deaths that year, 15 of them infants and children.[32] Working in the water year-round made slaves susceptible to cholera and other water-borne illnesses. The water was not clean, leading to gastrointestinal problems and deaths of children due to parasitic diarrhea. In Fanny Kemble's

Journal of a Residence on a Georgian Plantation 1838–1839, she recounts being horrified by the sight of enslaved women who convulse and have nervous breakdowns after being flogged by the overseer for requesting time to bathe their children, women who had spinal problems due to work demands, women whose insides were falling apart because of constant childbirth. Miscarriages, low-weight births, and stillbirths were common. Tiffany took me over to the infirmary, which was close to the dock. There slaves would be brought in and scrutinized for disease. In Fanny Kemble's words:

> I walked down the settlement towards the infirmary or hospital, calling in at one or two of the houses along the row. These cabins consist of one room about twelve feet by fifteen, with a couple of closets smaller and closer than the state-rooms of a ship, divided off from the main room and each other by rough wooden partitions in which the inhabitants sleep. They have almost all of them a rude bedstead, with the grey moss of the forests for mattress, and filthy, pestilential-looking blankets, for covering. . . . Such of these dwellings as I visited to-day were filthy and wretched in the extreme. . . . [33]

If you disobeyed, you were taken to a place called Five Pound Island, a punishment so cruel that it was dubbed Beyond the Whip. Tiffany told me a story of one woman who resisted Roswell King, a former manager of Butler Island Plantation, was whipped, then sent on a boat, where she was raped en route to Five Pound Island. The story is that she subsisted on large blades of grass for months, grass too tall and sharp for any slave to escape through without getting welts and cuts all over. In her journal, Kemble tells of three enslaved women, Sophy, Judy, and Sylla, who had each given birth less than a month before. Mrs. K, the wife of the father of Judy and Sylla's newborns, ordered that all three be whipped, then sent to

Five Pound, where they were to be beaten daily. As Fanny Kemble writes, "If I make you sick with these disgusting stories I cannot help it; they are the life itself here."[34]

While the Department of Natural Resources employees work around the plantation and both locals and visitors travel to this spot to hunt game, Tiffany conducts these tours independently, an activity that she says she feels is a privilege to do: "I feel honored to be here telling people about it, because there's nobody else to do it. I'd rather be doing that than it just being a desolate place like they mean for it to be, and just homes and deer and stuff all here. I'd rather it be something to represent who we are."

For the climactic part of our trip, Tiffany asked me to turn off my recorder and stow away my notebook and pen. She needed my undivided attention. I was not allowed to give the exact location. All she granted me permission to divulge was that we were at a place where the Altamaha meets the Champney River. She took a turn and traveled down a winding path. No one in the car spoke. The only noise were the tires crushing the gravel. The car gradually pulled to a stop, and Tiffany motioned for me to get out. When I did, she pointed at the murky brown water and told me that this is where the bodies of hundreds of Butler Island slaves were buried. I imagined their spirits drifting underwater in turmoil.

I don't remember how long we stood out there, but I do know that I was transfixed by the movement of the water. Before this day, I had never set foot on a plantation. I didn't believe such tours were meant for me. The horrors of slavery are too whitewashed on plantation tours for my liking. Like the Sapelo Island tourists, to whom there was no mention of the land-ownership struggles between black locals and white vacationers, plantation tourists are mostly white, and therefore the narrative is tailored to appease them. And who wants to listen to an hour-long recital of the brutal methods of punishment and the death rates of slaves while walking through beautiful sprawling estates and their magnificent trees?

But to distance ourselves from this history only reinforces the disconnect between our ancestral lands and those who moved away. Our enslaved forefathers and foremothers aren't the only ones forgotten. The resting places of ancestors from one or two generations ago are in peril too.

Dr. Edda Fields-Black, an associate professor in the History Department at Carnegie Mellon University, has been studying rice plantations for years. Both sides of her family were born in the Lowcountry. One of her cousins on her father's side was buried on a plantation in Colleton County, South Carolina, in the 1960s. Many of her relatives on her father's side, the Fields family, have been buried on this plantation for generations. She asked me not to disclose their names so that the owners of the property won't try to curtail her access for more research. When Dr. Fields-Black went to visit the area, which was full of unmarked graves, she found her cousin's grave with the help of another relative. The grave was underwater. His skull and other bones were floating inside the casket. "He was swimming in his grave," Dr. Fields-Black says. It is a moment that leaves her mentally and spiritually undone. To this day, none of his grandchildren, many of whom have migrated across the country, have done anything to restore his grave. Dr. Fields-Black argues that the reason for these underwater, unmarked, and relatively unknown graves is that, aside from climate change flooding, burial grounds are below sea level, the rice plantations have changed hands, and the owners don't have a connection with the family. She was right. The only other Butler Island descendant I found aside from Tiffany and Griffin Lotson (mentioned below) was a woman living in California, who had never visited the plantation. The unmarked, flooded graveyard made sense of Tiffany's decision to work outside of institutions. She has no connection to them nor they to her.

To understand how fear of water flows across time and space, I wanted to see how "higher powers," such as the state of Georgia, handle the narrative about plantations. To the unsuspecting mind, Butler Island was a place where rice was cultivated and where a famous actress and writer chronicled her time, because that's all that the plaque in front of the plantation indicates. There is no mention of who cultivated that rice or of the lives lost to make a profit for white people. Tiffany has received recognition from archaeologists for her work, yet she cannot get a Georgia historical marker to honor the slaves who were forced to sacrifice their lives for its wealth, those who made Butler Island what it is now. Hundreds of those slaves, who survived the horrendous journey across the Atlantic Ocean, now share the same fate as those who didn't—submerged and forgotten.

There was no justification for this underwater cemetery. There weren't any houses around. There was nothing but wildlife. Why have these bodies been deserted? Although I have read and studied many cases of the way black bodies are treated in life and death, I still expected to find compassion somewhere. Maybe that's naïveté on my end. Tiffany told me that I would be awakened once I traveled to the Lowcountry. When I did, I was made not only more conscious of our history, but also more sorrowful. I thought about the many near-drowning accidents that I had, growing up. This trip broadened my view of water from something to be enjoyed to something to be understood as a place holding all those who came before me. As Marquetta Goodwine perfectly stated, water was in fact the bloodline, not only for Gullah Geechee people, but also for many African Americans, like myself.

Fear of the water has been instilled in me for as long as I can remember. It was in Georgia where I realized that my fear is rooted in the historical fact that water has been a site for much black death. We were often kidnapped in water, we traveled through water to get here, we worked the water to produce crops, and many stipulations were put in place to keep us separated from it, lest we swim or sail to freedom. Many miles away, in my South Jersey hometown, I still felt the rawness of that fear and separation like a ripple effect. I thought of that little boy again. I never saw him again after that day when he almost drowned, but I think of his story as one within a larger story, of how an otherwise innocent pastime like swimming has never been so for black people. I found that his near-death experience with water, as well as mine, as well as my mother's, was such a routine occurrence because that was our unfortunate birthright as African Americans. To break the association of death with water in the African American experience would be to purposefully forget what has been done to us. Maybe that's why I was never able to forget that little boy. I knew, even as a child, that his saving was too clean, too matter-of-fact, that these adults had done this before, maybe even had it done for them.

Here I was in the Lowcountry, where the stories of drownings carried a more spiritual connection. Beyond the voluntary drownings at Igbo Landing, there were these countless bodies floating somewhere beneath the surface. I was ashamed that I had never heard of Butler Island before the making of this book, but then, this information was never readily available to me. There are many corners of black history still being uncovered hundreds of years later. This four-hundred-year-old pain we carry about the water was never meant to be ours. In a joke or story, we confess what the water has done to us. Naturally that memory is more visceral in the South.

3

LIKE MY FEELINGS about water, my conditioned attitude toward magic, especially "roots," was full of both ominousness and hilarity. Almost every time the root has been brought up by a family member, it was in the context of a woman, most likely single and older, who'd been suspected of hexing with herbs and roots, or planning to do so. I remember as a child, an older woman who liked to dress in vibrant colors came to our South Jersey church one day. In a matter of weeks, people suspected that she was involved with roots and witchcraft because she "kept doing things with her hands"—moving them around in circular motions and making designs with her fingers in her lap. Another single woman visited my church after the vibrantly dressed woman and people also suspected her of practicing witchcraft. There was never an explanation as to why. Once the rumor dispersed among the congregation, the woman left as unexpectedly as she came. Whenever someone in my community couldn't explain a sudden illness or a run of bad luck, it was assumed that someone had "put a root on" that person. I've used the phrase facetiously many times, but I never really understood what a "root" was. Was it something from the ground? No one in my community was a farmer, so why did they keep referencing something like this as though they were familiar with it?

I was traveling in the Lowcountry to reclaim some of what was lost along the migratory paths, but I met challenges, especially when it came to the root and all its properties. Tiffany told me that, besides the language and food, the healing remedies are vanishing, because the old people are dying off and young people are moving away to metropolitan areas throughout the country. But for those, like her, who stuck around, memories of the powers of those who practiced with a root are rich. Because Gullah Geechee people grew their own food, they also used the earth to assist in both healing and curses. Tiffany spoke of spirits as though they were flesh and blood, mentioned her ancestors in the present tense, and offered this anecdote: a healer helped an ailing woman by giving her a potion. The sickness left her body in the form of a scorpion crawling out from underneath her. Even though the results were sometimes said to be dramatically beneficial, my family spoke of these community healers with sharp condemnation. They were demonic and needed to be avoided at all cost.

The potential source of this disdain is embodied in one of my grandfather's most visceral memories while growing up in southern New Jersey. My great-grandparents were very religious. My great-grandmother, Gladys, was a born-again Pentecostal and attended church regularly. My great-grandfather, Fred I, was religious as well, though not as devoted. They were also hard workers. Fred I worked in construction and saved enough money to buy a large flatbed truck and chainsaws in order to start a pulpwood business. Gladys cleaned rich white people's houses five days a week. Fred was well known around town, because his business was successful. I suspect that he was good-looking, and maybe that's why he attracted the attention of one woman in particular.

Her name was Iris, and she wanted my great-grandfather badly. She was a dark-skinned woman whose eyes were said to have emitted a red hue. "Real devious-looking," my grandfather, Fred II, says. Iris migrated from Georgia and settled in a South Jersey town called Newtonville. The Jerkins family was one of many other families who lived in this predominantly black community in the 1950s. On one occasion, my mother, grandfather, and I drove through Newtonville as he regaled us with stories of how angels, demons, and other ghastly apparitions appeared alongside people and scared the daylights out of him and his siblings. Because I get frightened easily, I tried to tune him out. These stories reinforced my grandfather's belief that the spiritual and natural worlds interact with each other. The supernatural easily slid into the quotidian schedules of him and his neighbors.

Newtonville is an unincorporated town in Buena Vista Township of Atlantic County, New Jersey. It was founded by runaway slaves and began as a camp that made and sold charcoal.[1] Newtonville is a relatively rural town, surrounded by pine barrens, farmlands, and rivers. My grandfather and great-uncle can recall hiding in their neighbors' fields and devouring their raspberries.

But that Iris! My family can't recall if she had a husband or children, and in those days, being single was suspicious enough. She would tuck some kind of substance inside the band of a hat belonging to a man whom she desired. No one ever told me if my great-grandfather Fred had an affair with Iris, but I do know that my great-grandmother got terribly sick right around the time that Iris set her eyes on him. No one knew what the sickness was or how to cure her.

I asked my grandfather, "When your mom had to go to the doctor, did she go to a regular doctor? Or were people like, 'Hey, you just need some turpentine'?"

"In them days, the doctors used to come to your house."

"But this doctor—he wa'n't no real doctor," my great-uncle Curtis said. "He would ride around in the car with the top down and it don't even rain in the car. He was a different kind of doctor."

"He was a witchcraft doctor," my grandfather said.

After this doctor left my family's home, my great-grandmother was cured. According to Fred II, everyone in the community knew of Iris as a root worker. The only way to undo the root that Iris had put on her was to have a doctor of the same arts—who I later found out to be from Georgia also—perform a procedure. Why did my family abhor roots and yet rely on the power of witchcraft doctors to cure my ailing great-grandmother? I found this hypocrisy fascinating. Do its roots, so to speak, stretch farther than South Jersey? If so, could this hypocrisy have more to do with our movement away from the South and less to do with religious tenets within the black church?

I was raised in the Pentecostal Church, an evangelical denomination of Christianity. Its origins began with the collaboration of a black Baptist preacher from Texas named William J. Seymour and a white Methodist evangelist from Topeka, Kansas, named Charles F. Parham. Pentecostalism is largely characterized by three elements: baptism, speaking in tongues (glossolalia), and divine healing. Those who could speak in tongues, languages indecipherable to those who utter them, can convey prophetic messages, and those who've been blessed to heal may do so with the laying of hands on a sick person.[2]

It is arguably because of the Great Migration that my family is composed of Pentecostals. Many black migrants established their churches in storefront buildings or larger properties that white people used before they fled to the suburbs because of the burgeoning black populations.[3] Pentecostalism worked in urban areas as the overcrowdedness of housing projects led to an outpouring into churches, where congregants could find enthusiasm and relief through praying, singing, and shouting. In 1919, there were over a hundred storefront churches in Chicago, and in 1926, there were 140 churches on 150 blocks in Harlem.[4] My church, Evangelical Fellowship Church, is located in Pleasantville, and it faces the expressway that leads right into Atlantic City. Within a five-mile radius, there are several other black churches: Mount Zion Baptist, Grace Tabernacle, and Morning Star, to name a few.

As much as my family eschews superstition, I believe Pentecostals are some of the most superstitious people that you'll ever have the pleasure of meeting. Whenever a Pentecostal congregant moves into a new house, the elders of the church convene to pray so that they can drive out the spirits and energies of the previous owners. When I moved into my new apartment, my grandmother gave me a large bottle of anointing olive oil that she had prayed over. I keep it on top of my kitchen counter near the door for extra protection. That way whenever I enter and leave my apartment, I'm armored with an invisible shield to keep me from harm. When I'm feeling afraid, I pour some out and make the sign of the cross on my forehead for discernment and over my heart for love and vitality.

I'm also very particular about touching. I believe that someone can transfer their energy, by something as small as the brushing of shoulders or a huge embrace, to someone else through touch. I remember quite vividly one occasion, when my mother had a falling-out with a relative and that relative gave me a mug for my birthday. She and I never had any ill will toward each other. Nevertheless, my mother made me promptly dispose of the gift and made sure that I obeyed her order as we talked on the phone. In her mind, that's how people get sick: when they accept gifts or food from the hands of someone they do not entirely trust. She believed that if that relative couldn't get to her, she could still get to the closest thing to her: her daughter—me.

The women in my family always carry suspicion with them. My grandmother often dreams wild visions of birds and trees that are said to be premonitions. One time, an owl perched itself on one of my mother's trees in her backyard in broad daylight. Although owls can be seen during the day if their sleep schedules are off, my mother took the owl as a bad omen. The following day, a bishop and lifelong friend of the family was hit by a car and subsequently died.

If someone dies in the house, all the windows need to be open to let the spirits out. When someone is causing discord, they "got a spirit on 'em," meaning that a demonic spirit has taken possession of the person's body. Spirits hover among all of us but we generally identify them only when a situation turns adverse. We know that there are also good spirits, according to the Bible, but ironically, their invisibility and their immense impact on our lives make them all seem like a constant threat.

The spirit world is just as much in alignment with the natural world for black Northerners as for black Southerners. In the South, roots have a multitude of meanings. There was one person in Darien whom I *had* to meet to talk about the power of the root and how spirits intercede in the lives of black people. His name is Griffin Lotson, federal commissioner of the Gullah Geechee Cultural Heritage Commission and mayor pro tem of Darien. He spoke so much like my grandfather, it was eerie.

Born and raised in the town, Lotson emphatically and repeatedly told me that the song "Kumbaya," which in Gullah means "Come by here," was first recorded there by H. Wylie in 1926, an historical moment that was just recently recognized by Congress.[5] A seventh-generation Gullah Geechee, Lotson can trace his ancestors back to Sierra Leone, finding stunning similarities between their rice coasts and Georgia's. He admits that driving past rice plantations haunts him because of all the brutality that happened there. Like Tiffany Young, Lotson had ancestors who worked on Butler Island Plantation and later served in the Civil War. When it comes to survival through rootwork, Lotson said, "The root doctor and the root worker are sometimes the same person in our culture of Gullah Geechee. What it is, on the plantation of the slave masters now, you might find it interesting. We couldn't go to those doctors. That just didn't happen. So we had to figure out a way to stay alive as the Native Americans did and just about every other culture. You devise and you create a system where you learn about the things that grow around you." Because of black people's lack of access to proper medical care, they had to use what was readily available: the earth and whatever grew from it.

Every morning, Lotson drinks tea mixed with sassafras, the life everlasting plant, to promote longevity and thwart digestive problems. His family did not have much money when he was growing up. If someone in his family got sick, relatives would find a tall blade of a certain grass whose name eludes Lotson and suck the tart juice from it. When Lotson was a child, he had bronchial problems that threatened his life on a number of occasions. He says of that period, "Never was I suicidal, but if you've ever been in so much pain consistently . . . death was beautiful to me. If there was a plug to pull, I would have pulled it myself." Any time Lotson had a flare-up, his parents would bury a coconut in the ground for seven to ten days, dig it out, then guide Lotson to drink from the fruit. Lotson's father would also take him to a nearby forest and tell him to stand up against a hardwood tree. His father would drive a nail into the spot above Lotson's head. As the tree would continue to grow, so would the sickness grow out of the boy. When his grandmother Florence died, his father took thirteen-year-old Lotson to the funeral home where her body rested, opened the casket, and made Lotson talk to her. After that, his bronchial problems cleared up. At sixty-three years old, he can run seven miles when he's never at any time in his life before run more than two. He does see traditional doctors from time to time, while upholding his beliefs. He does admit that the practices are not as prevalent as they once were, because a lot of root doctors have died off. When Lotson spoke, he never coughed or touched his chest. His voice was as clear as a whistle and strong as a gong. *Wow!* I thought. I believed him.

Lotson's community is vital. The midwife who delivered him is still alive to this day. He remembers the elders warning him against pointing at a graveyard and that one would have to immediately put that finger into the ground, or else. But graveyards, particularly their dust, can also protect you. Lotson told me that he once collected dust off the grave of the last slave on Butler Island, Liverpool Hazzard. If a person was causing you trouble, you get a root worker to blow that dust into the face of the enemy. Lotson once found that he was being messed with himself. While living in DC, as he was entering his vehicle, he discovered a root on the mat near the brake and gas pedal and backed away from the car. "I was trying to lose my fear of this because once you get deep involved in this, it can overwhelm you. So, *phew*, I'm like, 'OK, Lotson, you have got to beat this, you have got to beat this.' Never can I forget all of those things that we did . . . this isn't one of those fake ghost stories, these are real things."

There was an evil that Lotson had to overcome because someone put a root on him by literally sticking a root in his car. He never found out who placed the root there—perhaps a root doctor. I found that many of the most famous root doctors came from the South Carolina Lowcountry. Many took the names of animals: Dr. Eagle, Dr. Hawk, Dr. Snake, Dr. Crow, Dr. Bug. But none of them reached the kind of international acclaim as Dr. Buzzard due to his extensive client list, signature tricks, and showdowns with the local enforcement (which I will describe later).

In her book, *God, Dr. Buzzard, and the Bolito Man*, Cornelia Bailey writes that they believed in the "properties of the earth and all forms of the supernatural . . . God, Dr. Buzzard and the Bolito Man . . . while people my age and older grew up praying to God, we also believed in Dr. Buzzard, the root doctor, whom people in other places call the voodoo man. . . ."[6] In the Lowcountry, God and roots were not in conflict with each other, as they were in the North. For those who are not familiar with the terms, however, I must emphasize that hoodoo and Voodoo are not the same. Hoodoo is a system of magic practices, and many of its practitioners are also Christians. Voodoo is an actual religion with loas (spirits), deities, and veves. The word *veve* is pronounced in two syllables with a short *e* in each. It's similar to a yantra, a mystic diagram used in several Eastern religions. Its purpose is to attract the spirits and focus the mind in interacting with them.

It is believed that Dr. Buzzard put a root on Daufuskie Island, where I went after my time in Georgia. Daufuskie Island was home to more than two hundred Gullah people until the 1980s, when developers decided to make it the Martha's Vineyard of the South. They didn't know that they were building on top of a slave graveyard. The locals consulted Dr. Buzzard for help.[7] Several of the plantations on Daufuskie Island were reconfigured into private-club resort communities. One of them is Melrose. Membership fees were to start at $50,000.[8] In 1984, there was a real estate office at Melrose Plantation that sat on top of a slave cemetery. Golf courses had been laid out over other cemeteries on the island.[9] Locals contacted the NAACP and the Christic Institute, a public interest law firm, for assistance in getting the Melrose Company developers to move the office elsewhere. A court date was set, but before the appointed time, a "flock of buzzards" swarmed the ferry landing. The developers ended up moving the office.[10]

But the Melrose developers did not give up on the land yet. Over twenty years ago, developers funded by institutional investors including International Paper, Halliburton, and ClubCorp decided to build luxury condominiums and gated communities on Daufuskie. But things started to go wrong quickly with what was supposed to be an exciting new resort. In 1997, ClubCorp, an international resort management firm, purchased the Melrose Beach Club of Melrose Resort, along with some properties from Bloody Point—also named after a plantation—in order to combine the lots as "Daufuskie Island, a Pinehurst Company Resort." At the Melrose Beach Club, ClubCorp developers projected that there would be thirty condominiums or ten single-family homes. The development would cost $30.1 million, and projected sales from the properties was $59.4 million.[11] Just two years later, in 1999, it was reported to the United States Securities and Exchange Commission that ClubCorp lost $13.5 million in impairment costs, meaning that they abandoned the land when they figured that it was no longer profitable. Besides these costs, in 1998 and 1999, Daufuskie Island Club and Resort had operating losses of $6.3 million and $6.7 million, respectively.[12]

The property changed hands several times, until its last owner, the Pelorus Group, filed for bankruptcy in 2017. The news was a repeat of 2008, when Bloody Point Golf Club and Beach Resort went bankrupt.[13] Though the Melrose case was dismissed and the property can be sold again, the resort is currently abandoned and has become a bit of a ghost property.[14] Some people believe that the failure of Melrose is due to the fact that Daufuskie Island, though only an hour outside of Hilton Head, is accessible only by ferry. Perhaps if there were a bridge, more people would have traveled there. Many locals, however, like Roger Pinckney XI, believe the downfall had Dr. Buzzard's work all over it. They believe the Melrose venture was cursed.

I had e-mailed Pinckney, a sought-after cultural historian, a month and a half earlier and was lucky enough to score an interview. He often rejected requests. Roger generally can't stand Yankees, so maybe my request was granted because I was black. He was once arrested for protesting efforts by Saudi oil barons to build an enclave on the island. At his home, he even has a sign that says DON'T TREAD ON ME, which to him means "Do not displace me for further vacation-property development on the island."

"The high priest of Daufuskie Island," Pinckney is white and the author of numerous books on African American religion, magic, and folkways. He knew all about Dr. Buzzard and his root. I drove by golf cart from Daufuskie's Freeport Marina to meet Roger and his wife, Amy, for lunch at the Old Daufuskie Crab Company. He greeted me with a bag of sachet powder that bore a graphic sticker of a man pursuing a woman. Sachet powder is common in hoodoo rootwork. It is often some combination of sand, salt, sugar, black pepper, sulfur, red pepper, and even graveyard dirt.[15] I was instructed to keep the bag inside my purse if I wanted to find love. I wondered if this was the same powder that Iris used to pull men to her. Inside a bag, inside a hatband.

The name Pinckney is very prominent in South Carolina. There is Pinckney Island, Pinckney Colony, Pinckney Road, and of course Charles Pinckney, the thirty-seventh governor, a member of the House of Representatives, and a signer of the Constitution. Roger was brought to Daufuskie as a toddler, and his father, also named Roger, a Beaufort County coroner, was partly responsible for bringing electricity there. As a child, Roger knew about root-work through his father's profession. As a coroner, Roger Pinckney X could not list "rootwork" as a cause of death, so instead he would write "dead of undetermined natural causes." When it comes to the protection of him and his family on the island, Roger believes he owes that to Dr. Buzzard.

For about two hours, Roger told me more about this island's ways. As on other Sea Islands, graves would face east, but if the people of the community believed you to be a bad person, you would be put in the grave the wrong way, facing south, to be directed toward hell or, more or less the same thing, to remain in the South. "Nothing normal ever happens here," Roger says with a squint, not to scare me but to underline his own inability to make sense of his environment.

I surmised that if nothing is normal, it's best to lean into the strange—all the rules enforced from the spirit realm. There is goofer dust, a mixture of graveyard dirt and other ingredients, like powdered snakeskin and salt. Your intention and the time of day you collect the goofer dust makes all the difference. Dead time is between 11:30 p.m. and 12:30 a.m. If you want to do good, you collect dust from the grave of a good person and leave coins as recompense. This has to be done before midnight. After midnight, the intention is for evil, and you collect dust from the grave of a bad person.

All kinds of tales circulate around the island. Cemetery watch-keepers say they see graveyards lit up like day in the middle of the night. People have experiences with ghosts, which locals like Roger just cuss out to leave them be. There are tales of buzzards hanging around developers. And there are plat-eyes. At mention of the word *plat-eye*, Roger and his wife shift uncomfortably in their seats. According to West Indian and Southern American folklore, plat-eyes are monsters, animals with glowing eyes or spirits that can pass through gates without opening them. One man, suicidal after breaking up with his girlfriend, took a bottle of liquor off one of the graves on Edisto Island at three a.m. and was found neck-deep in nearby rice fields the next day. Legend has it that after he took the bottle, a plat-eye took the form of his ex-lover and lured him to those fields, where he almost drowned, but he survived. Roger and Amy are thankful that they have never seen a plat-eye, but others have, and they say plat-eyes can take the shape of any-thing from a horse to a two-headed dog.

The shapeshifting narrative echoes across regions. The stories that my grandfather tried to tell to me as a child, the ones I tried to ignore, were similar.

"A demon followed him all the way home. People say it was a ghost, but it was really a demon," my grandfather said at his dining room table. He was sitting across from his older brother, Sam.

"What happened, Uncle Sam?" I asked and turned toward him.

"Mother sent me to the store. I just had a weird feeling and I didn't want to go. I had to walk down there at night. It wasn't dark until I got to that hill and it started getting darker and darker. I was coming through the woods and I was moving a little slower. I seen this great, big, white thing—bigger than any sheet. Maybe four or five sheets. I don't know how tall it was, but it was coming right for me. It kept on, kept on."

"Were you on your way to the store or coming back?" my grand-father asked Uncle Sam.

"On my way to the store, and I had to go the same way back. Boy, I prayed a prayer that time. It got closer and closer and I didn't know what to do. I was throwing dirt like crazy at him. Just throwing dirt."

"You never told us about this," my grandfather said.

"Scared me to death," Uncle Sam said.

My great-grandmother warned her children not to use the path that led to Iris's house. But my Uncle Curtis was what he called hard-headed, so he went down the path anyway. "That night when I left, I was coming back home, and I heard this"—he starts tapping on the table—"*tipping* in the woods and the leaves. I'm walking and I'm hearing these footsteps. Those footsteps and those leaves followed me until I got to the highway. Then when I got to the highway, it seemed like it was a dog following me, because you could hear its nails hitting the concrete. Then when I got ready to make that right turn and go down to Jackson Road to go to our house, I'm scared to death 'cause I don't know what this thang is that I'm hearing. I'm looking but I ain't seeing it."

"Wasn't it dark, though?" I asked.

"The moon was shining bright. So I'm coming down that road, and all of a sudden, when I get there to the house, I'm scared to run—and I could run pretty fast in those days. If I run, I might run past the house. But we had the light up. Just as I got to the house, this thang went through the woods. It was broomstraw grass, look like the broom that you sweep, and that thang went through the woods like that. You could see the grass parting."

"Curt made it home that night," my grandfather said. Everyone was silent for a moment. I was afraid to ask if they'd worried that Uncle Curtis wouldn't, or if anyone else's children weren't as fortunate. Their faces showed that they were indeed terrified.

Was it a dog? Was it a witch? Was it a spirit? Was it a demon? Uncle Curtis couldn't say. All he could rely on was his hearing. To be honest, I thought this story was funny. But then again, unlike my grandparents and his siblings, I have never lived in an environment where the supernatural injected itself into everyday living. My concept of the supernatural came from books, movies, and TV shows. I didn't know that world. Luckily, nothing happened to Uncle Sam, as nothing happened to Roger Pinckney and his wife. Back at lunch, Pinckney called over one of his friends, a black Daufuskie native, to talk about the shapeshifters on the island. He maintained a polite smile, but besides acknowledging and greeting me, he said nothing else. He obviously didn't want to talk about shapeshifters, perhaps out of fear that he would summon them or trigger some terrible memories.

As for my Uncle Sam, I found it odd that at the time when he saw this large, ghostly figure, he made no mention of screaming. Instead, he grabbed some dirt and flung it at the apparition, almost as if he instinctively knew exactly what to do. Nothing happened to Uncle Sam, either. Uncle Curtis's apparition fled once he made it home. Sam wasn't near home, but he could grab a piece of the soil and banish whatever spirit that was. In hoodoo, dirt, especially graveyard dirt, is used to ward off evil intentions and spirits. As Stephanie Rose Bird says in her book, *Sticks, Stones, Roots, & Bones*, "Graveyard dirt . . . contains the spirit of the ancestors, the folk who look after us and mediate the spirit world." Moreover, dirt in general is potent "because the earth is our mother . . . we can go to her for comfort, contemplation, and peace of mind."[16] Although my uncle Sam doesn't practice hoodoo and condemns it all as demonic, he still knew in a moment of fight or flight to grab for the earth as the only defense he had.

I often wonder how my family toggles between belief and disbelief, disdain and acceptance of spiritual forces. There seems to be no reconciliation between the two. Somehow, they believe that to acknowledge its strength and not immediately tie it to something evil would be to spite God himself. But in Uncle Sam's story, in that moment of fear, something instinctive was activated inside him, to use earth to protect himself. How was that any different from what Griffin Lotson or Tiffany Young did? Maybe his method was simple, because he didn't have time to do anything elaborate or he didn't remember, just as he didn't remember what exactly that root doctor did to cure his mother.

Maybe roots, like water, evoke disdain, fear, and loss. Maybe we were conditioned to stay away from them because no one could recall a time when rootwork was in harmony with the Bible. But when Uncle Sam said that he prayed and then grabbed some soil, I felt hope. God and the earth were never enemies. After visiting Darien and Daufuskie, I knew better. Uncle Sam's spirit knew better, and so did the ancestors.

I thought once more about Iris and how the desire for a man—someone else's man—can be the motive for rootwork. When I traveled to Saint Helena Island in South Carolina, I saw the outcome of said motive in real time. I met with Victoria Smalls, program manager of the International African American Museum there, who intimately knew about roots and the depths of their power when a woman—or women—are envious. Victoria is a light-skinned six-foot-four-inch woman with dark, curly hair. She gave me a warm hug, as if we were reuniting after a long absence. Spiritually, perhaps we were.

There is a difference between root doctor and a root worker. As Victoria puts it, "So there's root working, root practitioners, and root doctors, and root doctors can do 'em all. A root worker is someone who's maybe gonna put a spell or conjure something up. A practitioner is someone who can maybe also do some holistic care, and a doctor is someone that can do all of the above, and do [psychic] surgery and heal you."

Now things were making sense in my grandfather's story. There was a reason why he called Iris a root worker and the person who cured my great-grandmother a root doctor. Iris wanted a curse, and the doctor could heal and undo said curse.

Before Victoria had taken her current position, she was the director of history, art, and culture, as well as the director of development and public relations at the Penn Center, where we stopped first on our tour.[17] The Penn Center has been a National Historic Landmark since 1974, and two major buildings on campus were declared part of a Reconstruction Era National Monument by former President Obama just before he left office in 2017. It was a school for blacks that was begun in 1862 by abolitionist missionaries soon after the Union captured Saint Helena and gave plantation land to freed slaves. In less than seventy years, enrollment ballooned from eighty to six hundred students. From 1901 on, in addition to regular subjects, like math and reading, students learned industrial trades, such as blacksmithing, carpentry, and agriculture, as well as the requirements of land ownership. Tuition was twenty-five or fifty cents, depending on your family's income, and work-study was also an option: girls tended to do laundry or make sweetgrass baskets to sell, and the boys would cast nets. The Penn Center is also significant for its role in political activism. Members of the Southern Christian Leadership Conference (SCLC) would meet here in secret, and Dr. Martin Luther King Jr.'s early drafts of his "I Have a Dream" speech were written at the center. A cottage was built for him, but he was assassinated before he ever had a chance to use it.

Victoria has a personal connection to the center, as well as a professional one. After we drove through the forest behind the Penn Center and past Dr. King's cottage, we sat down on a gazebo that overlooks Chowan Creek, where she told me about her family. Her father, a Penn Center alumnus, was first married to a black woman, and together they had six children. His wife later passed, and her father continued to live with Victoria's grandmother on heirs property, land passed down from generation to generation, usually with no will. Her mother, Laura, who lived in Petoskey, Michigan, was a white woman, a widow with four children of her own. Laura traveled to the Penn Center for a Bahá'í Faith conference, where in the 1960s she met Victoria's father and fell in love with him. It was against the law for interracial couples to marry in South Carolina, so they traveled to Michigan and returned to Saint Helena as husband and wife. According to Victoria, her parents were the first to integrate the island, but that union came with a price.

You see, her father was well loved. He stood six-six, had a deep bass voice, and projected command in whatever room he entered. When his first wife died, there were many women waiting to be the new Mrs., but when he chose a woman outside of the community—a white one at that—the local women banded together and consulted Buzzy, Dr. Buzzard's son, another root worker. Buzzy told Victoria's father that he had some trouble coming his way.

Dr. Buzzy's curse was that none of Victoria's father's sons born within the next forty years would have a son with the surname Smalls. The only male family member to have a son was Victoria's younger brother, who became a father at forty-four. But the curse also claimed Victoria's son. At six foot six and 240 pounds, her son played football but also excelled in his academics. By the time he was in the tenth grade, he had scholarship offers from the University of South Carolina, Auburn, and Ohio State. But in the beginning of football season during his junior year, he tore his knee and had to get surgery less than two weeks later. Percocet and morphine plummeted him into depression. Her son was living with his father, whose gun he took to end his own life. It wasn't until the very end of our trip that Victoria paused and realized that this happened before the forty-year curse was over. She pinpoints the curse happening around 1968 or '69, and her deceased son was born in 1998. On his obituary, his last name is Jones, but he was born Julian Smalls.

Dr. Buzzard was known everywhere, but Saint Helena was his domain. His birth name was Stephany Robinson, and he was allegedly born with a caul, or within the amniotic sac. In African American folklore, those born with a caul are said to have psychic and healing powers. Victoria told me that native islanders would see him in a boat on Chowan Creek and a buzzard would be hovering over his body. To onlookers, it appeared as if the buzzard was moving the boat against the tide. It is believed among locals and historians that Robinson's father was illegally smuggled into Saint Helena from West Africa and passed his rootwork on to his son, who began making a name for himself in the early 1900s. His most famous specialty was "chewing the root." On the days of trials, Dr. Buzzard would chew a root in court in order to protect defendants from harsh sentences or guilty verdicts altogether. One of Dr. Buzzard's descendants, Mr. Gregory, who is a third-generation root worker and still alive today, helped Roger Pinckney with this "shut-mouth" special. When Pinckney was in court fighting with his ex-wife over property, Mr. Gregory gave Pinckney some roots for him to chew while looking his ex-wife in the eye. She ended up slobbering all over herself and couldn't testify. The cost for shut-mouth special was a little over a hundred dollars, which, according to Pinckney, was "cheaper than a lawyer." Dr. Buzzard's shut-mouth special was so well known that eight or nine cars at a time would be parked in Dr. Buzzard's driveway, each with a different state's license plate.[18]

One person who had had enough of Dr. Buzzard's meddling with the law was J. E. McTeer, a Beaufort County sheriff from 1926 to 1963. At first, McTeer tried to charge Dr. Buzzard with practicing medicine without a license. The first attempt led to a witness convulsing on the stand, foreshadowing the rest of the trial. In order to align the spiritual with the spiritual, McTeer began to learn rootwork himself. When I spoke to J. E. McTeer's grandson James, an author, he couldn't wait to regale me with stories of other root doctors of the time, especially Dr. Bug, who gave arsenic-laced cotton balls to his patients to give them heart palpitations and so they'd be passed over for the World War II draft. But Dr. Buzzard was the biggest root doctor, his legacy unmatched to this day. J. E. McTeer, like Dr. Buzzard, was born in the Lowcountry and raised by a Gullah woman. He had already had some familiarity with rootwork and became the only person in the McTeer family to practice it.

Dr. Buzzard and J. E. McTeer's rivalry came to a head when Dr. Buzzard's son mysteriously died in a car accident.[19] Some say that Dr. Buzzard's son lost control of the car and drowned in a nearby body of water, but Dr. Buzzard believed that the accident was J. E. McTeer's doing. In any case, the two men called a truce and Dr. Buzzard paid a small fine. Dr. Buzzard died of stomach cancer in 1947, and the location of his grave has been kept a secret for fear that his body would be dug up and used for magical purposes or simply desecrated altogether. After Woods Memorial Bridge was built, connecting mainland Beaufort County to the Sea Islands like Saint Helena, rootwork was pushed into the shadows as tourists came in and snapped up all the land that Gullah people couldn't afford.[20]

The Woods Memorial Bridge made a connection where the water once separated. That the water served as preservative for Victoria's people is what makes it special. I found my time with Victoria profound because she would not elaborate on her lineage and the stories attached to her family tree until she brought me to the water.

On the river, just a short drive away from the Penn Center, there was a slight breeze, and I was transfixed by the large cypress trees whose leaves swayed behind her. That breeze, along with her buttery voice, transported me to a faraway place. I wasn't in South Carolina anymore. I was someplace else entirely, ancient and foreign and yet present and familiar. It felt like what I would imagine the coasts of Western Africa to be: unadulterated and wide. I felt ensconced in protection from a place beyond what my eyes could see. I'm a petite black woman driving around the Deep South, so naturally there were moments when I felt that my safety was in jeopardy. Yet somehow, I also felt that I was being watched over. Even writing this confession of what I sensed feels embarrassing. I can't adequately explain feeling protected, but I was. My being here documenting all of this is proof of that.

Victoria brought me to the water to discuss roots in order for me to understand the process. In order to reach the root doctor, you would have to cross over multiple bodies of water because of its supernatural force. To Victoria, the soil and water are powerful, though she is at a loss for words to explain their strength. That power, she argues, comes from West Africa, but after African Americans were Christianized and Americanized, she says, we forgot how much memory the water and land hold. "We forget all of these wonderful powers of the forest and the land. We've forgotten a lot, but it sneaks out in the Gullah culture." *It sure does sneak out*, I thought. Iris and my uncle Sam were testaments to this—all the way from Newtonville, New Jersey. We're tethered to land and water—to Earth—whether we realize it or not. Yet despite this collective forgetfulness, Victoria believes that we receive reminders. The following privileged encounter was mine.

Here I saw two stories that brushed up against each other: my grandfather's and Victoria's. Here were two African Americans who knew about the power of the root. The former condemned it, and the latter exalted it. Their memories included blotches and omissions, but I wanted to create a bridge as strong as the one I stood upon at Chowan Creek. The truth is, in the nineteenth century, Christianity and conjuring, or rootwork, were most likely flourishing on the same soil . . . and in South Carolina at that. A folklorist named William Owens noticed that black people's superstitions combined with the Christian faith, resulting in "horrific debasement." Christianity and superstition, in his eyes, should be incompatible. But for black people, Christianity and conjure work were, at one point, congruent with each other. After emancipation, conjure did slip into churches, like those in Missouri and North Carolina. Dr. Buzzard financed the largest church in Saint Helena. Conjurers and black Pentecostals both practice faith healing. As Yvonne Chireau, professor of religion at Swarthmore College, puts it, "Pentecostal belief revolved around invisible forces, beings, and powers in the spiritual realm, and like Conjure practitioners, Pentecostalists viewed unusual events as signs of divine or satanic intervention in the spiritual realm."[21] When African Americans migrated to the North, many sought to change their lives not only economically, but also culturally. Some saw conjure as backward. Because of their better access to education and health care, many disavowed conjure as part of the past, an embarrassing remnant of their Southern heritage.[22] Our rejection of conjure was a by-product of our movement away from the South and into the middle class and cities.

Later that evening, I went back to my hotel room and checked in my bag for the powder that Pinckney had given me, only to find that the sachet had burst at the seams. "Oh, hell," I said to myself. What should I do now? I could either get a wet rag and clean up the powdered remains at the depths of my bag or leave it. I chose the latter. Then I felt bad about it. Then I questioned why. Did I expect to be in demonic possession? Did I leave myself vulnerable to bad spirits? I wasn't sure. All I knew was that I'd had a long day, I was tired, and I had been given a gift.

As I was drifting off to sleep, I did worry that I would be overwhelmed with nightmares or that I'd hear strange sounds in the middle of the night. Although Mr. Pinckney was kind enough to grant my interview request, I'd still accepted a gift from someone whom I did not intimately know. My mother would've been furious if I had told her. There could've been anything in that sachet powder, and if something were to happen to me, if I were to be hexed—a possibility that my mother and now I believe in—I wouldn't know whom to consult to undo the spell.

Luckily, I woke up the next morning feeling just the same as when I laid my head down on the pillow the night before. I slept so deeply that I couldn't remember my dreams. I packed my belongings and made my way to the airport, and in the days that followed, men would not leave me alone. Men approached me in random places and complimented my appearance in the South with such frequency that I thought I was back in New York. Despite that, I didn't feel hexed. I still don't. From that day on, I didn't fear conjure any longer, because I had seen what it could do for others. I am now uncomfortable with calling conjure demonic, because in invoking that word, I drive a wedge between me and those in the South, like Victoria Smalls and Griffin Lotson, who educated me on both its good and bad sides.

When I returned to New York, I researched the Book of Psalms and the spells that could be cast from it. I studied how honey jars could bring sweetness into my life, how roses can invite love, and how the lighting of different colored candles can yield different results, such as white for healing and purification and purple for spiritual protection. I have not done any spells because, admittedly, I'm uncertain—though how much different are these practices from eating collard greens for money and black-eyed peas for luck?

I have made a compromise between what I grew up with and what I witnessed on my trip. My grandmother's anointing olive oil still rests on my kitchen counter near my door. I bought a bottle of Florida Water, often used by hoodoo practitioners for home protection and energy cleansing. Florida Water, or Agua de Florida, smells wonderful. The aroma is light, based on citrus flowers, often with bergamot, cinnamon, or other scents. Before starting a writing session, I pray—as I've always done before my travels—then I spray Florida Water around my office for good measure. The ritual is very small, but it's my own way of realigning the past and the present, my Southern and Northern roots.

4

AFTER I SPOKE with Victoria Smalls, her words lingered in my mind: "We forget how much memory the water and land hold." I had learned something about how water and roots function in African American life, but now it was time to focus on the land itself and ask my grandfather the most critical question: "Why did you all leave?" I wanted to know more about the difference between what happened to those who stayed, like Victoria Smalls and Griffin Lotson, and what happened to those who left. I wanted to study the rupture of community and what it does to memory.

"I guess I can tell the story now," my grandfather said in a measured tone.

My maternal family's trajectory began with my great-grandfather, whose name was Fred Andrew Jerkins I. Five generations of men in my family bear his name. He was born in Americus, Georgia, and he married Gladys Wiggins of Andersonville, Georgia. The Wigginses were a well-to-do black family who owned a plantation near Sumter County; the Jerkins family were sharecroppers at first, before they were able to afford to buy their own land. Gladys bore sixteen children, but three did not survive into adulthood. From what my mother told me, she had a child every year; she passed in her fifties. There is about a twenty-five-year age difference between her eldest and youngest child, who is only a year older than one of their grandchildren, my aunt Sharene. Life was idyllic until the accident happened.

Fred was driving a car one night and hit a white man. No one in my family can confirm if that man survived. Fred jumped out of his vehicle and made a run for it through the woods where some of his relatives lived. Those relatives told him that he had to leave town or else he would be killed. News had spread fast. Fred I was no stranger to the threat of a noose. From 1877–1950, Georgia was second only to Mississippi in the number of lynchings.[1] As a teenager, he would hear other black people being lynched—their screams, their pleas for mercy—and he knew that there was nothing he could say to absolve him of hurting a white person, even if it was an accident. The white overseer of the cotton plantation was fond of my great-grandfather's productivity and hid Fred in the trunk to drive him as far as he could, while a mob was screaming Fred's name and vowing to string him up. The overseer drove him until the path was blocked by a body of water. Fred crossed that water by himself, traveled some ways, and found refuge with a relative near the border of Georgia and Florida. No one knows how long he was gone, but the coast was clear after another black man's body was found floating in the water near Americus. White people thought Fred had died—maybe some other whites got to him first, or maybe he just drowned. Either way, he was gone.

Fred returned to Americus and tried to continue his life as though nothing had happened. He worked in the cotton fields as he had before the accident. However, as soon as word got out that Fred I was very much alive, a white mob showed up at the plantation where he worked. His "employer," who my grandfather said was a mean man, invited the mob to kill him but then said whoever took the first step would get shot with his Winchester rifle. No one harmed him. Fred I stayed in Americus, settled down with my great-grandmother, and had children, but in the back of his mind, he was always worried that someone would find him hanging from a tree branch. Fred saved his money, and the Jerkins family left Georgia while my grandfather was still a baby, taking the railroad to Philadelphia, where over two hundred thousand black refugees, primarily from Virginia, South Carolina, Maryland, and Georgia, had already called the City of Brotherly Love their new home. Had my great-grandfather not fled from Americus, he might well have been murdered. My grandfather would have never been born, and therefore I would not be alive. The first time he fled was for self-preservation. The second time was for the preservation of his entire family.

The Jerkins family, which by that time was my great-grandparents and a few of their children, spent only two weeks in Philadelphia before they moved to Newtonville, New Jersey. There, Fred I taught his sons how to drive a tractor and fish for catfish, halibut, and bass. Their mother preserved watermelon rinds, peaches, and apples in a nearby cellar. If there was no food in the house, Fred I would tell Gladys to make the gravy and biscuits and he'd be right back. He'd take his shotgun, and after one *pop*, he'd come back with a bloodied blackbird in his hand. They grew all kinds of vegetables. "Anything you can think of," my uncles Curtis and Sam rhapsodized. Fred I trapped 'coons and possums, and he and his wife made wine and moonshine, an extra hustle that landed him in jail for a short period of time. "That's the thing about young people today," Uncle Curtis continued. "If something happened, they would not know how to fend for themselves. They wouldn't know what to do." Back then, the Jerkins family was self-sustaining. I asked my mother, Sybil, if she knew how to trap animals. She yelled, "No! Why in the world would I wanna do that?" My grandfather said that was mostly for the boys.

For two years, my grandfather lived in Springfield, Massachusetts, with an aunt while he went to high school there, but then he returned around the age of sixteen to wash dishes at an Atlantic City hotel right off Illinois Avenue. At the age of twenty-one, he got into construction work, went to a church service at Morning Star Baptist in Pleasantville, seven miles outside of Atlantic City, and immediately became besotted with my grandmother, sixteen-year-old Sylvia Lucas. They married soon after and lived on Bacharach Boulevard, where my aunt Sharene and my mother, Sybil, were born within nineteen months of each other.

My grandmother was a housekeeper for a wealthy white family in Margate, another community along the Jersey Shore, where racial covenants barred black families from buying or renting homes. Sylvia would frequently dress her children in the finest clothes, and it wasn't until years later that my mother realized that these were hand-me-downs from the Mitsons, one of the white families my grandmother worked for. My grandfather owned a Buick even though they lived in the projects. They worried about the safety of their family. Atlantic City was very dangerous at that time, so they decided to move outside of the city and into a quieter and whiter suburb in Atlantic County. At the time, lenders were charging black people 13 or 14 percent interest on loans to dissuade them from moving into two-level homes in residential communities. My grandparents were not dissuaded. My grandfather—who refused to take my grandmother's earnings from housekeeping—pooled his resources from construction work and savings, got two loans from two different companies, and paid close to five times more than their white neighbors to move into Pomona, the second black family on the block. The local KKK chapter got word of the new arrivals and burned crosses in their backyard. White kids threw mangled cats at my sister and mother. To this day, my mother harbors a fear of cats due to the trauma. To protect his children, my grandfather drove them to the bus stop to make sure they at least made it to school unscathed. But beyond that, my mother recalls that her parents did nothing else. "We were just scared," my mother says. And like her grandfather's fear in Americus, their fear was constant. It persisted in spite of their continuing to live in the place a long time, because their presence was not welcome. The fear became familiar, normal, and finally innate.

The middle-class lifestyle was what my family dreamed of back on Bacharach Boulevard. There were better schools, more stable residential communities, and greater safety in Pomona—or so we thought. The move was supposed to be a physical and psychic reset. Though Sharene and Sybil were taught to cook, they were not taught to hunt, fish, or make fruit preserves. They never traveled to Americus, Georgia.

It was only through the creation of this book that my mother, who is in her fifties, found out that her father wasn't even born in New Jersey. I'll never forget how my mother looked when she realized this. Her face sank. Her jaw went slack. Ironically, at the moment when our family history was being recovered, she was at a loss for words. She hardly blinked as we sat, stunned within the silence between us. I wondered if she felt disappointed in herself as a parent or in her own parents for not having passed these stories down in conversations over dinner or by a fireplace, before they would be presented to a wider audience in a book.

My grandfather had been to Americus only once, when he was six or seven. His parents brought him to the cotton fields, but he cannot recall anything else from his experiences there. Neither I, my sister, nor any of my cousins has ever been to Sumter County. We don't know what happened to the acres of land that my family was able to afford from their earnings as sharecroppers. All we know is that Fred Jerkins I was the last owner. I wanted to know more about the time when black land was vast and how the migration of blacks from the lands that they tilled led to an uphill battle for those who stayed put. In Gullah Geechee territory, I didn't have to look too far.

According to Leah Douglas of the *Nation*, "In the 45 years following the Civil War, freed slaves and their descendants accumulated roughly 15 million acres of land across the United States, most of it in the South." What this land meant for freed slaves was a chance for intergenerational wealth and economic mobility. But in the twentieth century, about six hundred thousand black farmers lost their land. Some of the reasons: systemic racism by the United States Department of Agriculture, the attraction of black Southerners to work in Northern factories, and thus the Great Migration.[2] My great-grandfather was one of those six hundred thousand. My great-great-grandfather was that sharecropper who worked within the forty-five years following the Civil War, and he was able to buy land so that my great-grandfather would own it outright. No one knows if Fred Jerkins I gave up the land willingly or involuntarily. All my grandfather and his siblings can tell me is that in 1944 or '45, they boarded a train from Georgia to Philadelphia, where relatives awaited them, and that was that.

In 1869 the Gullah Geechee people owned half of Beaufort County of South Carolina. Since then, they've lost fourteen million acres.[3] The best example of the rapid marginalization of Gullah Geechee people is on Hilton Head Island, one of the most lucrative places in the South.

In 2018, the *Conde Nast Traveler* ranked Hilton Head Island as the best island resort area in the United States for the second year in a row, and for good reason.[4] The island is full of world-class resorts, delectable cuisine, and sandy beaches, and it generally has idyllic weather. But beyond the optics of a wonderful vacation spot, there's a grim side. Although Gullah Geechee people are spread out all across the island, their biggest concentration is in the north end. Hilton Head Island was once one large plantation. After the Civil War, freed black people bought land from the United States government and settled into what was the first self-governed town of formerly enslaved black people in the country: Mitchelville. Other pieces of land were sold to (white) speculators or previous plantation owners, who settled on the south end. In

1956, Charles Fraser, the son of a well-off family who made their fortune in timber, started the "modern" era in Hilton Head by creating the first resort, Sea Pines Plantation, on the south end, constructing a bridge to connect to the mainland, and bringing air-conditioning to the island.[5] But over time, developers wanted to expand to the north, as well, and were ultimately successful. The lack of legal protection for those who had heirs property, the rising land taxes, and the exodus of African Americans leaving the South in general as a part of the Great Migration, all allowed Fraser to succeed in converting most of Hilton Head into a prime resort community.

Over 80 percent of "early black landowners" from the post–Civil War period and later did not have wills or clear titles. These landowners simply passed down their acres to their descendants or relatives as what is called heirs property. But families who have heirs property cannot get mortgages, do home repairs, apply for state or federal aid, get conservation funding, or take out loans available through the US Department of Agriculture.[6] My grandfather doesn't recall any kind of will or title that his father received from *his* father (my great-great-grandfather), so it is very likely that the land Fred Jerkins I inherited was heirs property.

Heirs property is one of the biggest issues when it comes to black land preservation and cultural heritage on Hilton Head Island.

I perused the internet to find Hilton Head locals who were outspoken about the effects of business expansion into predominantly Gullah Geechee communities, and found Taiwan Scott. Coincidentally, Taiwan—or Tai, for short—was born in New Jersey like me. But unlike me, Tai has traveled regularly to his grandmother's birthplace in Hilton Head and decided as an adult to move there to help preserve Gullah Geechee heritage. Unlike any other person I'd met from the Lowcountry, Scott was a real estate agent and therefore was willing to divulge his personal and professional stakes in Hilton Head. At the time that I was scheduled to meet him, Scott was in the midst of an ongoing battle with the town to run a business on his own property, and he believed the local media was not adequately covering the story.

I drove away from Savannah via I-95 North and then 278 through Jasper County and Bluffton to Hilton Head, and to this day, it is one of the most beautiful drives I've ever been on. The sun was shining, the trees flanked the streets, and I could see the glistening water from the bridges I crossed over to get to the island. But it was in Hilton Head where I soon learned how beautiful landscapes masked black carnage that was simplified and mocked at every turn. I saw the word *plantation* so much that I was starting to get a headache: Plantation Cafe & Grill, Plantation Cafe & Deli, Plantation Shopping Center, Paper & Party Plantation, Plantation Drive, Plantation Road, Plantation Club, Plantation Animal Hospital, Plantation Interiors, Plantation Cabinetry, Plantation Station Inc. . . . With every road I passed, there was another indication of a perverse symmetry between leisure and slavery. The Northerner in me was disoriented, to say the least. I had to keep focus and keep my hands steady on the wheel. I wanted to swerve my car into one of those stores, cut my eyes at an employee, and say, "There's blood running all over this fuckin' store. Tell your boss a nigga said that." But this fantasy only showed how strange Hilton Head's normal was, that a strip of land once worked, then owned and worked by Gullah Geechee people had now become a place where their kind was not welcome.

On the island's north end, I met Taiwan Scott on his property at 15 Marshland Road. We sat outside in the warm, muggy weather where Taiwan talked about himself and his family's history. Tai has invested time poring over archaeological studies on the island to match the locations of praise houses and cemeteries to new buildings and developments. He was stunned that anyone got clearance to construct, because these places hold such cultural and spiritual significance. Meanwhile, Tai's property sat languishing because there was what he believed to be miles of red tape for a Gullah-owned business to prosper or exist at all.

Tai claims that his business would have been the first Gullah native-owned commercial retail establishment to open on the owner's own land since the Town of Hilton Head Island was incorporated. The plan was to have a food-truck-style restaurant and a shop where fruit, vegetables, seafood, jewelry, and sweetgrass baskets would be sold. The food truck and kitchen were already DHEC (South Carolina Department of Health and Environmental Control) approved. Traditional Gullah food was to be served. Initially, he was told by the local government that they did not want food trucks on the island, but they wanted to see his development concept. His initial development concept would have cost around $50,000. After the town government's less-than-enthusiastic response to his plan, the concept escalated to nearly twice that amount because he was told that he was in a flood area and everything had to be elevated. He would also need to include a wrap-around deck. With the comments from the town government in hand, Tai began to read their rules and regulations book, and found a section that would allow his food truck without any of the flood-elevation requirements. After sitting down with local officials, he was given the OK to proceed. During the design-review process, he was told that his building was too orange, despite the color being a cedar natural tone with a transparent stain. On a trip around town, he spotted a building within Shelter Cove Harbor, a newly developed upscale waterfront community, with bright orange awnings over the door and windows. Afterward, Tai consulted his white next-door neighbor, who owns a successful honey business. This neighbor showed up to a town meeting and went on record supporting Tai and his business plan. They even established a working relationship, because up to twenty cars at a time would be parked on Tai's property, and those visitors could be potential patrons for the neighbor's business too.

"One week later, the town officials call this guy in to this meeting about my establishment. The guy comes back out of this meeting and says, 'I don't want anything to do with you or your property, and I don't want to smell *any Gullah fried chicken.*' I said, 'What do you mean? What happened?' He says, 'Well, I just don't want to be a part of this.' I said, 'What happened in the meeting?' When I cut my grass, I used to cut this guy's grass. Our daughters were on the same soccer team for three seasons."

I wondered why Scott didn't know what happened in the town meeting; these kinds of meetings usually have someone recording what happens. "They didn't have minutes?"

"No minutes. I did a freedom-of-information request. They said they weren't obligated to take any minutes to this meeting . . . because it wasn't an official public meeting."

"Oh, OK. So once it was discussed, it wasn't open to the public."

"They had a closed door meeting . . ."

". . . that they didn't invite *you* to."

". . . about my establishment."

Upon further research, Tai found that at one time, members of the Gullah community owned all kinds of businesses, like a seamstress shop, gas stations, and fishing co-ops. If an establishment like Ruby Lee's—a Gullah-owned restaurant that was once in the community but moved to the South End near the vacationers' stomping grounds—is in a plaza, the people do not own the land itself. What has happened to Tai and his business has caused a shock wave among the native islanders, since Tai spread the word about what's going on. Some elders have encouraged him to stop pressing the local government to make things right. Others' hopes are dashed for any economic mobility.

Tai says, "We have people in the back right now. They're in the back of their houses doing the cooking or whatever, and they're afraid to come out. It's like . . . we should not be afraid thinking that the town's gonna come and shut us down."

"Mmm-hmm. Now, when you say they're in the back, what do you mean?"

"When I say they're in the back, that means they're not publicly letting people know that they're open for business."

"Why? What are they afraid of?"

"The town shutting them down. Because they live in an area that's zoned residential, but they want to do some type of commercial establishment. See, at one time, we owned a piece of property. We had our business in the front, and we lived in the back. So what has happened to me, a lot of people are saying, 'No, we don't even try. Here it is. Tai with the paper route trying to do it, and they're stopping him and they won't even answer him.'" His persistence has come with a cost. He fears for his wife and children. In 2017, a white pickup truck often circled around his home. Banana trees that grew on his property were dug up, and the security camera on his Marshland lot was smashed.

Though Scott purchased 15 Marshland Road back in 1997 as a single-family residence *and* commercial business, he's still mindful of those whose land is considered heirs property and as a real estate agent tries to help them make the best decisions. He's one of only a handful of black real estate agents on the island. Ideally, Scott would like Gullah people to keep their heirs property but if they cannot and are forced to sell, he wants them to get the best offer available. Hilton Head is continuing to develop, and therefore the property taxes are going to steadily rise. He said to me, "I had one client—seventeen thousand dollars a year in taxes. I mean how can they afford to keep that? So they're forced to sell it."

To give me a more well-rounded sense of this divided place, Tai took me on a tour around the island. Within a half hour or so, I was able to distinguish between Gullah land, with its mobile park homes and weeds growing wildly on the lawns, and the plantations—or gated communities—where a pass is required for entry and we could only see an entrance sign with a long trail to the security booth behind it. Today the word *plantation* is code for luxury, and gated communities have caused the natives to become purposely displaced. These homes are in the plantation communities, whose names are Hilton Head, Indigo Run, Long Cove, Palmetto Dunes/Shelter Cove, Palmetto Hall, Port Royal, Sea Pines, Shipyard Plantation, Spanish Wells, Wexford, and Windmill Harbour. In 2016, 77 percent of the Hilton Head population was white and under 7 percent was black. Over 10 percent of the population was in poverty, but of those in poverty, 30.6 percent were black, whereas only 5.4 percent were white.[7]

The way the plantation system works down here is that the people within it literally reside in a world apart. On Hilton Head Plantation, two patrols are on duty twenty-four hours a day. They provide home checks when residents are away, medical assistance, and alarm response. In other words, when something happens behind those gates, residents don't call the county; they have their own policing inside.[8] Gated communities like those on Hilton Head exist nationwide and are set up to quell white people's anxieties about having contact with what transpires beyond their neighborhoods. In the 1860s, there were twenty-four plantations on Hilton Head Island.[9] In a *New York Times* op-ed, contributor Rich Benjamin writes, "No matter the label, the product is the same: self-contained, conservative and overzealous in its demands for 'safety.' Gated communities churn a vicious cycle by attracting like-minded residents who seek shelter from outsiders and whose physical seclusion then worsens paranoid groupthink against outsiders."[10] The rebranding of plantations as gated communities also appeals to the white imagination. An adjunct professor of anthropology at the University of Tennessee–Knoxville, Melissa Hargrove wrote in her PhD dissertation on this spatial segregation. "For the Gullah, this practice has translated into a reinvention of history that denies the collective memories intimately linking them to these recently appropriated spaces."[11]

One of these collective memories is of the way the Gullah people honor the dead. Alex Brown, chairman of the Hilton Head Town Planning Commission, whose family has been in Hilton Head for eight generations, knows of Gullah burial grounds within three plantations: Hilton Head, Sea Pines, and Indigo Run. About five years ago, one of Brown's closest friends passed away and was set to be buried in Indigo Run. Because that friend was a motorcyclist, Brown and his social circle decided to ride motorcycles to the funeral in his honor. However, the bikes weren't allowed. Brown isn't sure whether this restriction was discriminatory, but demonstrates that the gated communities make rules independent of the town. Whereas the Butler Island Plantation slaves were underwater, Taiwan's family is buried underneath a prestigious golf course. His ancestors and countless others are buried in Harbor Town Cemetery on Sea Pines Plantation where South Carolina's only annual RBC Heritage PGA tournament is held, a renowned event that Taiwan aches to see. He's even been a part of protests during this event to call attention to Gullah displacement.[12] With regard to preservation, the state of South Carolina, SC Code of Laws 27–43–210 states:

> This law grants family members and descendants limited access to graves on private property. It requires owners of cemeteries on private property to provide reasonable access to family members and descendants of those buried in the cemetery. The law requires the person wanting access to the cemetery to submit a written request to the property owner.[13]

Descendants of someone who's buried in a cemetery on private property must rely on the goodwill of a property owner and petition said person, whether they're natives or visitors, to pay respects to their own people. Furthermore, one may have to pay a fee, as is the case with Sea Pines Plantation. There is a three-dollar fee, like the entrance fee to a state park, for locals to visit their deceased relatives. That alongside having to explain themselves to security guards makes it hard for the Gullah people to maintain their connection to the land.[14]

Tish Lynn is director of communications and outreach for the Center for Heirs Property Preservation, a Charleston-based nonprofit organization working to help heirs retain their land. In a phone interview, she said, "All of these developments that have become gated communities on both Hilton Head and along the coast of South Carolina have cut them [the Gullah Geechee] off from their traditions, their culture, and their way of life. It's more than losing land. It's heritage and culture as we know it. It's the loss of access to water as a means of transportation, to fish and oyster, and make a sustainable living."

I thought of my family and how suburbs were supposed to be the dream. If we could have been living in a gated community, that would have been even better than living in a house on a cul-de-sac in some hostile neighborhood. To us, a gate represented the highest echelon of residential living. But now I was seeing that the planning of gated communities, especially in the South, was at the expense of black people, their ancestors' bodies, and their customs. In the places we left behind, like Americus, what happened to our former neighbors? Did they get uprooted too? Did they stay and have to fight along the margins for what is rightfully theirs, like Tai Scott? That day I felt that the black North and the black South were in conversation. I, the Northerner, was face-to-face with a man who lived in the North but came back to the South to fight for his people. Both of us were effects of migration. Arguably, if more Gullah Geechee people had stayed in Hilton Head, Tai would not have faced so many challenges with his business venture, because there would have been more of them to claim their stakes in the land. Arguably, if my grandfather and his father had kept returning to Georgia with their children after moving up north, then maybe I would've never felt that my connection to the South had been severed. But this day felt like a meeting in the middle. No matter where we are along the coast, we are a vulnerable people, prone to cultural erasure and amnesia.

"This is the hardest part right here," Tai said with a smirk. Tai's grandparents, Daniel and Geneva Burke, once owned the largest oceanfront tract of land on the eastern shore of the island. They had twenty-seven acres of land, which they sold for $3 million. The attorney who represented them had once represented Marriott, but that fact was never disclosed to his grandparents. Marriott now owns those twenty-seven acres. To give you a sense of the loss, Marriott paid $2 million for the next oceanfront lot that he pointed out to me, then flipped it, selling it for $5 million. The company then purchased the Burke family land—$3 million for those twenty-seven acres. When I asked Tai how much twenty-seven acres was, he replied, "The sale should have never happened." It was the perfect example of the loss of generational wealth. The beach on this lot is named for the Burke family. Years ago, the now defunct Burke's Hideaway was a famous nightclub that once hosted Ike and Tina Turner.[15] According to Alex Brown, any resorts on the north end of the island, such as the Marriott, Westin, and Sonesta, were once Gullah-owned.

Michelle Aiken is a member of one of the first families of Hilton Head. The Aiken family lived in Mitchelville after emancipation and remained in the north end to the present day.[16] A street not too far from Marshland Road in Hilton Head bears their name. When Michelle's grandfather, William Aiken, passed away, he had acres upon acres of land, though she can't give an exact number. He left his children and grandchildren land as a way to remember him. Michelle is the youngest of nine siblings, and though most of them have remained in Hilton Head or in neighboring counties, her brother Marian chose to leave for California back in the eighties for better job opportunities. The decision is one that Michelle teases Marian about to this day. Still, jobs on the island are few and far between, especially outside the tourism business, and even then, discrimination is blatant. When Michelle interviewed for a job at the Marriott Surfwatch in the early aughts, her prospective employers asked her if she wanted to be a housekeeper, though she'd applied to be a child-care coordinator. "For black people . . . they always want us to do housekeeping. They always like to put us in the back area," Aiken says. "Many of us black people, when we work in these places, we would be in the corner and the white people would be in the front."

Still, Michelle doesn't want to leave and encourages her daughter to stay on the island as well. She feels lucky. Her family with one accord agreed to keep the property and had the money to do so. Over two hundred members of the Aiken line descended on Hilton Head for the annual family reunion, and Michelle emphasizes that they always have a place to come back to.

Alex Brown, chairman of the Town Planning Commission, also considers himself fortunate to have stayed in Hilton Head. His family has two pieces of land, one of eight acres and the other of fifteen. The fifteen acres, however, is what Brown calls infiltrated. Heirs property is divided among siblings, and a few of Brown's relatives were not keeping up with the payments for their parcels, which have been up for auction. Thankfully, they haven't lost any property . . . yet.

Alex's father had nine brothers and sisters, many of whom migrated to cosmopolitan Southern cities, like Atlanta, or to places as far away as New York. "Missed opportunities" is what he calls their migration. They didn't make the land work for them and so sought a home elsewhere. Growing up in the 1970s and '80s, he had seen neighbors give up and move to other parts of the country for easier living, never to return, and this pattern convinced him to dig his heels deep into the soil and fight.

Speaking of the black land loss in Hilton Head, Brown says, "It has been a devastating blow to our community. But we haven't lost all. We're trying to bring awareness to this issue." That's why Brown is a part of the Planning Commission and speaks regularly to publications, such as *Hilton Head Monthly* and *The Nation*. Such hope and persistence has enabled some, like Taiwan Scott, to finally win against the Town of Hilton Head. In March 2019, Beaufort County Judge Marvin Dukes III threw out a motion filed by the town government that would have forced Scott to move his buildings within a certain buffer zone if he wanted to designate one part of his property as residential and another as commercial.[17] The people of the Gullah community, whether they stayed or left and came back, realize the stakes involved—their heritage on Hilton Head and in all of Beaufort County.

I started to think about my family, whose lives in South Jersey began only because my great-grandfather left Americus. Even if that land in Americus had still been in the family name, I wasn't going to pack all of my belongings and move there. I don't know how to ride a horse. I don't know how to grow cotton or any other crop. Did my family, in the words of Alex Brown, miss an opportunity to stay where they were planted, to persevere and band together with other black people to hold on to their community? What really is home for me? When my grandparents die, there will be no land in their name, passed down for generations. I don't blame my late grandfather for the decisions he made. He was afraid to take his chances and stay. And maybe what pushes previous generations to leave is what paradoxically binds us African Americans together as we search for community and press forward to maintain our sense of identity, our culture, and our heritage. If he had stayed, I might now be in a hopeless, treacherous situation. How could I maintain a living if the taxes continue to rise and white people are circling my land, ready to snap it up if I miss any payments? In that situation, under constant racial intimidation, how would I maintain peace of mind?

My grandparents worked in Atlantic City and saved up enough

to move to the suburbs. That socioeconomic shift changed the course of all of our lives. Nevertheless, because Fred Jerkins I moved away, we, his descendants, have lost our familial networks. On this part of my trip, I was face-to-face with islanders who never left or left and came back. I was their opposite. My grandparents left and never returned. They didn't bring my mother to their original homes, and therefore my mother never brought me there, either. I am the embodiment of that abandonment of land. I am the result of those who never went back. Before this moment, I thought gated communities were enviable places to live for any family. In Hilton Head, I saw them as a vulgar barrier between Gullah lands and Gullah people—a constant reminder of black land loss.

The threat of displacement or forced removal by white people was a major impetus for the millions of African Americans who left the South, and I was able to see the effects in real time. As a woman raised by a woman who prided herself on continual movement, I had a change of heart. Maybe staying in one place does not mean stagnation. There can be opportunity for economic growth, though one will have to fight for it, as those on Hilton Head are, because whatever was once ours—whether as abstract as oral histories or as tangible as land—is worth saving. The land is everything, and without it, our culture is in peril. We once worked the land, we bought that land, and we prospered on that land. Although I feel quite unmoored that I have no ancestral home in the South, at least the name Americus can rest on my tongue, letting me know that New Jersey is neither the beginning nor necessarily the end of my family's story. I learned that there is always a deeper story. No matter how many times one moves away from one's original place, somehow one will be called back, as I was.

Though I may not have been actually related to any of the people I met, in a sense all black people are related to Gullah Geechee people. They are our oldest African Americans, the source of so much of our history. We are related despite our differences, tied to one another in the midst of systemic and personal forces that may tear us apart as we try to survive. On this journey, I found the links between the reverence and the contempt for root work, found how water has both nourished and harmed us, and found the cause and effects of black land loss with respect to our sense of community. Our migrations from the South and subsequent adaptation to our new surroundings fermented these disparities, but there is room for reclamation and understanding.

If we can meet each other in the middle, as I and my new acquaintances had done during this journey, then we can understand that distance is moot. Speaking about our lives and those of our deceased relatives, as my grandfather finally did, reminded me that I am much more connected to others than I ever could have imagined. Our people are powerful. I carried all of these stories, in journal entries, photographs, videos, and recordings, to immortalize them in some way. If I cannot pass down land, I can pass on words that will live on after I'm gone to remind other African Americans that they, too, are much more connected to the rest of us than they could have ever imagined. My maternal line stretches over 940 miles, and that makes me feel hopeful that there is more for me to uncover as long as I pose questions and listen.

And that I was, for so far I had researched only one side of my family.

PART II

Louisiana Creole

I

—————

WHEN ONE WRITES about one's own life, I believe there are many doors through which to enter. Before I started to write about my mother's family, I felt confident as to which doors might be the best. Their history felt more like a long and winding road and less like the labyrinth of my father's side. Obviously, that's because I lived with my mother and had access to her relatives and their conversations. Moreover, both of my paternal grandparents are dead.

My father is fifteen years my mother's senior. He is closer in age to Pop-Pop, my grandfather Fred, than to my mother. I never met my paternal grandfather, Cleveland Jr. He died a year after I was born, and I met my grandmother Gladys—"Gram-Gram"—only once or twice before her Alzheimer's and dementia worsened. They were born in 1919 and 1918, respectively. Before I began this book, the only keepsakes I had of Cleveland and Gram-Gram were two photos and a letter. Cleveland was a handsome, dark-skinned man with a disarming smile, a thin moustache, and a slight gap between his two front teeth. Gram-Gram was very fair with gray eyes, her paternity catalyzing family lore that has persisted for over a hundred years.

My strongest memory of Gram-Gram was our first time laying eyes upon each other. I was around four or five and she was around seventy-nine. I was on her lap and she was jubilant. She wrote my mother and me two separate letters soon afterward. To me, she wrote about how proud she was of me; for my mother, she wrote of her gratitude for getting us together and how praying could help get us through the "odd situation" of my dad balancing two families.

When I say that there are many doors through which to enter a personal story, I mean it. I could start by telling you how my sisters innocently giggled when I called our grandmother Gladys instead of Gram-Gram till I was a teenager, which made me feel embarrassed that I didn't know the Regis sisters' ways of addressing her. I could start with the disappointment my dad felt when I refused to apply to any colleges and universities in North Carolina, where he was born—a firm stance that essentially meant that I did not want to be connected to the South at all (which I didn't). I didn't have any family there, and the family that I knew about through my father were abstractions. I was never close to any of them. His home was not my home.

I could start with my first trip to North Carolina, for Gram-Gram's funeral—seeing her home and experiencing the solemnity of a Catholic ceremony, which was quite foreign to me. But instead, I'm going to start with the easiest door: my father, Jon. Unlike on the Jerkins side, where I had to skip over my mother's generation to gather some threads about our past, I could go directly to him.

My dad is the first complicated love of my life. He's the most charismatic man I've ever met—when he walks into a room, he commands attention. He loves to dance, drink mojitos, and talk business. One of our favorite things to do together is to debate—because we both love to talk about any and all things—and sometimes, he will troll me just to make me smile and break character in the midst of an otherwise serious conversation. Yet ironically, he had been an enigma to me. My mother, on the other hand, was extremely vulnerable and transparent during my childhood, as most Jerkins women are. The anecdotes she told me about her life growing up always came out whenever we took a drive down the Black

Horse Pike in New Jersey. My dad wasn't the same. He shared anecdotes whenever he felt like it, and I could never anticipate them. Then again, New Jersey wasn't home to him, so maybe the recollection just wasn't natural. The roads and landmarks simply didn't inspire the same feelings in him.

My dad hasn't lived in North Carolina, his birthplace, for over thirty years. I thought homesickness might drive him to be more open about his life in North Carolina, but that's not what happened. He mentioned small things about Gram-Gram, but he never really spoke about his father, almost as if Cleveland were a stranger, almost as if Cleveland only picked my dad up on the weekends, as he did me. I wondered if he thought of his father as an enigma too.

When I called Aunt Pammy, my dad's older sister, on the phone and asked about my grandfather, she hesitated in describing him. For that brief moment I was stunned. The Regises were, to me, the quintessential family unit. They were supposed to be cohesive. Unlike me, most people I knew grew up in two-parent households. There shouldn't be any gaps or holes in the history of a two-parent household, right? Wrong. "I wish I could say that I really knew him," Aunt Pammy said. "When you're a child, you just grow up knowing that it's your father. He goes to work, comes home, and we had dinner together every night."

As for his life in Houston, according to Aunt Pammy, he never went into detail. I descend from a line of shadowy men whose mouths were citadels guarding their past lives. In these omissions, I found that my Jerkins and Regis sides were not as different as I once thought. And like the Jerkins side, the Regis line stretched deeper than I initially thought. My father's line didn't begin in North Carolina either, but in a place over nine hundred miles away, beyond the Mississippi River. I had to travel there, not only for me, but also for the fathers I wanted to know—to, I hoped, feel more grounded in who I was and my place in the Regis family tree.

Here are the pieces of my paternal line that I have: Cleveland Jr.

was born and raised in Frenchtown, a subcommunity within the Fifth Ward of Houston, Texas. He attended Our Mother of Mercy Catholic Church. His father, Cleveland Sr., was terribly strict, and his iron-fisted rule led the son who carried his name to run away from home and join the army. He was only seventeen years old. He was either a first sergeant or sergeant first class, a part of the Eighty-Second Airborne Division, stationed at Fort Bragg, where he met and eloped with Gram-Gram, whose family was many generations deep in and around the Sandhills region of North Carolina. He had an eighth-grade education but completed the *New York Times* crossword puzzles for fun. He had a drinking problem. He didn't speak much about his own father. He loved making chili con carne with pinto beans and couche-couche. He was a devout Catholic and oftentimes, he'd say phrases in French. I still remember the first time my dad alluded to the fact that the Regis side had many more branches and splinters than I thought. We were at Applebee's for dinner, and that was the first time I heard my paternal grandfather described as Creole. He was a Creole man, but he never identified as such. His family was from Saint Martinville, but like my mother's family, neither my dad nor his relatives or their children had ever gone back home.

The only Louisiana Creoles I'd ever seen were on-screen. Once, when I was a preteen flipping through movies to watch on HBO on a quiet weekend afternoon, I stumbled upon *Eve's Bayou*. A film directed by Kasi Lemmons, *Eve's Bayou* is about family secrets, the power of words, and the fallibility of memory. One of the main characters, Louis Batiste, played by Samuel L. Jackson, is the town doctor. Thinking back on this film, my heart flutters. Louis is exactly like my father: a tall, wealthy man who entertains the community. These weren't regular black people to me. I wasn't even sure they were black, because their many gradations of brown said otherwise. They spoke French, like Cleveland Jr. and possibly like his father, too. Their house was large, and the land surrounding it was sprawling. White people didn't terrorize them. White people didn't exist in this world.

Shortly before my trip, during a phone conversation, my dad emphatically told me of his family's socioeconomic and educational privilege. Gram-Gram's family was comprised of landowners. Her mother's house was a gift from the Rockefellers, but Dad wasn't sure how the rest of the family was able to have land in the late 1800s and early 1900s. Though my aunt Pammy remembers times when her mother didn't have two coins to rub together, they mainly lived a comfortable middle- and upper-middle-class lifestyle. Cleveland Jr. was in the military, and the respect he received from the town as a result also improved their lives. The confidence in my dad's voice gave me the impression that the Regises weren't new to social status. While my mother had leaped to higher status through real estate, the Regises had been perched aloft for decades, maybe even centuries longer. What if the Regises' prized social status ran much deeper than I thought? A voice-over of Eve in *Eve's Bayou* says, "Memory is a selection of images. Some elusive, others printed indelibly on the brain. Each image is like a thread. Each thread woven together to make a tapestry of intricate texture and the tapestry tells a story and the story is our past." All I had were a selection of images that I conjured from what my dad and his siblings could remember. But the French, the couche-couche, the Regis name, the parish, and that intergenerational privilege were all the threads I needed to return to the original ball of yarn.

Cleveland Sr., my great-great-grandfather, lived on 2828 Davis Street. Davis Street was within the four square blocks that comprised Frenchtown, a subcommunity of the Fifth Ward that was created in 1922 when five hundred Louisiana Creoles migrated to Houston in search of better economic opportunities. Frenchtown locals worked in many different professions, such as carpentry, mechanics, sawmill work, and bricklaying. Cleveland Sr. worked, like many of his cohorts, at a railroad company. The Great Mississippi

Flood of 1927 displaced some two hundred thousand African Americans, and part of this black population, the Creoles, poured into Houston and many other cities in search of safer ground. Our Mother of Mercy Catholic Church was the social hub of Frenchtown, and those within this community often distanced themselves from other black people with segregated streets and neighborhoods based on their lighter skin. At the same time, Frenchtown residents refrained from teaching their children French, because they were teased for it by other black children.[1] This may be why neither my father nor his siblings grew up with French being spoken in the home.

To this day, my dad facetiously refers to Creoles and our culture as "Creole crap," believing the Creole label is a thinly veiled attempt by black people to disavow their blackness. Perhaps to him, Creoles don't need their own label. It's a subset of African American, not a separate category. After all, my grandfather never defined himself as a Creole man yet brought elements of his Creole heritage to North Carolina. From the little bit that I learned of Creoles in New Jersey, I assumed that they were nothing more than uppity, light-skinned blacks who thought they were better than everybody else. There were no Creoles I knew of in South Jersey, so it was easy to make this assumption and maintain it all the way to adulthood. But such a framing is far from the truth. Not all Creoles are light-skinned, but there was no one up north to tell me that because Creoles aren't common where I'm from. I had to go to Louisiana to get the nuance. But before I could travel there, I needed to understand how unique Louisiana was *before* the land became American and its people were subjected to binary rules of racial classification.

In America, black and white are polar opposites. Though race is a social construct, we assume someone's race from their parents and phenotype. The "one-drop rule" meant that one black ancestor anywhere in your family tree—one drop of black blood or DNA—ruined your chances of being considered 100 percent

white and placed you among the oppressed so as to maintain social order. Even Ivory soap, "99⁴⁴/₁₀₀ percent pure," was technically
black. Whites were at the top of hierarchy of institutional power
and privilege, and blacks were at the bottom. But in the beginning,
when Africans were first brought to the English colonies in the seventeenth century, this disparity was less extreme. Blacks and poor
whites were indentured servants. Black and white women worked
side by side in the fields, and black and white men who broke their
contracts were given the same punishments. After indentured servants served their time, they could move on and buy their own
land. This ability threatened to dilute the elite. And the wealthy
whose servants had moved on needed replacements for their lost
laborers. In 1641, Massachusetts became the first colony to recognize slavery; others followed.[2]

Race then started to take precedence. The poor whites, whom
the black, formerly indentured servants once worked with, were,
before their voyage to the colonies, a part of the English working
class. The black people, however, were seen as outsiders under
English colonial law, so no one knew how they should be treated
with respect to everyone else. In 1654 a black indentured servant,
John Casor, was bound to his master for life in a civil suit, *Johnson v. Parker*. This decision solved two problems: (1) It ensured that
black people could not become wealthy property owners, like
their white counterparts. (2) It maintained the control by wealthy
whites of their black, non-English constituents. The courts then
made this fate hereditary, beginning with the Virginia colony
in 1662. Because of the courts, if you were black and brought to
the colonies by force, you were a slave. If you had children, they
would be slaves, too. From then on, the terms *black* and *slave* were
interchangeable.[3] The Fugitive Slave Act of 1850 is a prime example of how the judicial system made the two synonymous. Free
black people could not provide documentation that they were legally free, as in the famous case of Solomon Northup recounted

in Northup's book *12 Years a Slave*, and if they were captured, they were denied rights to a trial.

Furthermore, in 1676, a wealthy white planter in Virginia named Nathanial Bacon rebelled against Governor William Berkeley's policies, particularly with regards to Native Americans. Bacon gathered both black and white indentured servants and enslaved blacks to fight. Although the rebellion famously known as Bacon's Rebellion was ultimately unsuccessful, Virginia lawmakers legally separated whites and blacks and gave poor whites more rights and privileges in hopes that they would never band together to challenge the colonial government again.[4] In grade school, I was never taught about the different social milieus that black people occupied in nineteenth-century America and earlier, and I was definitely never taught that free black people existed prior to the Emancipation Proclamation. My parents never spoke of such a thing either. But in Louisiana, there were many free blacks, because the racial and ethnic classifications were different than those elsewhere.

It is important to remember that Louisiana was not originally a part of the United States. The territory exchanged hands between the French and Spanish until 1803, when the US government acquired the land via the Louisiana Purchase. European settlers poured into the territory and purchased African slaves. The children that resulted from the relations between European white settlers and enslaved African women were caught between two worlds, creating a need for a social category between white and black. Although white settlers couldn't marry their slaves, some did end up freeing them and buying property for them. Both white and black, their children were called free people of color, *gens de couleur libre*. Their whiteness allowed these people to learn to read and write, testify in court, take up a profession, and own property.[5] But their blackness excluded them from other opportunities, such as owning businesses that sold alcohol. Separate railroad cars also had to be used to transport corpses of different races.[6] Because these free people of color oscillated between white and black spaces, never entirely fitting into one or the other, they often married other free people of color and created their own communities.

To define Creole is to invite ambiguity, because the definition has changed over time and across different cultures. In 1929, a Creole was defined in the Larousse French dictionary as pertaining only to white people. In 1992, the *American Heritage Dictionary* gave five definitions:

1. a person of European descent who was born in the West Indies or Spanish America
2. a person descended from or culturally related to the original French settlers of the southern U.S., especially Louisiana
3. a person descended from or culturally related to the Spanish and Portuguese settlers of the gulf states (such as Mississippi)
4. a person of mixed black and European ancestry who speaks a creolized language
5. an enslaved African who was born in the Americas

In Louisiana, a Creole person was one of distinction. As long as you were not a slave and had at least one parent of Spanish or French parentage, you were entitled to social rank and considered a Creole. By this logic, many white people and *gens de couleur libre* were Creole. Later on, the term was expanded to mean anyone of mixed heritage, including any Native American ancestry. In other words, anyone born in Louisiana, whether white or black, enslaved or free, could be Creole.[7]

After learning this, I was confused. If a Creole could be anyone born in Louisiana, then why didn't my grandfather identify as one? Why did my father and I believe that Creoles were just uppity black people? *Uppity* implies that black people considered themselves superior, but if any Louisiana person, irrespective of social status, could be Creole, then where did this idea of uppityness come from? Maybe it was because the Creoles I'd heard of—though never met—didn't identify as black people despite blackness being a part of their ethnic makeup. The Gullah Geechee people owed their retention of West African customs to their isolation from the mainland. In Louisiana, this retention was due to the instability between white masters and black slaves. The waterways in lower Louisiana helped slaves escape through the swamps; moreover, the black slave population vastly outnumbered the elite who controlled the colony. Because of this imbalance, Africans were able to have cultural autonomy,[8] and yet also have relations with Europeans and indigenous people, giving rise to the people we now know as Creole. I suppose my indignation toward Creole people arose from the idea that by asserting the Creole label, they were implicitly trying to separate themselves from their blackness, and that meant they didn't want to carry the weight of being black in America.

When I started searching for interview subjects, I thought this desire for separation was confirmed when I reached out to Alexandre Guillory, who I later found to be a distant relative of mine. A Louisiana Creole man and genealogy researcher, Guillory disavows his Americanness and went so far as to say that Creoles were a non–African American ethnic group. I was gobsmacked. He sounded ridiculous to me. Since he wasn't born prior to the Louisiana Purchase, didn't that make him an American? Creole culture is part African, and since Creoles are a part of Louisiana, which has been American since 1803, Creole culture is by definition part of African American culture. Creole people are not a race—at least not in the way America defines race. They are neither white nor black. But I now believe Guillory was trying to express his need to define himself as just Creole, not a compound nationality like African American, in order to not feel erased. Perhaps being Creole did in fact hold different social, legal, and cultural implications than being African American.

Other Louisiana Creoles and academics, such as Andrew Joli-vétte, professor in the department of American Indian Studies and the College of Ethnic Studies at San Francisco State University, dispute this complete separation yet still emphasize that Creoles are a very distinct people: "I'm from the region—on my father's side—but I think this is true of the South in general but very much so in Louisiana, that Creoles are a very particular culture. While I would describe it as being a part of the African diaspora and African American culture, it also has its own sort of distinct culture as well, and so I think that creates or adds to the complications there. But, you know, generally in the United States if you're not white, then you're black, and if you're anything else, then you kind of don't exist.

"Up to the 1850s maybe, or the 1890s, a lot of Creoles didn't identify as being American because they weren't, actually. So they felt the same way as Native American people. Treaties were signed, and then all of a sudden they were forced into a country they weren't a part of, and they didn't identify as Americans for a long time. Now I think if you talk to contemporary Creoles in 2018, you're not going to hear very many say they are not American."

Another assumption from non-Creoles that Professor Jolivétte and I discussed was that Louisiana Creoles are defined by their skin color and language. Some people assume that Creoles are just French-speaking black people, but Jolivétte believes that's an oversimplification. While Creoles may also speak French, they speak Louisiana French Creole, a mixture of French and several West African languages, including Mande, Ewe, and Yoruba.[9] Creoles are also distinct in terms of their religion. While many black Southerners are Baptist or African Methodist Episcopal (AME), most Creoles are Catholic. As a child, the only black Catholic I knew in my close circle was my father. As he lived in New Jersey, my father mainly went to nondenominational and Pentecostal churches, but I never asked him why. I made yet another assumption—that he may have found it easier to commune in Pentecostal congregations because there were more black people there than in Catholic churches. He was probably more comfortable worshipping in a black Pentecostal church rather than a mixed-race Catholic church.

As for the appearance aspect of Creole communities, Professor Jolivétte explains that the colorism runs deep: "I've met other people who are Creole and darker, and they go down there, and they're like, 'Oh my God, your family, they're going to judge me' or something. I'm like, 'No, they're not." In fact, they're from the country. They're not from New Orleans, and they say they're where the real Creoles are. They very heavily identify as black and they're as white as—in complexion anyway—as you might want to think." Professor Jolivétte himself is not one who I would consider light-skinned. He's a rich brown, like my mother, letting me know that Creoles, like other African Americans, come in all different shades and hair textures. How could they not? They've been mixing with other races and ethnic groups for centuries.

The conversation with Professor Jolivétte gave me one of what would become many humbling moments. I wanted to get to the root of why I made assumptions about my own people as though they all looked and acted the same way. Aren't these the kinds of assumptions that I've been fighting against in my own life and through my writing? The truth is, leaning on assumptions is easier than doing the work necessary to understand a difficult and multilayered subject. For me, unpacking this was important not only for the work itself, but also for me to unlearn what I thought I knew about my ethnic identity. I was nervous because I would be going into new territory, and if I couldn't rely on what I thought I knew about myself, what else would I have?

At least this time I had a place of origin, a beginning. No matter what, I could use Saint Martin Parish as an anchor throughout this trip. When I asked Professor Jolivétte about Saint Martinville, he told me that it was the heart of Creole country, an acknowledgment that brought a smile to my face. I wasn't confident in my connection, though. I'd never been there. Neither had my sisters, aunts, or uncles. It had been far too long since family had been in that area—two or three generations at least. I am fully Americanized. I'd never had gumbo or crawfish étouffée (crawfish cooked in roux then served over rice). I didn't know what a krewe was, never listened to zydeco, and had never seen a bayou. I existed in that black-white binary because it was easier. If you looked black, you were black, no matter what ethnicity and nuance came along with it. But on the Regises' side, in one generation, Cleveland Jr.'s generation, his relatives represented a full range—from the darkest brown to white-passing. Creoles weren't all light-skinned blacks. They were much, much more. Toward the end of our initial conversation, Professor Jolivétte knew exactly whom to connect me with for my field research in Louisiana.

The field researcher's name is Tracey Colson Antee. She is the seventeenth descendant of Marie Thérèse Coin, a woman whose power and wealth is responsible for a whole community of Creoles of color near the Cane River. Marie Thérèse was born in 1742, the fourth child of first-generation slaves. No record of her parents' names has been found. Researchers have claimed that she was a part of the St. Denis family, but because Marie Thérèse was a common name and the St. Denises were the largest slave owners in the county, her ties to this group are debatable. Her biological family's origins are also disputable. Some say they came from the Congo or Angola, from which many captured Africans landed in the Lowcountry. The most widely accepted story of Marie Thérèse's history is that she was owned by Louis Juchereau de St. Denis. Claude Thomas Pierre Metoyer, a bourgeois French merchant, became attracted to Marie Thérèse, and Louis Juchereau rented her out to Metoyer as a housekeeper. Several children resulted from their relationship. Religious authorities tried to break up their union by threatening to sell Marie to someone in New

Orleans. To thwart this transaction, Claude manumitted, or freed, Marie and gifted her with sixty-eight acres of land, on which she cultivated tobacco. One of her sons, Louis Metoyer, was deeded over nine hundred acres of land, which became Melrose Plantation.[10] The Metoyer line became the wealthiest free people of color in the nation.[11] Because Marie Thérèse's grave is unmarked and its whereabouts are unknown, she has been the focus of much imagination about Creole people for centuries. It is a fascination that puts those like Tracey Colson at odds with the general public.

Tracey's mother, Janet Ravare Colson was assistant director of the Louisiana Creole Heritage Center at Northwestern State University in Natchitoches. The center was founded in 1991 by Terrell Delphin Jr., an icon whose efforts to promote Cane River's culture and history through ethnographic studies and organizations greatly benefited the community. Janet got involved with the center, along with the Saint Augustine Historical Society, her church, and other organizations responsible for maintaining the cemetery, where many Metoyer descendants are buried, and other sites in and around Cane River. Because more and more visitors began to visit Natchitoches, she and others created a proposal for the potential center to the state Board of Regents and were able to secure funding.

Janet's steadfastness is due largely to her concern that Creoles would be erased from the public landscape and collective memory. Janet's apprehension has been passed down to Tracey, who recalls an earlier time, before the center was created, when Creoles and their culture were invisible in other institutions, such as the school system. There were few documents on their history. Tracey told me that ever since turning forty, she has lost her filter, a disclaimer that only excited me. To elucidate the complications of her ethnicity, she refers to an anecdote from her childhood:

"When I started seventh grade, I had to do my little papers. I was in my homeroom class, and my homeroom teacher was a middle-aged black man. It was the little card where you put your name and address and all that. It said gender, and it said race, and I was like, 'Hmm,' and I remember the panic started. My heart started beating really fast. I was like, 'What do I put?' because I literally had never thought about it. Never. In fact the conversation had never happened. I just knew that we were Creole, but I didn't know, like . . . do I put that? So I put *tan*."

"OK."

"He looks at my card and starts yelling at me. 'You goddamn Geechees from down the river. I can't stand y'all. Pretending to be somebody else, with your light skin and your good hair. Y'all just think this and you think you better than everybody else, and you ain't.' I'm scared to death, trying to be a big girl."

And then, the class proceeded normally. As it turns out, my rebuff of Creoles as a distinct people is not only because of my Northern upbringing. No, this condemnation persists even in Louisiana. Tracey and her mother's worry was justifiable: people in their own birthplace were trying to erase them. And if a teacher could get in on it, who knows what other people could do?

Throughout Tracey's life, there was an emphasis on ethnicity, not race. Her Creoleness was at the forefront. A certain grooming was expected from someone whose earliest ancestor was responsible for an entire Creole community, but to call her a Geechee was an insult, as JR Grovner had mentioned to me back on Sapelo Island. This pejorative spanned several states and African American ethnic groups. The belief that Creoles think they're better than blacks is persistent, no doubt because they were in fact higher in social rank. Tracey never tried to deny her blackness, but often Creole and black are an either/or when they should be a both/and.

Creoles are indeed between two worlds. Tracey says, "I couldn't date nobody. I wasn't black enough. I wasn't white enough. Or I was too black or I was too white. People get mad at you if you say you're black. People get mad at you if you say you're white. People get mad at you if you say you're Creole. They want to argue with you all the time. I'm Creole. I am black, but what I am is African, French, Hispanic, and Native. I'm a whole lot of different things, and if I say just one of these things, I'm denying so many other parts of myself."

Over the years, Tracey has been passionate about genealogical research and Creole culture preservation. She and her mother travel throughout the country to make presentations and create events to show that Creoles still exist. There is often a voyeuristic quality to interest in her people, which she detests. One of her colleagues, who is a tour guide, was once asked by white tourists if Creoles still existed and where they could see some. Such tourists travel down to Natchitoches just to drive past a group of Creoles and point at them.

Stories about Cane River were published without the Creoles knowing that they'd been interview subjects. Allegedly, there was a nun who hid a tape recorder in her habit to collect stories. Rumors circulated that some white people would go as far to steal artifacts from families, some of which would wind up in museums.

I said to Tracey, "You had these self-contained communities that didn't bother anybody. Nobody bothered them. Then you started having these outsiders coming in and taking people's possessions without bringing them back. That created tension."

"Yeah, it was much more of a paranoia, like, 'What are you here for?' You know, people are very skeptical. They were not open at all. People wanted to know, how come these colored people are so light-skinned? How come these colored people got all this land? This is why so much of Creole culture has been lost and people are scared to share anything."

What fuels her persistence in spite of even other Creoles jokingly asking why she keeps doing her "Creole stuff" is the way the antebellum era is overly simplified as being everywhere a strictly binary white-equals-master, black-equals-slave system.

Tracey wants to dispel myths like the one that says black people were never slave owners. Some even owned family members whom they eventually set free. Much of the region where her parents live is stuck in a cycle of sanitization for the public. In any case, white people hold most of the capital, and the Creoles who gave Cane River its prominence are pushed toward the margins. At the end of our conversation, I realized that this trip was more than a reclamation of the Regises' past and my own. It was also a disentanglement of black ethnic identity as it twists and turns under the powers and laws of white supremacy.

2

ONCE I WAS able to understand Creole identity and its flexible definitions across centuries, it was time for me to assess how much
of that heritage and history have been erased, using the Metoyer
line as the example. I wanted to know more about the robust Creole communities of the past, their collapse after the Civil War and
during Jim Crow, and the consequences for those who stayed and
those who moved away. First, I was going to dig into my father's
history by talking with my great-great-aunt, whose life combines
migration, Creole elitism, and disappearance in the twentieth century. It was through her life, connected with the lives of the Metoyers, that I was confronted with my own hesitation to tell the truth
about Creole people's vested interest in white supremacy.

Evelyn Jewell Regis Navarre was a beauty for the ages. In the
only image I could recover of her, from a cousin, she's dressed up
in a Glen plaid two-piece outfit. Her jet-black hair is styled in a
smooth upswept roll in front while the rest falls past her shoulders. She's sitting on top of her ottoman with her legs swung to the
right side as though she wanted the photographer to get the scale
of her body more accurately. Born in 1922 in Harris County, Texas,
one of my grandfather Cleveland's younger sisters, Evelyn had
dreams of being a movie star and singer. Maybe that's why in this
photograph she is looking beyond the center, smiling at an imag-

ined future that only she can see. She married Henry Navarre, who also migrated to Texas but from Lafayette, when she was eighteen and he twenty-one. The name Navarre belongs to one of the oldest Creole families originating in New Orleans. One of the many neighborhoods in New Orleans is named in their honor. I am related to the Navarres in two ways: (1) through my great-aunt Evelyn and (2) through my great-great-great-aunt Rose Rochon, née Regis, who married Honoré Rochon, a grandson of Charlotte Rochon and Jean-Baptiste Navarre. I'm not

My late great-aunt Evelyn Jewell Regis Navarre. *Janice Bradley*

sure if Evelyn and Henry knew that they were distantly related, but that's what certain Creoles did in those days.

One of my late cousins, David DeWitt Turpeau, wrote in his autobiography, *Up from the Cane-Brakes*, about the Creole caste system. Remember, many Creoles married among themselves, and because they were mindful of social status and rank, the stakes were high to ensure continued prominence and wealth:

> . . . the one upon whom the caste is practiced as well as the one practicing it are all the victims of a superstition that deprived them of the natural process of a free choice of their associates and kept them within the narrow limits of a prescribed circle. . . .
>
> . . . when ever you meet a Creole you know him by his rigid adherence to some phrase of the caste system and if he

is not too far removed by years of different culture and other habit forming influences, he still is a strong believer in some form of caste. . . . [1]

I don't know if Henry went through an intense screening process, complete with thorough family trees and pedigrees, to receive Evelyn's hand in marriage, but I do believe that their respective families were familiar with each other, whether or not their links were fully known to both parties.

Lafayette, the town Evelyn moved to, is less than twenty-five miles from Saint Martin Parish. As Evelyn and Henry were growing up in Houston, the Fifth Ward was flourishing with Creoles who sought to re-create the communities they left back in Louisiana. This reconstruction of community came through zydeco music, the accordion-based dance music of Louisiana Creoles, and through cuisine and architecture. It wouldn't be too much of a stretch to believe that these storied families from the distant past wanted to maintain their caste system by marrying people with names that they already recognized.

I couldn't find any other documentation on Evelyn, but I did find a death certificate for Henry in Santa Clara. The missing pieces between their move to California and Henry's death made me feel as if the young couple had vanished after beginning what was supposed to be a new and exciting chapter of their lives together. Evelyn and her children's fate have been whispered about throughout my family across generations. Evelyn's father, Cleveland Sr., had a strict personality that motivated not only my grandfather— Evelyn's brother Cleveland Jr.—but also Evelyn to flee. Though instead of migrating east, she went west to California, like many other Creoles during the early to mid-twentieth century. She never became a movie star or actress. She died at the young age of forty-seven after spiraling into alcohol and drug addictions. Though Henry and Evelyn both identified themselves as Negro, in 1930 and

1940 respectively, in the US Census, many in the Navarre family were classified in their day as mulattos, including Evelyn, who was very fair. Evelyn and Henry's daughter Gwen chose to pass as white, and because of that decision, that part of my family has been severed with no possibility of reconciliation. Years later, one of my cousins tried to reach out to Gwen's children, who had been hurt in that their family had been ravaged by substance abuse and parental neglect. They became even more hurt that their black family came looking for them when it was far too late and the wounds were far too deep.

Many Creoles left Louisiana for better economic conditions, but better conditions were easier to attain where they were recognized legally and socially as Creole rather than black. After migrating, they re-created their cloistered communities in hopes of resurrecting this advantage, but their sense of Creoleness could dissipate if they didn't have a tight-knit community where they landed. A prime example was Anatole Broyard, author and *New York Times* book critic, whose family migrated from New Orleans to the Bedford-Stuyvesant area of Brooklyn. His family was Creole with mixed-race ancestry, and his blackness was an open secret in his circles. In other words, he was passing. Even his daughter, Bliss Broyard, didn't know about her black lineage; she wrote about discovering it in *One Drop: My Father's Hidden Life—a Story of Race and Family Secrets*. The reasons why he was coy about his blackness are still speculative. Perhaps he didn't want to be labeled a black writer instead of just a writer, or maybe he never saw himself as black but as Creole. Whatever the case may have been, to some, like one of Broyard's friends, black scholar and dramatist W. F. Lucas, "He was black when he got into the subway in Brooklyn, but as soon as he got out at West Fourth Street, he became white." Never Creole. There was no comfortable space for the in-between, no relief from the pressure of a migrant to conform to a racial binary.

According to Professor Andrew Jolivétte, there were many

Creoles who abandoned their culture the farther they moved away from Louisiana. It doesn't surprise me that Cleveland Jr. never really identified as Creole to my father and his siblings. How would they make sense of it? They were North Carolina–born. The number of people of Louisiana Creole descent in North Carolina was negligible. Their only link was Catholicism. Creoleness became an abstraction. Even my relatives who remained in Houston don't live in the Fifth Ward. After World War II ended, Frenchtown began to lose its core identity, especially as segregation ended in the sixties. There was a time when there were certain avenues that darker-skinned black people could not cross over unless they wanted a swift rebuke. When speaking with relatives as they drove me around the Fifth Ward, they categorized where they'd lived as separate from Frenchtown and dubbed Mother of Mercy a black church. I'm not sure if they misspoke or if it was an example of how this community had fallen since it "became" black.

The further I delved into genealogical studies, the more questions I found. Yes, the Regises were descended from Louisiana Creoles. But if they sought to distinguish their community from black Americans, they must have thought they were different or socially distinct from them. If they thought of themselves as separate, even in a black-and-white world, maybe they once had a higher social position. An uncomfortable thought crept into my mind. Was my family once composed of free people of color who wanted to maintain their social advantage over (other) blacks after migration? The idea seemed perverse. I was never taught, either through family oral history or educators, that free people of color existed. The known story was simple: we were captured from someplace in West Africa, enslaved, emancipated, and so on and so forth. To harbor the possibility that my family was once free on American soil before the Civil War would be to undo twenty-something years of indoctrination as to who I am as an African American. I didn't want to be the descendants of free people of color. Wouldn't that mean my family was what I detested, what I assumed Creoles to be—uppity? I wanted to be part of the burden of being black. My blackness is as much tied to my phenotype as my systemic disenfranchisement. If at one time some of my ancestors weren't as disfranchised, then that would make me unravel. But then again, why was I binding blackness and oppression together? The more I pondered these complicated relationships, the more I found myself speaking and note-taking in circles that returned to the original point: me. Reconsideration is what history is all about; history doesn't care what you feel. I had to be OK with being uncomfortable with whatever I would find out about my family.

Ultimately, I decided that I needed some help. I didn't know how to juggle the contradictory, interrelated identity markers of my family genealogy, that of the Colson family, and the history of Cane River. I reached out to black academics who had experience with ethnography and historical research. I connected with Antoine Hardy, a black Southern professor with a deep affinity for black ethnic studies and a gift for using Twitter as a resource. Every day, Antoine and I researched and exchanged and reviewed articles about the Metoyers, the social milieu of Creoles, and how racial binaries threatened their lives. From his experience I learned which questions to ask, how to keep my mind and heart open for my upcoming trip, and some note-taking skills for fieldwork. While preparing for this ethnographic research, I also searched the Regis surname and Saint Martin, Louisiana, in the Ancestry.com search engine and found a distant cousin, Janice Bradley, in a matter of minutes.

Janice is a Turpeau and related to David DeWitt Turpeau who wrote an autobiographical history of the Regis and Turpeau lines. She had a long, extensive family tree, one she worked and reworked over decades. I took a deep breath and sent her an e-mail. She responded within a few hours, and we hopped on the phone that same night. Toward the middle of our conversation, she told me that my earliest ancestor that she could trace was Maturin Regis Sr., said to be from Virginia. He was manumitted, moved to Louisiana, and fell in love with and married a Creole woman named Carrie. She said, "They once all lived along the Cane River."

"Cane River?" I asked. *That's absurd*, I thought. No way could I have a link to where I'd be traveling. No one would believe me. Hell, I didn't want to believe it myself. Saint Martinville isn't near Cane River, so unless Maturin or Carrie traveled or there were other family members I had yet to learn about. . . . As Turpeau mentioned in his characterization of Creole communities, how connected we were, it was beginning to feel too coincidental for comfort. I thought I was kidding myself when I saw how quickly the threads were weaving themselves together in front of my eyes. But I soon learned that I wasn't.

*   *   *

I FLEW INTO Alexandria, Louisiana, at the end of April 2018, right at the peak of crawfish season. It was an auspicious arrival, one of many to come. As my plane pulled into its gate at the airport, I notified Tracey of my arrival, to which she responded with an enthusiastic "Welcome home!" I couldn't help but feel a sliver of happiness alongside a more overwhelming sense of uneasiness. I'm a New Jerseyan through and through. But New Jersey is not my ancestral home. Tracey told me that it is not uncommon for people to scrutinize one's face and guess the parish where that person's family is from. Even though I was a few generations removed from Louisiana, I wondered if someone would recognize me. Then I silently admitted to myself, as I walked to baggage claim, that I actually did want someone to recognize my face and tell me something I didn't know about myself. Maybe then I would feel less uneasy and more accepting of my lineage. After all, I was in the Deep South now. It would be much more difficult for me to remain in denial in the land of my people.

Because Louisiana was not far from where Antoine was based and spring break was on, he agreed to meet me in Alexandria to help me with the ethnographic research. Just as I had done in the Lowcountry, I wanted to have notes, video, audio, and photography. I would primarily take the notes and Antoine would do some of the notes alongside the visual component.

Tracey picked Antoine and me up the following morning at eight thirty. The closer we got to Natchitoches, the more the streets began to change. The street signs were in French and adorned with the fleur-de-lis. Magnolia trees were everywhere. Scenic roads were paved with cobblestones, and the buildings reflected Spanish and French architectural styles. The downtown district was full of restaurants, galleries, mom-and-pop shops, and fashion boutiques. When Tracey drove over the Cane River Bridge, the view of the town reminded me of when I first walked across the Pont des Arts in Paris, looking toward the first arrondissement.

There is no mention of Marie Thérèse, Tracey's great-grandmother, anywhere in the heart of Natchitoches. The average visitor does not know who she was. The parish is most famous for *Steel Magnolias*. The worldwide attention that the film brought to this otherwise quaint town caused a boom in the tourism industry, especially for the hotels and bed-and-breakfasts.[2] Tracey spoke to us along the waterfront of the downtown district, where she expressed her main critiques about the town. "When people come here [to Cane River], when Creoles come here from California or from Chicago or wherever they're coming from, this is their Mecca. This is where everybody wants . . . this is home, this is where they want to come to, because everybody has that connection to their particular family—and then they walk away feeling kind of left out." The Creoles, those who have ties to Cane River, are all over the United States, and yet when they come home, there is very little reflection of themselves in the landscape.

I got a severe sense of this erasure when Tracey took me on

a tour of Melrose Plantation, right off Highway 119. When Marie Thérèse died, she left Louis, one of her sons with Claude Metoyer, 912 acres, upon which he began to build Melrose.[3] Along with the typical features of a plantation, such as pecan trees, colonnades, and monochromatic tones, there is a structure called the African House, built by slaves, whose purpose remains unknown. A two-story hutlike structure, it has a roof of Cypress shingles, floors of brick and hand-hewn timbers, and a twelve-foot overhang.[4] Nowadays, the African House is home to the murals of Clementine Hunter, the community's most famous artist of folklife from 1940 to 1980. Much reverence was paid to her on the tour but not much to Marie Thérèse. To understand this, one must understand the Metoyers' loss of affluence.

To put into perspective just how wealthy Cane River Creoles were compared to other free people of color in the South, in 1860 the average free black person's wealth was $34, whereas a Cane River Creole's was $1,875. The region took two hits in the 1830s and 1840s. In the 1830s, property costs were rising as people speculated, and too much credit led to a decade-long depression. When the Depression ended in the 1840s, a flood brought an influx of caterpillars that ruined half of Cane River's crops, causing the price of cotton to drop from nine to four cents a pound in two years. Unlike the white people of Cane River, the Metoyers did not have any Creole peers in their income bracket, so even though they produced more than the whites, their per capita wealth continued to decrease, because they married and had children with those who made less than their family.[5]

As Louisiana became more Americanized and it became a black-and-white binary, Creoles were not as distinct a class as they once were. As new white American settlers came into the parish and not only depleted the available land and finite food supplies, there was a level of tension played out differently among the Cane River whites and Creoles. While the Cane River whites often amicably associated with the incoming whites—and eventually subsumed their identities under these newcomers—to maintain social and actual capital, the Creoles of color soon learned that their friendship was of interest to whites only if there was a profit involved, which usually led to legends of property loss. While white people were able to rebuild after the Depression and the Civil War and emancipation, the Creoles of color were not. In a sense, they had been blackened.[6]

Melrose Plantation passed into white hands when brothers Henry and Hyppolite Hertzog purchased it for $8,340 in 1847. After Reconstruction, the Hertzogs sold to the Henrys. The Henrys owned Melrose from 1884 to 1970. From 1971 till the present, the Association for Preservation of Historic Natchitoches (APHN) owned the plantation.[7]

Despite Tracey having a stake in Melrose Plantation, this was her first time going on a tour there. From the moment it started, I thought this whole event was a masochistic experience for her. Our tour guide was a white woman who could not have been any older than twenty-three. Though friendly, she had a bubbliness that seemed ill-suited to a plantation tour. Unsurprisingly to me, almost like a repeat of Sapelo Island, there were no other people of color on the tour. The guide began with the story of Marie Thérèse, who she said got her name Coin Coin, the onomatopoeic French equivalent of Quack Quack, because she allegedly talked too much. I shot a glance at Tracey, who smirked and swayed from side to side, her bottom lip eventually tucking into her mouth. "Don't say anything," I whispered.

The guide did mention Marie Thérèse Coin Coin's relationship with Claude Thomas Metoyer and the singsong tunes she sang to describe their bond did convey the illicitness of that union. Yet beyond mentioning her eventual freedom and the birth of her son, who was responsible for building the plantation, nothing else was said. There was no mention of her wealth, land and slave ownership, or descendants. Her life story was packed into a one-minute introduction. I learned more about the Hertzog family and about Cammie Henry, who turned the plantation into an artists' retreat, than about the Metoyer family, despite the fact that paintings of Marie Thérèse Coin Coin's children and grandchildren still hang in one of the dining rooms.

You are a descendant of Marie Thérèse Coin Coin if you live in and around Natchitoches and your last name is one of the following: Metoyer, Antee, Hamilton, Sarpy, Roque, Severin, Conant, Colson, Rachal, Dupre, Balthazar, LeComte, LeCour/LaCour, or Llorens. I don't think their absence from Melrose was out of ignorance. The vast majority of the extended family members did not want to be a part of the APHN and their cultural tours. On one hand, I can see why they wouldn't feel welcome if their *grand-mère* is characterized as a talkative whore. They shouldn't want to be a part of APHN. They should have control over these tours themselves. And since these descendants knew their own history, there might have been no purpose to be included. Would they be participating for themselves or for an outside audience? If Creoles were being exoticized, there was too much at stake; their whole lives and histories would be stamped into gimmicks and cheap thrills.

Cultural dissonance defines Natchitoches. There is no one meaning. There are multiple voices that clash over Marie Thérèse Coin Coin and her legacy. The academics who visit Melrose deny that Marie had any architectural say over the plantation, particularly the African House. The APHN is a not-for-profit group whose members are mainly affluent white women, who center the narrative of Melrose Plantation on three women: Marie Thérèse Coin Coin, Cammie Henry, and Clementine Hunter, the self-taught black artist. The problem with focusing on a black woman like Marie without any of her children's children involved in these preservation groups is that doing so drives a wedge between us, the descendants, and them, the tourists and conservators. In an earlier

Melrose brochure, Marie Thérèse Coin Coin is written about as a legend, not an actual person. The fact that there are no pictures of her only adds to her mythical aura. The Cane River Creoles are not exactly pleased with others telling a story that they themselves know. One of them asked me, "Why should the largely Anglo members of the APHN tell their version of our story for the benefit of their organization?"

One voice dominates and inadvertently silences the others or pushes them to the periphery. The Cane River Creoles argue that the APHN directors are cherry-picking certain parts of Marie Thérèse Coin Coin's story to suit their purposes; thus her life becomes inauthentic. Marie Coin Coin wasn't just a strong woman—a crutch that I believe white folks use when they're at a loss how else to compliment us—but the founder of a community. The omission of oral history leads to erasure altogether. A Cane River Creole once attended a Melrose Plantation tour on which an APHN member mentioned twice that Cane River Creoles had been "wiped out by Jim Crow."[8] On *our* tour, the guide never said anything that was blatantly untrue, but neither was there any mention of Cane River Creoles and their influence. Toward the end of it, I felt bad for Tracey. I could imagine what thoughts must have been coursing through her mind as the half-truths were spoken with no acknowledgment of her large family tree in the area.

When we were back in downtown Natchitoches, Tracey told me a beautiful metaphor for her identity: "There's this huge tree, and it's got these big huge roots, and if you're only watering one side of the tree and only one side of the tree is getting the sunshine, then the rest of it's gonna die. So I choose to water and give sun to my entire tree, not just to the parts that make everybody else feel comfortable or the side that they like the most." How much water and sun can a Creole woman give if the tree's not on solid ground? What good are water and sun if people believe that that species of tree is extinct?

Nevertheless, there is still a large part of Natchitoches Parish that has yet to be flooded with tourists: Isle Brevelle, an 18,000-acre stretch of land between Cane River and Bayou Brevelle; 16,000 of those acres are still owned by Creole families. It was at Isle Brevelle where I got to see a possible precursor to cloistered communities like Frenchtown in Houston, where Creole families like the Regises migrated. The original owner of all 18,000 acres was Nicolas Augustin Metoyer, one of Claude and Marie Coin Coin's sons. A blacksmith and businessman, he petitioned the Spanish Crown for land in 1795 and received 395 acres. He and his brothers came to Isle Brevelle and cleared the canebrakes and prepared the land for tobacco and cotton cultivation. With each new harvest, they would buy out their neighbors, who also had received grants from the Spanish Crown but did not maintain the land. By the mid-1800s, Metoyer's family held those 18,000 acres and five hundred slaves. When his wife, Agnes, died, Augustin divided his estate among his children; it amounted to over $140,000, an incredible figure in the midst of a worldwide depression. Whenever his children married, they would receive land, cash, slaves, or all three. Like his mother, he eventually freed the slaves he bought, rendering a complicated portrait of those people of African descent who participated in the plantation economy.[9] To this day, Metoyer descendants and their extended-family members still live in the area.

While there, I was able to see just how wide and pristinely blue Cane River is. We toured the Badin-Roque House, the former residence of Marie Coin Coin's grandson Augustin Metoyer, later turned into a convent for a few years before passing through several hands to the Saint Augustine Historical Society. We toured the house with Tracey's eighty-year-old father, Oswald Colson, who is one of the few remaining people who still know how to maintain a house with *bousillage*, a mixture of clay with grass and/or retted Spanish moss used to fill the spaces between the timbers of the building's walls. Then we traveled farther down Highway 484 to Saint Augustine Church. Like Our Mother of Mercy in French-town, Saint Augustine was the Creole social hub. The connection reaffirmed to me that Catholicism was one of the strongest ties that my father's family had to their heritage.

The origin story of Saint Augustine Roman Church goes like this: Claude Metoyer sent Nicolas Augustin to France, where he was enchanted by the way churches were the center of social life. Nicolas Augustin donated the land, and his brother Louis built the church for free people of color. The exact date still unknown. It was the first church in the United States built by nonwhites to be used by nonwhites. In 1856, the year of Nicolas Augustin's death, the parish was established, as well as a mission to serve an all-white congregation on Old River. Saint Augustine was the first nonwhite church in the states to have authority over a religious mission of whites.

Although I could see paintings of Marie Coin Coin's descendants at Melrose Plantation, they were smaller than what I was about to see next. Unlike that plantation tour guide, Tracey wanted to draw my attention to her family's most famous artifact: a large portrait of Augustin Metoyer. One can find Augustin on the left side of the church upon entering the sanctuary. The life-size portrait hangs on the right-hand wall of its niche, adjacent to photographs of the filth in the barn where the painting had been left to spoil. The only other time I had seen an image that large and overwhelming was at the Louvre. Nicolas Augustin Metoyer stands on a blue-checkered floor dressed in a black coat, suit, bow tie, and leather shoes. He is holding a top hat in his left hand. His skin is light brown, hair thick and gray, and dark eyes unyieldingly confident. His right hand is presenting his church in the background of the painting. The size of the painting alone demonstrates wealth. Augustin's prominence is most likely the reason why the Cane River Creoles have this memory of what he looked like.

Tracey stood underneath the painting with her hands on her

hips in contemplative and reverent silence. She is at home in this part of the sanctuary.

"It was very significant for people to come to actually see the painting. One of his Metoyer descendants, Mr. Charles Metoyer . . . they took a picture of him standing next to this painting. He looks exactly like him. The hair—everything. He looks exactly like him. It's scary how much they look alike." She showed me a picture of Charles, and I was at a loss for words. "But it means a whole lot to a whole lot of people because they have a picture of him and you can look at him, which is different than a lot of these other free people of color. You can see that he was brown and looked like us."

"This is what we look like. We're not white Creoles. This is who we came from. More than anything in this life, just like they [Augustin Metoyer's grandchildren] were tired of people coming and literally taking stuff. His grandchildren had a right to it. That's like somebody coming into your apartment and saying, 'This table would look really good in my house' and taking it. It's the same thing, to me. So that happened a whole bunch of times. We ain't bothering y'all. Don't come here and bother us. This is an emotional experience for people to finally come here and just be in this space when you know that you have that connection. My daddy said we are "the Man without a Country." We don't come from anywhere. And that does make us feel lost and forgotten sometimes."

Tracey gave me some time to sit in front of the painting, and I was thankful for every moment of that solitude. I looked up at Nicolas Augustin with his self-satisfied smirk and felt small underneath the grandeur of this painting. Of course, I knew that Tracey was telling the truth about her family history. I had been studying the Metoyers through censuses and books for months. But being in Saint Augustine Church and observing this painting gave me another level of understanding. It wasn't enough to believe this history of Cane River Creoles. I didn't just believe, I was confronted and cornered. There was no physical space within those sixteen thousand acres of land where I could run away from the influence of black slave owners. My internal dialogue was filled with questions that looped on repeat. Why was I wrestling with the truth that black slave owners existed? I couldn't handle the idea that there *were* black people who benefited under a white supremacist system by enslaving other black people. But this isn't new. West African elites sold other black people into slavery. Sometimes slavery was an equal-opportunity atrocity. I was gaining a history lesson and maturing as a person and researcher all at once. I could grasp how Creole history became erased in the binary system by first abandoning that binary in my mind. I felt able to shed these polarities when I saw this painting. I'd never seen a painting of a black man that was this large. Even if I had no idea who Augustin was, I would have known, just from the sheer size of it, that he was important. Men of importance usually are wealthy, and if he was wealthy when this portrait was painted, then that undermined part of what I "knew" about slavery. I was staring directly into history as he stared at me, an African American woman whose tongue was gradually becoming strong enough to hold the word Creole in her mouth.

According to historian R. Halliburton Jr., black people have owned slaves in each of the thirteen original colonies as well as all the states where slavery was allowed. Sometimes black slave owners obtained slaves through inheritance or as gifts from white or black relatives. Some bought women with the intent to marry them, and others bought family members with the intent to free them. But not all black slave owners participated in the system out of the goodness of their hearts. Some were in it for profit just as much as their white counterparts. In 1830, in twenty-four states, including Louisiana, New Jersey, Alabama, and New Hampshire, there were 3,775 black owners of 12,760 slaves.[10]

As Tracey said, it's important for Marie Coin Coin's descendants to return to this church to remember who they were—a mélange of brown-skinned slaves and slave owners—and how much their ancestors had achieved. Just as in the Lowcountry, I learned that coming back home is a crucial healing pilgrimage. Today the Metoyers are spread out all over the country, especially in New York, Pennsylvania, Ohio, Texas, California, and Illinois.

Upon further research, I've found that much of their land passed into white hands during the Great Migration. After the death of her husband, John, in 1918, Cammie Henry turned Melrose Plantation into an artists' colony. When Cammie's son, the manager of the plantation, died in 1970, usually considered the last year of the Great Migration, the plantation was sold at public auction, and all of Clementine Hunter's murals, except those in the African House, were stripped and sold as well.[11]

Tracey herself is the daughter of those who migrated but came back to Louisiana. Her father, Oswald, an olive-skinned man whose eighty years were belied by his irreverent jokes and sharp memory, is known around Natchitoches mostly for being the filé man. He plucks, destems, and pounds leaves from sassafras trees, then sifts and bottles them for three weeks. He uses it to make gumbo, adding it just before serving to thicken the stew and impart a spicy, earthy flavor—a process that he learned from his mother, Veronica Metoyer.[12]

Oswald Colson crossed color lines wherever he moved. He reminded me of a slightly darker-skinned version of the late actor Anthony Quinn, whose long career was partly attributed to his being racially ambiguous. Oswald left Louisiana when the price of cotton per pound dropped precipitously. Agricultural mechanization led many like him to flock to the West and North before and after World War II for better opportunities.[13] His parents let someone else take care of the land. He first moved to Chicago, where he was often mistaken for Italian; he made car parts. Then he drove his '55 Ford from Saint Louis to California, where he claimed that there was no job discrimination. On his off days, he'd play guitar and piano on La Cienega and Sunset Boulevards.

Oswald's wife, Janet, was born and raised in Los Angeles, where hordes of Creoles migrated, starting in the 1920s. On what was supposed to be a simple trip back to Louisiana in March, she met Oswald, and they got married in July. I was able to meet Tracey's parents along with her extended-family members at Mass. I gathered that, like Our Mother of Mercy and Saint Augustine, Saint Anthony was central to the Creole community because Tracey's relatives swarmed her in the parking lot. One parishioner mistook me for kin: "Are you Agnes's daughter?" My eyebrows curved inward in confusion, though I smiled and politely told her no. Tracey told me that Creoles can recognize their own, and though that woman mistook me for someone else, she wouldn't have made that mistake if she hadn't thought that I resemble another Creole person, maybe even someone connected to Cane River. But I've been in many situations where I remind someone of a loved one, so I didn't think much of it. At least, not at that moment.

I was too focused on the larger picture, seeing quite a few of Marie Coin Coin's descendants together in one place and knowing that they weren't all erased, no matter what tour guides said. They were here and lively as ever. They carried themselves with pride in a way that could only come from those who knew their history well. They all looked well-to-do. They walked with a certain command, like my father.

I wondered if these Cane River Creoles still conducted themselves as though they were socially different, despite the much different racial legal system in the twenty-first century. This Catholic church was their social hub, and they were a cohesive bunch. Yes, Natchitoches is a small town, but the ambience was distinguishable here. They were united by a single woman, her blood running through their veins, no matter if the dominant narrative about her life downplays her influence. But I noticed—and maybe this is why someone mistook me for another—that every last one of them was quite light, doubtless a major factor behind their wealth and power. I felt as if a thorn had pierced my side, forcing me to confront a long-standing pain about my complexion and how it relates to my father and my identity as a whole.

3

NOW THAT I had learned something about Creole identity and the social stratum Creoles occupied in the plantation economy, I had to deal with skin color. Although I wasn't told by my parents until I was older that my father called me "the milkman's baby" because of my lightness at birth, my light skin had always intrigued people in South Jersey. Whenever my mother would introduce me to friends, black or white, they would assume that my father was white. Friends from church joked that I was white, and their playful jabs bothered me because, unlike them, only one of my parents sat in a pew every Sunday morning. I couldn't show the actual proof to the skeptics. I knew exactly who I was, yet I hated when people would ask what I was mixed with, as if my skin couldn't be the product of two black parents, as if blackness always looks a certain way, as if two black parents having a child lighter than either of them was an aberration in the natural order of things.

No one ever doubted that I was black, but *how* black was up for debate. However, tomorrow I was going to learn how color is wielded at the opposite end of the spectrum, where blackness is invisible. I assumed that Tracey would take me to visit another cultural landmark, but I couldn't have been more wrong. In fact, this day was going to further unravel my preconceived notions about Creoles, what they look like, and how they relate to my ideas about blackness, but in a much more intimate setting.

I suppose Tracey wanted me to see how consequences of the American way of defining race stretch into the present day. She introduced me to her friend Kelly Clayton. We drove out of Natchitoches, made a pit stop in Opelousas to see Tracey's husband and children, then continued to Lafayette. Kelly lived on a quaint street corner on the North side of the city, the predominantly black side, and all sorts of herbs and fruits grew in her yard. Originally from Baton Rouge and New Orleans, Kelly had a long stint in Brooklyn before returning to Louisiana. When she emerged from the back porch, I was confused. Did Tracey take me to a white woman's house? Kelly was very pale and slender with an aquiline nose. Maybe in her youth she could have been a model. But her hair was the most peculiar attribute about her. She had gray dreadlocks that reached down her back. I had never seen a white person's dreadlocks that neat and maintained, especially around the edges. Then it hit me: this woman was not white.

Kelly's dog, Maybelline, who was about the same size as me, greeted us. She steered Maybelline to the side and yelled for her son to come and get her. As she guided us into the kitchen, I saw an immaculate altar next to her work desk. Morris Day was playing from a stereo in the kitchen. There was Obama iconography behind the dining-room table. Two magazines, one *Vogue* and the other *Allure*, had women of color on the cover (Amal Clooney and Zoe Lane, respectively). She fixed me a strong mint julep before pulling a chair beside mine, readying herself to be interviewed. I scooted farther to the edge of my seat to hear about her earlier, runaway life.

"Mmm! We can unpack that one. Well I married somebody really young. First of all, I was a very, very young mother. I have a thirty-six-year-old son, a thirty-year-old son, a twenty-eight-year-old son, and that's the babiest of babies," she said as her fifteen-year-old son moved in and out of the dining room, preoccupied with all he had to do for the Festival International de Louisiane, an annual francophone arts and music festival in town.

Kelly was talking a mile a minute, as if she'd been waiting for me. Turned out she *had* been following me on Twitter for quite some time and was a fan of my work. Needless to say, I was relieved. I knew I could expect Southern hospitality but not this depth of vulnerability. Kelly told me that she married into an Italian Catholic family, though she wasn't a great pick because of her background. I didn't understand. She *looked* white to me. Many Louisianans, like Italians, are Catholic, and those who aren't are familiar with the protocols and rituals of the faith. Her relatives didn't understand why Kelly wouldn't pass and have an easier life. The older folks, Kelly said, would "break you down" with their swipes about how ethnic you looked: "I wanted an ass I could carry a beer on. I was so disappointed in my allotment of features. But my grandmother used to say, 'Look at her. She's got good hair and she's so pale' but then she would say, 'But that nose. I'm sorry about that nose.'" Tracey interjected to tell me that the older generation would celebrate if a child looked light enough to pass, and Kelly admittedly felt that pressure. If she ever wore braids, her mother told her to take them out. Her hair was constantly "ironed," as she called it, to smooth out any kinkiness. I could relate to that hair story, though I cannot pass. I realized again how much bullshit race is. The more I try to make sense of who is black or white, the less sense it makes.

Before sitting down and speaking to her, I thought this white woman was *performing* blackness—playing black music and adorning her walls with black iconography—just because I couldn't see any reflection of my physical self in her. The humbling truth is that I don't know all black people. I haven't traveled to every state and met every black person in every town. I'm sure if I did, I would come away with the same impression that I had upon meeting Kelly: blackness is complicated by one's sense of place and history. Kelly was pressured to be respectable and assimilate, as I was. Why else would her family want her to change her appearance, if they hadn't thought it would be easier for her to survive in this world by hiding? While Kelly does enjoy certain privileges due to her skin color—and most likely had been socialized as white for the majority of her life—I could relate to the pressure to conform as a black woman.

Then I pondered some more when I realized I *was* black. I knew that the community in which I was raised was brown, but I didn't know the full weight of being black until I was compared to an animal as a preteen. I didn't make the all-white cheerleading squad, and a friend told me it was because "monkeys" like me didn't make the team. That was my entrée into what blackness meant in the larger sense. It was not the reflection of my beautiful family but rather the constant reminder of being misunderstood and mislabeled or in need of correction. I didn't grow up in a family where white-passing children were celebrated. I am the lightest person in my immediate family on my mother's side. I seldom encountered other light-skinned people. One aunt even encouraged me to date and marry a darker-skinned man—to balance me out.

I have spent my career trying to tease out the interwoven threads of who I am as a black woman. Kelly has tried to become a writer to explore her own identity, but with much trouble: "I began to teach myself how to write, and I spent my life in libraries and applied to Hedgebrook and VONA [Voices of Our Nation's Arts Foundation], and I got in. I was gonna write about what it feels like—this Creole heritage. I had a story. But I got scared. When people look at me and say something on Twitter, they get savage, and I didn't want to explain like, well wait a minute, I'm not exactly what you think I am. I didn't want to live my life defending myself, and I backed up and I stopped writing for a long time." Kelly embodied what Tracey told me back on the waterfront in downtown Natchitoches—the exhaustion of having to explain herself over and over and over again. It didn't matter whether the people who harassed her were white or people of color. We all have our preconceived notions of what people of the diaspora are supposed to look like, and often we don't admit that our sample sizes are way too small to support these assumptions.

"There's only one Creole and that's mixed. The end. You Creole, you black. There is no white creole. That's a stupid, stupid designation, and you know . . . We're mixed people, and once you see that in your genealogy, what is the problem? I don't get it. It's important to me. It's important because it's not stamped on my face. It's not stamped on my skin. I have to make a statement. Otherwise I disappear." I noticed Kelly's word choices. Creoles are black people *and* they're a mixed people. There is no either/or. There is no black American who is 100 percent black because blackness has nothing to do with blood purity. We became black through systems. *New York Times* opinion columnist Jamelle Bouie once said, taking from W.E.B. Du Bois, with regard to one of these systems, namely Jim Crow, that "people weren't subjected to Jim Crow because they were black. Rather, what made them black is that they were a subject of Jim Crow."[1]

It would be intellectually irresponsible for me to suggest that my blackness could be separated from systems in America. But I hope that there is space to discuss the "lost ones" in this system, those like Kelly who benefit from their light or white skin yet want none of its privileges. Blackness is not static: I may travel to another place and be considered something else *in addition to*, not *in lieu of*, black. If we could consider blackness not as a zero-sum experience, then that discomfort can give way to understanding and healing.

I thought about my great-aunt Evelyn and her daughter Gwen, who chose to take advantage of her privilege and call herself white. As Kelly fought to define herself, did Gwen ever struggle on the other side of the color line? I could not assume either one had it easier. Both were affected by the tough racial stratifications of American society and made separate choices for a better life or a sense of peace. Maybe if Gwen had "stayed" black, I would've gotten to know her, and the Regis family would have been less fragmented. Suddenly, I began to feel pity for those relatives.

After we finished discussing Kelly's identity challenges, Kelly wanted to show me a part of Creole and Louisiana identity that sent a chill down my spine: Voodoo. Louisiana Voodoo is a syncretized religion that combines French Roman Catholicism and West African spirituality and religions via the transatlantic slave trade. Not every Creole person is a Voodoo practitioner, but the religion is a vital element of Louisiana Creole culture. The faith's most powerful leaders were those of African and Creole descent, such as Marie Laveau, whose story has been popularized most recently in *American Horror Story*.

I was raised to believe that, like the "root" in my mother's house, Voodoo was demonic and something to be feared. But in conversations with my cousin Colleen, our family's relationship with Voodoo was more complicated. Colleen was born and raised in Lafayette, the city where Kelly is based, and though she identifies as Christian, she tells me that our family was familiar with Voodoo and its power. She wasn't sure if any relatives practiced at all. She can recall two brushes with the religion. One of them was either a relative or neighbor who suddenly died. When the body was sliced open, there were snakes inside. Another was a next-door neighbor who ceaselessly slobbered. He could not speak well and was mentally challenged. Word around the neighborhood was that he broke a woman's heart and she fixed him good, though no one knows what ritual or spell she performed. When Colleen and her family migrated to Philadelphia, Voodoo didn't occupy the same space as it once did in Lafayette. They didn't talk about it unless prompted, as when I interviewed them. There weren't any anecdotes of vengeful spells and whatnot from spiteful lovers. Philadelphia was a new landscape and the old ways weren't relevant up north. Consequently, those like me who had never lived in Louisiana were not as attuned to how seamlessly Voodoo was woven into our family's lives.

Because Kelly wanted me to understand the connection between Creoles and Voodoo, she showed me both of her altars—a gift that I did not take for granted. She had had requests from white women who wanted to stop by her home and take pictures of the altars for artistic research, but she turned them down. She knew what the game was. But after learning that my ancestors were from Louisiana too, she wanted me to see them. I was Creole, and I needed to know about not just Catholicism, but also the other religious and spiritual practices of our people. The ancestor altar was in the upper right-hand corner of her living room facing the kitchen. There are pictures of her grandmother and her child's dog, who recently died, the key to her aunt's house, a doorstop from her grandmother's house, a ram's horn, some of Oswald's filé, her brother's ashes, and a bottle of whiskey from which she fills a shot glass every evening. When it has evaporated by the morning, she knows that the ancestors have had their fill. A few pieces of cotton are placed on the altar in memory of those who were enslaved, and offerings need to be given to them: a piece of peanut butter–chocolate candy or some mints will do. Before she starts to cook, she lights the candles on the altar. She did so before teaching me how to cook crawfish étouffée. Whatever she prepares, she portions some in wooden bowls to give to the ancestors. Whenever there's a crisis, her family will lie down beside the altar, watch the candles glow, and talk to the ancestors in regular conversation.

Without prompting, Kelly echoed what I'd learned in the Lowcountry: "My mother . . . she's terrified of storms, and she's terribly afraid of water, and she can't swim, but she has never been traumatized by any storm. Nothing's ever happened to her. There's no reason for these fears; they're just genetic memory—that's all." But genetic memory is only half of her family's history. A relative of hers committed suicide by throwing himself into the river. Her mother was a guard at Angola, one of the most notorious prisons in the world. Angola comprises four plantations and is almost surrounded by a bend of the Mississippi River. Many of the black men in there can't swim, and even if they could, gators would await them.

But water is also a vital resource and an aspect of Kelly's spirituality and reverence for her heritage. Her ancestors lived along the Atchafalaya River, a 137-mile-long tributary of the Mississippi that runs through south central Louisiana. She gathered water from it as part of her vow-of-renewal ceremony. Resa, Tracey's sister, performed traditional Voodoo rites. For the ceremony, Tracey, Resa, and Resa's boyfriend drew veves using cornmeal on the pavement. Veves are Voodoo geometric designs or symbols each corresponding to a different loa, or lwa—one of a group of spiritual forces recognized by the faith. In Kelly's words, "It's the act, not the result. The symbol is [the doing,] that you take the cornmeal in your hand and then you're leaning down and you're creating the [physical] symbol with your hand. It's the action of your body and the intent in your mind that makes whatever it's going to make. It's not about the final result." There are different families of loas called nanchons, which are said to have come from different tribes in Africa. Papa Legba of Rada nanchon was the one called upon in Kelly's ceremony. He is said to speak all human languages and serves as an intermediary between this world and the souls of the dead. Syncretized with saints Peter, Anthony, and Lazarus, Legba often appears as an older black man with a cane or crutch, smoking a pipe. Resa took a mouthful of whiskey and blew it in the direction of Kelly and her husband. Together, Resa, Kelly, and her husband petitioned for Legba to open the door into the spirit world. Resa doesn't remember a word she said during the ceremony, because she was absent and a spirit took her place.

For Kelly's personal altar, located in her studio, she has her grandfather's rosary and rocks and mineral specimens, some of which her sister gave after a jaunt in Egypt. The four corners of her altar need rocks to ground it. Then there is the dirt. Hers is from Poverty Point, a UNESCO World Heritage Site of prehistoric earthworks and mounds. There's also a bird's nest and some water, which she charges every full moon. If the water isn't charged, the energy, she says, can make you depressed. The water cannot get stale either. The renewal is a commitment. If there is dust anywhere on the altar or the water is stagnant, the lack of maintenance affects her emotional health. She regularly prays to seven African deities. Her personal favorite is Oya, the goddess of winds, who creates cataclysmic change, especially when it comes to career paths and anything concerning women. La Sirène is another she points out—a mermaid goddess associated with wealth, beauty, and seduction. Also Baron Samedi (Saturday), god of the dead but also a giver of life, who can cure any ailment—if he so chooses. This ritual acknowledgment of spirits is a dedication. If one is not consistent and faithful, all kinds of doors will close. Kelly is not sure if she comes from a line of Voodoo practitioners, but she suspects she has, because of the customs she's learned:

1. A split cow tongue on the kitchen counter can bind the tongue of someone who's talking negatively about you.
2. If you have an enemy, do a ritual. Write down your grievances. Wait until midnight. Walk down the block from your place to an intersection, leave that note in the middle of it, and walk away without looking back.
3. Another alternative is to put the note in a little bottle, like a baby food jar, and throw it into the Mississippi.

This part of my trip was both different from and similar to my learning about the root in the Lowcountry. I learned about the powers of the spiritual realm there, but here in Louisiana, this kind of devotion was much more tangible, with altars and sacrifices.

It reminded me of similar practices in my family, like a prayer closet in one's home, crucifixes or paintings of Jesus, portraits of deceased family members, and biblical sayings as artwork on the walls. Weren't these all examples of our gratitude to God and the ancestors? Didn't we have these adornments as a way to remind ourselves, like Kelly, that we were being watched over? And as for my father, he always had photos of his ancestors. He even gave me snapshots of my grandparents—his parents—to put up in my own home. At first, I thought these were just gifts, but after visiting Louisiana, I knew that these images were charged with my ancestors' presence, which would always be with me, no matter what.

Later that day, I attended the Festival International de Louisiane with Kelly. One woman looked at me and asked, "Are you from Saint Landry Parish?" I blinked. Saint Martin Parish is an hour southeast of Saint Landry. I shook my head, smiled, and said no, as I had done before at Saint Anthony of Padua Catholic Church. I told this woman the correct parish, and Kelly chimed in, "It's those half-moon eyes." I was stupefied. I never liked my eyes, the way they curled upward whenever I smiled for photographs. "Open your eyes," my mother would say as she grew impatient behind the camera. Though I tried my hardest, I gave up after a while.

My half-moon eyes are one of the biggest indicators that I am my father's daughter. When my father and I smile, often you can hardly see our irises, but we are exuberant. These weren't stubborn eyes; they were my father's eyes, and now they had a name. It was only after I came to discover my family history in Louisiana that someone identified these eyes for what they were: half-moons.

4

ALL I COULD think about for the rest of that evening en route to Tracey's home in Opelousas was half-moons. It was the first time in my life that I truly felt like my father's daughter without having to explain who or what I was. I had a name for one of the characteristics that I once thought of as a physical flaw in need of correction. Now I felt transformed, but not into someone new; rather, I was looking at myself with a different degree of magnification. My eyes weren't small. They were half-moons that waxed and waned. The beauty of the label stuck with me and announced in a subtle way that these people in Louisiana were *my* people, no matter how long I had been away and how little I knew about my own culture. The power of three is no mistake. I was recognized at Saint Anthony and at the Festival International de Louisiane by both Kelly and another woman. And now half-moon eyes. It was the eve of the day when I would finally return to Saint Martinville. After I had spent all this time listening to everyone else's narrative, it was now time to excavate my own.

I asked Tracey if my last full day in Louisiana could be spent going to Saint Martinville; otherwise my father and cousin Janice would be livid. She agreed, and hence my previous days were jam-packed with activity about Cane River Creoles. Going from Natchitoches to Lafayette to Saint Martinville made the most sense geographically. I was looking for my great-grandmother Carrie. I didn't know Carrie's maiden name, but her son Armstead's surname was Hamilton, and Hamiltons were related to the Metoyers. Was this what Janice meant when she mentioned our connection to Cane River? I wasn't too sure. I wanted a stronger link. I found marriage licenses, both in English and French, from Maturin Regis's children, but couldn't find anything about Carrie. Sometimes marriage information will include the names of the parents of the bride or groom, but there was nothing.

My dad messaged me very frequently, asking me when was I going to Saint Martinville and whether I'd found anything interesting so far. I would send him pictures of the Acadiana landscape, and Janice would send me a list of surnames to look up in the records. I was nervous that I'd let my family down, especially my dad, if I couldn't find any substantial information. This trip was unexpectedly bringing us closer together because I was returning to a past that he never knew about in a place to which he had never traveled. He was hungry for details, feeling empowered for when I would tell him about our history.

The third oldest city in Louisiana, Saint Martinville is a part of the Acadiana region, just eighteen miles southeast of Lafayette. With its mossy oaks and picturesque street corners, Saint Martinville was the place where people from New Orleans escaped to, calling it Petit Paris because of its good French-language theaters.[1] Many residents are descendants of Beausoleil Broussard, who led the Acadians, French people who settled in what is now Canada and northern Maine, to southern Louisiana after the British occupied their land and expelled them from Canada. Others are descendants of the bourgeois Bienvenu and Duchamps families, who fled after the French Revolution. Others are from Senegal.[2] Acadiana's most famous landmark is the Evangeline Oak in the center of town because it was the inspiration for Henry Wadsworth Longfellow's poem *Evangeline*.

Our first plan was to go to the African American Museum just a few steps away from the Evangeline Oak, but it was closed. There was a number to call for someone across town to open the door for visitors, but that woman never picked up the phone. Our next stop was the City Hall, but a woman there told us our best bet was the Saint Martinville Public Library if I was interested in genealogical research. If it weren't for Tracey, Antoine, and Richie, I would have remained paralyzed at the threshold of the door leading to the records section. I'm not a stranger to libraries and archives rooms with rows that exercise my eyes to gauge their lengths, but this expedition was different. My family was in there somewhere. I didn't know where to look, much less where to begin. I tried to pace myself.

"Do you need some help?" A small, bearded man with glasses peeked out from behind one of the columns.

"Yes," I said exasperatedly. I repeated all the loose strands of my family history to him, and he said, "Well, I don't have much time, but I'll see if I can help." He adjusted his glasses on his face and began to go down the aisles, pulling out books the size of his chest and handing them to Richie and Antoine. He directed them to search through them to find a Maturin Regis or Armstead Hamilton. We hit a brick wall: one of the large books that included my family's name was inexplicably missing. But that was OK. This stranger, who was neither a librarian nor a genealogist, was undeterred. He placed his finger on a few property records and saw that Maturin Regis Sr. was listed but never Carrie, causing him to conclude that they may have never been legally married.

"Succession records. We have to look in the succession records." The stranger moved past us and pulled out another big book in a different row. As he flipped through the pages for Armstead Hamilton's name, the room felt eerily still. All of us leaned forward. What was he going to find? Could the missing link really be in succession records? I tried to make excuses for why it wouldn't work out in order to avoid disappointment. Sometimes succession records don't exist for black landowners. I knew this from my time in the Lowcountry. What if it was heirs property? We hadn't been in the library long enough. There wasn't enough time. I was supposed to fly back to New York the next afternoon. This was too good to be true.

There was a loud tap on the page. His finger was underneath a line that told me that Armstead, listed as a free man of color, was given a plantation by his mother, Carrie. I squinted at the document, and it read exactly as the stranger said. Antoine pulled out his camera and asked the stranger to repeat what he just found. My family was not made up only of free people of color; some of them were slave owners, complicating what I thought about my own history. There it was: a decree in cursive handwriting. A plantation. I didn't know what to do with that information. Tracey and Richie urged me to find out which plantation it was, but then what? Would I go visit? Would I subject myself to a plantation tour as Tracey had done back in Melrose and listen to some white girl gloss over the history of my family?

I wrestled with what to do, long after I returned to New York. Months passed, and then those months turned into a year. I could not find Carrie, my great-grandmother, anywhere. My only talisman was *Up from the Cane-Brakes*, in which Turpeau—a grandson of Maturin Regis Sr.—writes:

> While working for the Labbes, he [Maturin Regis Sr.] had a wife who gave him a child, Aunt Rose by name. He had two sons, Uncle Sanfore and Uncle Alexandra [*sic*], and judging from the ages of the following children, he also had Uncle Louis, Uncle Matt, Aunt Virginia, Aunt Amanda, and Uncle Jimmie besides my mother whose name was Isabelle, all about the same period. Of course a man's wife or wives in those days were quite a matter of taste. There seemed to be no special limit. . . . In my grandfather's case, he had a family on the east bank of the Teche and one on the west bank of

Teche. He lived on the west bank; Uncle Sanfore, Uncle Alex-
andra [*sic*], and Aunt Rose lived on the west bank.

This section I found incredibly intriguing. I am a product of
blended families. My father lived in one county in South Jersey
while I lived in another with my mother. But in this particular time
period, in the mid-nineteenth century, why did Maturin Sr. have
some of his children on the west bank of the bayou and some on
the east? Was it a matter of arrangement or something deeper?
Turpeau goes on to say:

A rather significant thing to be noted here. My grandmother
whose name was Carrie always lived on the east bank of the
Teche . . . my grandfather never lived on the east bank of
the Teche. There seemed to have been a mutual understanding between them and when my grandmother Carrie died,
which was in my day, I only saw my grandfather at the gate
of the cemetery.

This was even more strange to me, for several reasons. For one,
Turpeau names Maturin's children but does not specify which children belong to which mother. I know Isabelle Turpeau, his mother,
was a child of Maturin and Carrie, and through process of elimination, she lived on the east bank of the Bayou Teche at one time, according to him. For a man to have had children with a woman but
to be at the cemetery gate and never venture in when his beloved
died seems intentional. And if it were intentional that he could only
be at the cemetery gate, could this be the same reason as to why
they lived on opposite sides of the bayou? Was their affair illicit?
The family lore is that Maturin Regis Sr. was a manumitted
slave from Virginia, although when David DeWitt Turpeau Sr. did
his research, he found that neither Maturin nor the Regis name was
common in the state. He believed that Maturin may have picked

up an alias once he came down to Louisiana and met Carrie, a Creole woman. I didn't know why Turpeau says these lines: "Maturin did not work on the plantation known as Keystone as might be supposed; I learned from his own lips that he was 'no plantation nigger.' He was employed by a Mr. Labbe . . . They [the Labbes] were a very prominent family in our section and people of money." Turpeau devotes ample space to the surnames of many families in Saint Martinville, but not once does he mention Carrie's maiden name. He does, however, state that he has omitted certain names out of respect. To me, this was a cop-out. My intuition told me that he was omitting names to protect people, and I began to wonder if he was protecting Carrie.

I tried everything. I scrutinized the lines of his autobiography, hoping that Carrie's identity would emerge somehow from the titles of sections or the page numbers. I pored over census after census, contacted Louisiana genealogists—who never responded to my requests for help—and attempted to extract whatever crumbs and threads I could from the oldest members of my family. The search began to turn into an obsession, and the only mantra that kept me from floundering was this: *Question everything.* Then I came up with a hypothesis. Let's say that Maturin and Carrie's union was not socially acceptable. That would explain why I couldn't find their marriage record at the Saint Martinville Public Library and why Maturin didn't attend Carrie's funeral. If their union was taboo, would it be too far-fetched to believe that they tried to hide or obfuscate parts of their lives, even to their grandchildren, like David? At least with Maturin I had a last name. With Carrie, I had nothing. Her name sounded too informal in comparison to Maturin or Isabella or Amanda. Was Carrie a nickname? Was Carrie even her real name?

Then, in the midnight hour, my cousin Janice sent me an 1870 census page that I had glossed over umpteen times and thought nothing of it. The census form documents a woman named Constance Deblanc. She was a white woman whose occupation was "keeping the house," and there were several white people listed underneath her with a different surname, suggesting that they were her children. Then, there was a black man listed as Carry Love, who was born in Virginia. The three children underneath him were Amanda, Virginia, and James Regis. James had to have been my Uncle Jimmie. Those three children were listed as mulatto. I was overwhelmed. First, what kind of name is Carry Love? That sounded fake. Second, he was listed as being born in Virginia, and according to Turpeau Sr., Maturin Sr. was born in Virginia. If the children underneath his name were mulatto and Constance was listed as white, could it be that Carry Love was Maturin Regis Sr. and Constance was grandmother Carrie? Did Maturin take on the name Carry to hide his identity and Constance then become Carrie to their children and their children's children? Was Constance Deblanc my grandmother?

An 1870 United States federal census that lists some of the Regises—Virginia, James, and Amanda—a man whose name, Carry Love, I believe to be an alias for my great-great-great-grandfather Maturin Regis, and the one who is the head of the household and the potential mother of the Regis children, Constance DeBlanc. *Martinville, Louisiana Post Office, June 13th, 1870*

David DeWitt Turpeau Sr. said that Maturin never lived on the east bank, but how would he have known? He was born in 1874, and this census was taken in 1870. Carry Love is listed as a laborer. Why would Turpeau Sr. mention Maturin working on Keystone Plantation when Keystone Plantation was formerly known as Deblanc Plantation?[3] *Deeper*, I told myself. Deeper. Upon further research, I found that the Deblancs owned much land, many plantations from Saint Martin Parish to New Iberia. Maturin was not a slave in Louisiana, but he could have worked on Keystone, or any of the Deblanc properties, where he met and fell in love with Constance. But the Deblancs' story didn't begin there. No. The Deblancs in Louisiana began in Natchitoches, of all places. One of Constance's ancestors, Caesar de Blanc, married Marie Des Douleurs Simone Juchereau St. Denis. She was the daughter of Pierre Antoine Juchereau de St. Denis. Pierre's father, Louis, was said to have been the first owner of Marie Coin Coin. One of the De Blancs, Louis Charles, son of Caesar and Marie, was a commandant of the post in Natchitoches before serving as commandant of the post in Attakapas, also known as Saint Martinville. Legend has it that he was the one who granted Louis Metoyer title to the 912-acre tract of land known as Melrose.[4] The Deblancs were connected to the Metoyers not only professionally but also personally. The Deblancs are also linked by marriage to the LaCours, one of the earliest families of Cane River. When I reminisce on being mistaken for Agnes's daughter back at Saint Anthony of Padua Catholic Church, perhaps I wasn't being mistaken for someone else at all, but rather being identified. I'm a half-moon child, the daughter of a Regis, the great-great-great-great-granddaughter of a Deblanc, whose lineages are indelibly woven among those of the Metoyers.

I wish there were a word to adequately describe the ecstasy that happens alongside a sense of mourning for what was lost. I could now trace my father's line back to the 1700s, all the way to Natchitoches, where my fieldwork in Louisiana began. But the longer I sat in that happiness, the more I tried to force myself to feel shame, too. Why should I be relieved and happy that I found this information, knowing that one of my ancestors, Louis Juchereau St. Denis, leased a black woman, Marie Coin Coin, to a French merchant, Claude Thomas Pierre Metoyer? Yes, she was manumitted and became wealthy through land and slave owning, but shouldn't I be upset that the foundation for this history of Cane River Creoles was rape? I've always been told that any sexual relationship between white slave owners and black enslaved women was rape. When Beyoncé, a fellow Creole and African American woman, wrote an essay in *Vogue* stating that her family line began when a white slave owner fell in love with a slave and married her, I watched as the internet attempted to correct her on her own oral history.[5] But no one can say for sure what happened. Rape of enslaved black women was rampant, but we cannot assume that every relation between a white slave owner and black female slave was nonconsensual.

Such a thought is explosive, however, and ruffles a lot of feathers. According to Treva B. Lindsey, associate professor of women's, gender, and sexuality studies at Ohio State University, and Jessica Marie Johnson, associate professor of history at Johns Hopkins University:

> Despite the increasing rigor with which scholars are approaching slavery and erotics, the pervasiveness of intellectual skepticism reflects how deeply entrenched narratives of violation, violence, and trauma are to our understanding of black female sexuality. Emphasizing subjugation, exploitation, and dehumanization, however, cannot preclude fuller incorporation of pleasure and erotic possibility in the lives of enslaved black women. Sex acts happened often during slavery. Political goals of the moment do not rewrite the sexual lives, desires, and choices of enslaved and free women of color, but they can obscure those lives to our detriment. . . .

To search for this in chattel slavery by interrogating these possibilities . . . does not lessen the traumatic, terrorizing, and horrific nature of slavery. Such inquiries allow for the interior lives and erotic subjectivities of enslaved blacks to matter.[6]

No one can ever know if a specific woman like Marie Coin Coin was a victim of rape. From a historical standpoint, it's very likely. However, my trip to Louisiana taught me that intimate details may vary from historical norms. With the story of Tracey and her family, history was more personalized. I wasn't reading about these people in textbooks. I was seeing them up close. I was seeing Marie Thérèse Coin Coin and Claude Thomas Pierre Metoyer's descendants in the flesh, walking along the fields their children once owned. I can't slap labels on relationships hundreds of years prior. All I can do is give what I've found of the true and complicated intimate lives of my family and black people in general, testifying that we're more connected than we think. I was afraid to write about this part of my father's family, because I didn't want to ruffle feathers. But that's what historical research does: it makes a person uncomfortable. I can't be beholden to an unknown's feelings, because unlike facts, emotions are fickle. All I can ask is, did I tell the truth? Did I tell *my* truth? And I did.

To add to these family surprises, I learned that Maturin Regis's story didn't start in Virginia. Maturin Regis was born in Saint Lucia, where he joined his mother, Angelique, and his sister, Maturine, under the ownership of Reverend William John Jolliffe. From an English political dynasty, in 1822 Reverend Jolliffe owned 249 acres and 250 slaves.[7] I am not completely sure where his plantation was, but his name is associated with Balenbouche, which is now a family-run guesthouse in Laborie, on the southeastern coast of the island. Maturin is listed as being seven months old on an 1819 slave register. The Jolliffe family also owned land in Virginia. Maybe, just maybe, Maturin told his children and grandchildren that he was from Virginia because he didn't remember Saint Lucia and because neither his mother nor his sister followed him on his journey north.

The slave register of Reverend W. J. Jolliffe of London. Thirty-one-year-old Angelique Regis, the earliest ancestor that I can trace on my father's side, is listed third from the bottom on the left. Her children, three-year-old Maturine and seven-month-old Maturin, my great-great-great-great grandfather, are listed beneath her. *Legacies of British Slave-ownership, University of College London Department of History*

There you are, ancestors, I said to myself. There you are. I was both elated and sad at my discovery. I don't believe Constance ever wanted me to find her. I believe that there were elements about my family history that were hidden for a reason. The aliases shared between Maturin and Constance changed the course of their descendants' lives for centuries. The love between a white plantation owner and a manumitted black man—two Creoles, one from Louisiana and the other from the Antilles—changed their families forever. Amanda and Virginia Regis disappeared after that 1870 census. James, on the other hand, lived with his older brother, Maturin Jr., and was recategorized as black in 1880. Depending on the household, one's identity changed along with the times. Maybe Amanda and Virginia changed their surnames or names entirely and chose to pass for white like the daughter of my great-aunt Evelyn. Maybe that's why my grandfather Cleveland Sr. didn't speak much about being Creole. Whether or not he consciously knew of the divide, our family story was fragmented before we left Saint Martin Parish. Though Cleveland Sr. left Frenchtown, he would inadvertently re-create its caste system by marrying a North Carolina woman descended from free people of color on both sides of her family.

I was meant to meet Tracey Colson and to uncover how she and I were linked centuries before our time on Earth. It is nothing short of divine. I entered into Louisiana as Morgan Jerkins. I returned to New York City as Morgan Simone Régis Jerkins. I am a black and Creole woman, a descendant of slaves, slave owners, and free people of color. I need to say this not only for myself but for those fighting for Creole preservation and for my numerous family lines out there, those whom I may never meet due to racial boundaries or lack of time or travel opportunities. I know my father, my father's father, and the fathers before him. As for Maturin Régis Sr., juggling multiple families like my own father, my cousin Janice laughed and said to me, unprompted, "He was definitely the milkman."

And I am his baby.

PART III

Oklahoma

I

WHEN I RETURNED to my mother's side of the family to gather more oral history, I thought I was back at square one. As I mentioned earlier, I learned about Creoleness first through disdain. I assumed that Creoles identified themselves as such because they didn't want to be black. I assumed this partly because I didn't grow up around any other self-identified Creoles. New Jersey, unlike Louisiana, had existed in a strict black-white racial binary. But there was a greater contradiction. While I was conditioned to feel that all African Americans disdained Creoleness, I found that every black family I knew, including my own, claimed that they "had Indian in 'em."

So many African Americans have shared oral histories of their part-indigenous relatives that I couldn't help but wonder if our elders were often making things up, yet I refused to believe that everyone was suffering from some collective delusion. Hundreds of thousands of Native Americans were forcibly removed from the Southeast to the Midwest, to Indian Territory in present-day Oklahoma. Since about 1.5 million black people[1] were enslaved at the time of this Native American migration, could there have been intermingling along the Trail of Tears? When, a century later, millions of African Americans moved from the South, did they have some Native American ties, whether they knew it or not? Maybe that's why I heard such assertions so often.

But when families like mine made these claims, generally the remark wouldn't go any further than that, for two reasons: (1) the usual response was admiration rather than a request for more information, and anyway (2) no one in my circles could test the claim by anything other than looks. If and when you claimed indigeneity, looks were everything.

Growing up, my mother, Sybil, and her sister Sharene were assumed to have Native American ancestry because of the hue of their brown skin and slick, dark hair. Other relatives of mine were assumed to have Indian in 'em because they had reddish-brown skin and high cheekbones. But growing up, I saw Native Americans only in history texts and Hollywood movies, and no one in my community looks like the ones depicted in book illustrations and on-screen. But then again, I was operating under the assumption that Native Americans all look like actors Wes Studi or Eric Schweig. Louisiana taught me that race is arbitrary and appearances are deceitful. Indigenous people, like black people, do not have one look.

I never fully believed that my family was part indigenous, but after my Louisiana fieldwork, I found it interesting that one label (Creole) is downplayed while another (Native American) is flaunted. Perhaps this is because blackness is part of Creole but native seemed entirely separate, more exotic. I didn't speak any indigenous languages. I didn't know of or wear any regalia. Moreover, I thought that any African Americans who claimed indigeneity were trying to renounce being "just black" in the belief that their lineage wasn't interesting unless mixed with something else— even though no American is 100 percent of anything.

If more black Americans have Native American lineage than I initially believed, then perhaps there was a place I could go to find people to tell me what happened during and after these migrations, which kinships and customs were kept and which were lost. It was a formidable undertaking, because I didn't have many threads to follow starting out from my family, but I always say gaps can be passes instead of impasses. If many blacks have this claim in their family stories but no substantive proof, could that history have been erased or altered to force us further into a narrow, binary understanding of our identities?

I came across a blog by a man named Terry Ligon, who wrote about the connection between black and indigenous people. I e-mailed him and we soon connected in a phone conversation. The son of a migrant, his father, Warren, told Terry that when Terry's grandfather passed away, Warren and his brother went down to the local courthouse because they had heard through other family members that their father had land. But when they inquired about this supposed land at the courthouse, officials told them to "get away from here," that nothing belonged to them. They weren't even allowed to look through files to prove or disprove this rumor, and the officials weren't about to do it either. When Warren thought that he was dying, he wanted to leave family heirlooms to his children. At the time, Terry was into photography and found boxes of those heirlooms: pictures, obituaries, and documents. Warren figured Terry would be the most responsible sibling to handle all of his archives. In the process of sorting through the photos and negatives—a task that took over a year—Terry came across a picture of a woman he considered to be white. When Terry described the picture to his father, his father told him that the woman in the picture was in fact his Indian grandmother. Initially, Terry dismissed the claim: "Being a student of African American studies, I took the position that black people were always trying to distance themselves from slavery." I've also often assumed that black people have claimed other races and ethnic identities as a historical buffer against the horrors of slavery. The response shows how often black identity is demonized and denigrated, even in our own communities.

Terry and his family migrated to California in the 1960s. The racism that led black Americans to flee the South combined with the rise of black communities and ghettos in the North provided the perfect climate for the civil rights movement, which began in 1954.[2] As a teenager and then a young adult, Terry was empowered by all the activism and wanted to firmly root himself in a strong African American identity. Besides, his father had never discussed his indigenous background to Terry before. Terry didn't even know his paternal grandparents' names. His belief that the Ligon family was black and nothing else persisted for decades, until he found those heirlooms.

Terry decided to look into the photograph and discovered that his grandmother, Bettie Ligon, was a Choctaw freedwoman. Along with two thousand other freed Choctaw and Chickasaw descendants of the enslaved—or freedmen—she filed a lawsuit in 1907 in order for them to be transferred from the freedmen rolls to the rolls of the Choctaw and Chickasaw by blood. She refused to even accept a freedmen land patent until the courts decided if she was a freedwoman or a citizen by blood. In 1911, the case made its way to the United States Supreme Court, where it was ultimately dismissed because "the appellants failed to file printed briefs."[3] For over thirty years, Terry has been telling the story of Bettie Ligon and mobilizing efforts to connect descendants of other Choctaw and Chickasaw freedpeople throughout the country. Had Terry not found those photos, he would have thought of himself as African American only, with no ties to other cultures or identities. If Terry hadn't pushed past his initial disbelief, he would have never discovered the indigenous background that rooted him to a specific time and place in Indian territory. Before the end of our conversation, Terry said to me, "What you're doing is very important, because it's all tied together. We tend to see ourselves so apart that we don't see how closely we're related. It's the fallacy of race."

Terry informed me his late father, Warren, was from Oklahoma and left that state because he couldn't stand the conservative

Southern attitudes any longer. I decided that Oklahoma was the next stop for me. If blacks and indigenous people were as tied together as Terry claimed, then maybe that was the place to unearth those connections.

Upon further research, I came upon an NPR feature on a group of Oklahomans fighting to be recognized by the Cherokee nation. They looked like regular black people to me: no high cheekbones, and not all of them had slick, dark hair. But they *were* native. And they were also black. And they, like the Creoles of Louisiana, were fighting to be able to exist, legally as citizens of both the United States and the Cherokee Nation. Their ancestors were categorized as freedmen. But that label historically was the beginning of a long, cruel road of separating black people from their indigenous heritage, negating their blood connections, and seizing the lands that they had claims to; such treatment eventually induced some families, like Terry Ligon's, to abandon the continual struggle to possess what was rightfully theirs and migrate instead.

Many Americans have some familiarity with the Trail of Tears, but I'd like to back up a bit for context. In the 1830s, about 125,000 Native Americans lived on millions and millions of acres throughout the southeastern United States in Georgia, Tennessee, Alabama, and Florida. As one can imagine, these millions of acres were worth an inestimable amount, and the United States government wanted all that land to grow cotton for slaves to line white pockets with. But white people weren't the only ones who owned slaves. In terms of hierarchy, enslaved black people were the lowest of the low—subhuman and possessed. Indigenous people, though inferior to whites, were superior to blacks, which gave them a chance to be groomed and refined into mainstream society.

George Washington believed that the best way to correct the "Indian problem"—for he thought of them as savages—was to civilize certain tribes through education, conversion to Christianity, English language proficiency, and slave ownership. These tribes, known as the Five Civilized Tribes, were the Cherokee, Seminole, Creek, Choctaw, and Chickasaw. The United States government encouraged the Five Civilized Tribes to participate in chattel slavery for two reasons: (1) to interbreed the native population with their white fellow slave owners, diluting Indians' undesirable "primitive" traits, and (2) more important, to dissuade the Native Americans from protecting runaway slaves.[4] But even assimilation didn't protect these tribes from white atrocities. Because whites didn't see indigenous people as equals, they dispossessed and massacred them at will. Before Andrew Jackson became president, he led wars against the Creeks in Georgia and the Seminoles in Florida, transferring many thousands of acres from natives to white farmers. And then in 1830, when Jackson was president, he signed the Indian Removal Act, which forced these tribes to move west of the Mississippi into what is now known as Oklahoma. The brutal journey they took is known as the Trail of Tears. A little-known fact about the Trail of Tears—one I never learned in grade school— was that both free blacks and enslaved blacks accompanied the Five Civilized Tribes on this journey.[5]

Historians, such as Dr. Henry Louis Gates Jr., professor and director of the Hutchins Center for African and African American Research at Harvard University, consider this journey westward to be the Second Middle Passage.[6] For the second time in history, enslaved black people were forced to leave their homes and the lands they knew, to cross another body of water into unfamiliar territory. Instead of being crammed into the holds of ships, they had to walk thousands of miles without enough wagons to carry the sick, elderly, and young. Instead of suffocating heat, they died of bitter cold, disease, and malnutrition.[7] This forced migration was a precursor to the Great Migration.

By the mid to late nineteenth century, the ideas surrounding blackness, indigeneity, and blood purity all became contentious points. Once enslaved blacks were emancipated, these categories began to take on a more capitalistic and therefore more racially segregated meaning. The question for both the United States government and the governments of these five tribes was this: What was to be done about the blacks, all of them now free? Were they American citizens, citizens of the native nation, or both? In 1866, treaties with the United States government and the Five Civilized Tribes were signed saying that all people of African descent would be able to vote and would be afforded the same rights and privileges as everyone else.

In order to "civilize" these tribes even more, the government wanted to switch them from communal to individual land ownership.[8] To implement this, the Dawes Act of 1887 empowered the president of the United States to divide tribal land into individual allotments. The Dawes Commission was responsible for carrying out these orders. The commission separated people into categories and allocated the land differentially. The citizens and freedmen were different categories. If you had African ancestry, you weren't a citizen; you were a freedman.

White clerks dispatched from Washington set up offices in Oklahoma towns and villages to categorize people. Because most of these clerks did not speak the languages of the tribes, they relied on sight. If you "looked" black, you were placed on the Freedmen Roll. It didn't matter if you had an indigenous parent. If you looked black, you were; you weren't given a blood quantum, like full-blood or half-blood. If you "looked" Indian, with typical Indian features, such as high cheekbones, reddish skin, and silky hair, you were placed on the By Blood Roll. As you can imagine, this procedure led to an imbalance of rights and privileges among relatives. Members of one family would be on different rolls. Indigenous women married black men, and their children suddenly became freedmen. Blacks free prior to emancipation were grouped with the formerly enslaved blacks.

With the exception of the Choctaw and Chickasaw, everyone

in the same tribe received the same land allotment: Cherokee, 110 acres; Creek, 160; and Seminole, 120. The Choctaw and Chickasaw by blood were to receive 320 acres, while the Choctaw and Chickasaw freedmen were to receive 40.[9] But freedmen were often disenfranchised of even that land. Unlike the by-blood people, they didn't have to clear their land transactions with the Indian Bureau, making them vulnerable to unscrupulous white settlers migrating from the Deep South. Many freedmen, fresh from the throes of slavery, could not read, and it was not uncommon to hear of a freedman selling his 160 acres for a measly fifteen dollars.[10] At the same time, white people were paying clerks five dollars to put them on the By Blood Roll to get the land allotment. So many did this that they came to be known as the Five Dollar Indians.[11]

I was *meant* to believe that blacks and natives were always separate; the Dawes Rolls enforced this separation. It's no accident that I believed blood determines one's race or ethnicity and that blackness precludes any claim to be partly anything else; that's the ghost of the one-drop rule. It's no accident that I thought blacks should look a certain way despite having mixed and intermarried with other groups for centuries. These misconceptions that my family held to be true had historical precedents, even though we weren't aware of the Dawes Rolls or any black people in Indian country. This expulsion across the Mississippi was a direct cause of our narrow ideas about black identity.

After absorbing this information, I returned to that NPR article and found out that the leader of the fight for Cherokee freedmen to be recognized by the Cherokee Nation of Oklahoma was Marilyn Vann. Marilyn Vann is a distant descendant of James Vann, one of the largest slaveholders in the Cherokee Nation. At the time of his death, at age forty-three, he was said to be one of the richest men in the Cherokee Nation as well as the eastern United States. Two decades later, under the Indian Removal Act, James Vann's family and their two thousand slaves marched to Indian territory.[12] I e-mailed Marilyn through her contact information on the website of the Descendants of Freedmen of the Five Civilized Tribes—of which she serves as president—and she responded to me within less than forty-eight hours.

During a lengthy introductory phone call, she told me that her family has been in Oklahoma since the early 1800s, but she can trace her line back even further. Her late father, George Musgrove Vann, spoke Tsalagi, the official Cherokee language, and attended stomp dances. He was awarded 110 acres as compensation for the United States government forcing his family to move to Oklahoma from Georgia on the Trail of Tears.[13] *Hmm*, I thought. *My maternal line is full of relatives who claim Indian. My maternal grandfather is from Georgia. Could Cherokee be the Indian that my family thought was in 'em?* This wasn't enough to go on, though. Not yet. I listened to Marilyn as she talked and kept my assumptions to myself until I had more information.

Vann has ancestors on the Cherokee Freedmen and By Blood rolls. Back in the late aughts, she applied for tribal membership in the Cherokee Nation but was denied. Like other black and native people, she had been unaware of the term *freedmen.* "I called the Bureau of Indian Affairs, and they kind of blew me off. I called the tribal registrar's office, and they kind of blew me off. I was not aware of freedmen. Up till that time that term had not meant anything to me. The only thing that I knew was that my father had been a member of the tribe and he had received a land allotment at some time. But I didn't know that he had status of freedman—him and his parents, grandparents, everybody.

"I don't know what happened to my father's allotment. The majority of allotments were stolen from freedmen people. They were stolen from other tribal members too. One of the freedmen on my mother's side was Choctaw and Chickasaw. They said that their elderly relative had died and they found some oil on his land. They said a white man showed up and demanded they leave the property that day. They squatted on the land and were eventually able to get it.

"You have all these kinds of cases with people—murders. You've probably heard of the Osage murders. You had some of those. You had a lot of just outright murders, intimidation, harassment—white men showing up with guns, you know? And telling you to leave. Outright murders, you know—people disappearing. Being persecuted. Bodies disappearing. Or whites filing false papers in the courthouses saying that they had been sold this land for ten dollars—160 acres." Just to be clear, 160 acres is approximately 121 football fields. "There's just not many people who still have their valuable land."

Marilyn Vann was one of the plaintiffs in the lawsuit against the Cherokee Nation. After a decade of fighting, in 2017, a US district judge ruled that Cherokee freedmen must have citizenship rights. Vann called the decision "groundbreaking." In an interview with NPR, she says, "What this means for me, is the freedmen people will be able to continue our citizenship . . . and also that we're able to preserve our history. All we ever wanted was the rights promised us to continue to be enforced."[14]

The turning-point period between black and indigenous families was 1890 to the late 1950s—Reconstruction and the Great Migration. Whites were threatened by the influx of black people pouring into Oklahoma because of the promise of land and so enacted Jim Crow to curtail their movement. The first bill passed in the Oklahoma Senate stipulated that if you had a drop of African blood, you were black. If you were indigenous, especially if you were white-presenting, you were legally defined as white. Vann said to me, "You have a lot of people in these former slaveholding tribes who now think they're better than their Negro relatives and neighbors."

"So they were identifying as white?" I asked.

"Yes! I've heard stories of how some would hide their black grandparents in the back of the house so people wouldn't see them. All people of African descent know about having family members who pretend like they don't know you in certain places. Oklahoma is full of that."

During the second wave of the Great Migration, from about 1940 to 1970, Oklahoma lost 14 percent of its black population, much of it to the West.[15] One of Marilyn's cousins was part of that group. In 1940, he moved to Los Angeles, where he still lives. There isn't as much scholarship on the black-and-indigenous mixed-race people who fled the South during the Great Migration as there is about black people specifically, doubtless due to the strict racial binary dictated by the one-drop Jim Crow laws, which said there *was* no black-plus-something-else. But if Marilyn had a family member who left, could it be that many of those who fled Oklahoma during this time were mixed black and native? Then that could mean that African American and Native American people are spread out all over the country. I contacted Andrew Jolivétte again, to ask him if my guesses were a stretch. He replied succinctly, "Not a stretch at all." If in Oklahoma legally white indigenous people were forsaking their own black relatives, and then those black relatives also fled to greener pastures with less racism, who's to say how many families were splintered with no clear way to suture those old wounds?

After my phone call with Marilyn, I contacted my mother again. I thought maybe I needed to pay more attention to what she was saying about our family, no matter how farfetched it had once seemed to me. After all, laws had erased other parts of black people's lineage. From our chat, I soon realized that I'd been wrong in my own assumptions. My mother and Aunt Sharene, or Reenie for short, were assumed to be part indigenous not only by black people, but also by indigenous people when she traveled to the South. She told me that it happened on more than one occasion, and, growing up, she heard it from her father, my Pop-Pop, too.

"Which tribe was it, Mom? Do you remember which one it was?"

"Well, Dad always said that we were Cherokee Indian."

I asked Marilyn if she would be my liaison if I traveled to Oklahoma. She agreed, but with some stipulations: she wanted to meet with me the first night I was in town, and she wanted me to stay in a hotel that was close to her home. I was shook. None of my previous liaisons had cared where I stayed. Was I in danger? I had never been to Oklahoma, and no one in my immediate circle ever had either. When I told Tracey, back in Louisiana, that I would be going to Oklahoma, her mood changed and she looked down before asking, "You gon' be goin' by yourself?" I knew Oklahoma was more conservative than New York, but now I started wondering if I should learn how to shoot a gun. If murder and fraud were happening to black people with land claims, then what the hell might happen to me investigating the freedmen's legacy? I complied with Marilyn's requests. We met on a quiet evening at a Saladworks in Oklahoma City, only a ten-minute drive from my hotel.

She came prepared with all sorts of documents—forwarded e-mails, political ballots, advertisements . . . During our meeting, she told me more about all the resistance she and her supporters had encountered as they fought for freedmen to be recognized by the Cherokee Nation. One of the biggest opponents of the court ruling that granted freedmen tribal citizenship is David Walkingstick, a white-presenting tribal councilor of the Cherokee Nation. About three months after the US district judge ruled in the freedmen's favor, Walkingstick sought to appeal, citing as grounds not race but the fact that tribal councilors had been left out of the process. He said he wanted to uphold democracy according to the Cherokee Nation's constitution. In 2007 the tribe had voted to deny the freedmen citizenship, and its members were dismayed by the extra program dollars it would cost to recognize them.[16] Walkingstick introduced a bill before the Cherokee Tribal Council to appeal the judge's decision, and soon a petition was circulated to get him to step down from his position as the Muskogee Public Schools director of Indian education.[17] In January 2018, he reached a resignation agreement with the Muskogee Board of Education, whereby he received his salary plus $17,528 and the board was "released of all claims and liabilities."[18]

Marilyn also showed me e-mails from officials who argued that freedmen are not Cherokee by blood and that Joe Crittenden, a deputy chief, derisively dubbed the Freedmen's Friend for giving them citizenship, is seen as the enemy. The worst of them was a widely circulated e-mail from Darren Buzzard, a Cherokee Nation tribal member and son of a council member, who asked, "Why do Freedmen want to be Cherokee? Why don't they develop their own culture? Do African-Americans not have their own culture? . . . Could it be that they want the monetary benefits? . . . Don't get taken advantage of by these people. They will suck you dry." For her own safety, Marilyn does not post her whereabouts on social media until after the fact. Luckily, nothing has ever happened to her.

No sooner had I returned to the hotel than Marilyn sent me a list of names and phone numbers of black and indigenous Oklahomans categorized as freedmen. She must've alerted them that I was coming, I assumed. No matter which tribe they came from, legally they were all connected as being of African descent. My meeting with Marilyn was both a primer and a warning: Stay open. Listen carefully. Be careful. Question everything. My family's oral histories hadn't failed me yet. I wasn't sure I'd have as much luck as I'd had in Louisiana, but in spite of the racism, the displacement, and the length of time that had passed, for all the black people in Oklahoma, for my mother and her family, I was damn sure going to find out.

2

WHEN MY MOTHER told me she'd heard that our family had Cherokee Indian heritage, I groaned. I didn't want to hear that. *Everybody* claims Cherokee. No one claims Lenape, Wampanoag, or Apache. It is always Cherokee, as if it's a placeholder for any kind of indigenous ancestry, never mind the more than five hundred Native American tribes in existence today. The Cherokee *is* the third-largest tribe, after Navajo and Sioux,[1] but Cherokee was the one most often claimed by people I knew growing up. According to Gregory P. Smithers, writing in *Slate*, the 2000 census found that over eight hundred thousand Americans claimed one Cherokee ancestor. About 70 percent of them claimed to be mixed-race Cherokees. On the one hand, Smithers argues that the claiming of Cherokee blood speaks to "the enduring legacy of American colonialism" as a way for people to absolve themselves of the crimes committed against the Cherokee people. But the benefactors of colonialism were white, not black, and the Cherokee also had a vested interest in white supremacy, for they too enslaved African Americans. Furthermore, Smithers argues that a claim to Cherokee ancestry reflects the tribe's "wide-ranging migrations throughout North America."[2] So if the Cherokee and African Americans accompanied each other on the Trail of Tears and then dispersed throughout the country, maybe our kinship wasn't as fictitious as I once thought.

The Cherokee tribe wasn't the only one that my family claimed. My mother heard of a Cherokee kin on one side of her father's family, but Pop-Pop and his older brother Curtis spoke of Seminoles in their father's line. In fact, the relationship between my family and the Seminoles showed how strong the bond between black and indigenous people could be. When my great-grandfather was running from a lynch mob, a Seminole woman probably saved his life.

"He left and went on down to Okefenokee Swamp. When he came out on the other side, he saw a lil' ol' Indian woman, who was your great-great-grandfather's sister," my Uncle Curtis said. Okefenokee is over two hundred miles from Sumter County. Neither my grandfather nor my Uncle Curtis knows how he got there or where he stopped along the way.

"Which kind?" I asked, in reference to this sister's tribal heritage.

"He never said, but through my research, the Seminoles were prevalent in that area."

According to Uncle Curtis, my great-granddad couldn't remember the last time he'd seen her, but she remembered him and was delighted that he had come to visit. While he was living with his aunt, he helped her with her cornfields and most likely planted other crops, such as peanuts and soybeans. To my surprise, my Uncle Curtis was right. The last tribe to seek sanctuary in the Okefenokee Swamp were the Seminoles.[3]

"You know," Uncle Curtis continued, "the Seminoles were one of the Twelve Tribes of Israel." The Twelve Tribes of Israel were said to have descended from the twelve sons of Jacob, who was the father of the Israelites, God's chosen people, according to the Old Testament.

Oh, brother, I thought. He's about to get a little bit too woo-woo on me. Though I didn't agree with him, there was a reason behind this claim. He and Pop-Pop believed it because the Seminoles were different from the other four of the Five Civilized Tribes, in that they did not enslave black people. In fact, they participated in slave revolts alongside African Americans. The Seminoles' assistance in protecting enslaved blacks explained why people like my grandfather and his brother held them in great esteem, even granting them biblical status.

If this Seminole woman did in fact take in my great-grandfather, there was precedent for her hospitality. The Seminoles were the tribe best known for providing sanctuary to black people. They lived in what is now Georgia and Florida, where many of the Jerkinses reside to this day. In the seventeenth century, their land became Spanish territory. Before 1693, when slavery was outlawed there, the system was much different from the system developing to the north. Slavery in the Seminole tribe was not a lifelong sentence of unpaid labor. Slaves merely had to pay a percentage of their annual harvest to the tribe. This apparently seemed like a better deal to plantation slaves.[4] Many Gullah slaves escaped from the rice plantations of coastal Georgia and South Carolina to Seminole communities in Florida. At that time, Florida was a wilderness frontier full of jungles and malaria-ridden swamps, thus the landscape made it easier for fugitives to get gone and stay gone. These fugitives created free communities as far back as the 1700s and often intermarried into the Seminoles until their communities merged. When the Indian Removal Act took effect, some fled to Mexico, which had abolished slavery in 1824. Others moved right along with the rest of the Seminole Nation to Indian Territory, and the rest hid so that they could remain in the only territory that they knew.[5]

Ironically, the tribe that was friendliest to blacks then is anything but in the present day, and I was certain that this rupture indicated much violence and whitewashed history. Determined to discover more about the relationship between African Americans and Seminole Indians, via Marilyn Vann I contacted a Seminole freedman activist named LeEtta Osborne-Sampson. I was afraid to ask her about my possible Seminole links to Georgia and Florida, worrying that I'd offend her for trying to claim Indian like everyone else, but I realized that I'd never have an opportunity like this again.

I told LeEtta the story of my great-grandfather and asked, "Do you or anyone you know have ancestors who were originally from Georgia or Florida?"

"Yes, many of us. My grandfather owned land in Georgia." I grinned. She was the perfect link.

Born in 1962 in Sasakwa on an Indian reservation, LeEtta recalled a time when blacks were entirely accepted in the Seminole Nation. Despite their different classifications on the Dawes Rolls, from her vantage point, there was no hostility between blacks and natives. Those who had one black and one indigenous parent were considered mixed-breed, and it wasn't until LeEtta was twenty-four that she heard the term freedmen and learned all of its implications. The discrimination, she argues, happened when the US government began to provide the Seminole Nation with money. Seminole representatives would annually travel to Washington to give a tally of all the Seminole citizens, because the financial allocation correlated to the population. According to LeEtta, the Seminole Nation would include freedmen in its tally but would never allocate their share of the funds to them. On top of that, Seminole freedmen land was more likely to be repossessed. If you are listed as full-blooded or half-blooded on the Dawes Rolls, your land doesn't get taxed, but LeEtta's land is taxed because she is neither full- nor half-blooded. If she were rightfully registered as a Seminole citizen, she would not be getting taxed because she would have the same rights as those on the By Blood Roll. Remember: according to the Dawes Act, if you're classified as a freedman, you're all black; you have no native blood regardless of your actual ancestry.

LeEtta is one of four black council members out of twenty-eight and has held this position for seven years. She is considered a member of the tribe but with only one privilege: the right to vote.

Seminoles with the freedmen card do not get help with housing, health care, job placement programs, or other benefits from the federal funding pool that the tribe receives. LeEtta can trace her line back to Minerva Moppins, listed on the Freedmen Rolls of Seminole Nation,[6] and the "voting privileges only" citizenship card she carries, which she calls a token of apartheid, has been ruled illegal by a federal court. She emphasizes that she will not deal with tribal government anymore because of the discrimination. Her cousin passed away a few years ago because he could not afford the dialysis he would have received free of charge had he received medical benefits from the nation. Freedmen are often denied medical services outright or told that if they don't have a CDIB, or Certificate of Degree of Indian Blood issued after Dawes Rolls verification, they cannot be seen. "A silent massacre," is what LeEtta calls it. Extended families had to resort to begging the nation to put holes in the ground for their loved ones; otherwise they would receive no help for proper burials. Freedmen who work at the casinos on Indian reservations are in another world of danger. The women are sexually harassed and the men are accused of sexual harassment. No one who has had these experiences wanted to take part in my fieldwork.

During one disagreement, a fellow member said maybe LeEtta needed to take a trip to the whipping tree that stands in front of the courthouse. There is an image of a lynched black man in the council house.

I said, "I was going to ask if someone could take me to the council house so I could take a picture of it."

"I'll take you right there."

I was stunned. If LeEtta was threatened, what the hell might happen to me—an African American author and journalist with no clear ties to that place? Of course, I wanted to see the image, but I also did not want to see it. But I had to see the image in its setting to experience it as both a historical artifact and a present-day warning. I was not used to that kind of intimidation. Sure, I have read of nooses hanging on the doorknobs of offices belonging to black employees in companies all along the East Coast, but reading is not the same as seeing. I needed to see this threat of racial terrorism up close.

LeEtta has been told by council members to relent with her activism in order to not fan any flames. Still she does not budge, in spite of her fear for her life and the lives of her family: "As long as the river flow and the grass is green, we are one people. No matter what color my skin is or what creed I am, we are one people: Seminole. There's enough blood in my [council house] seat that I drown every time I sit in it, because these people are ignoring us, because they don't even look at us as human beings."

LeEtta was in charge of organizing a freedmen's protest outside the Bureau of Indian Affairs office in Seminole County, about sixty-five miles southeast of Oklahoma City. She picked me up from my hotel on Northwestern Boulevard, and when I opened up the passenger-side door, I beheld a woman who was all of four foot nine, with a grin that was both friendly and mischievous. As she pulled out onto the expressway, she said, "You know, you're pretty brave for coming out here by yourself. If I had a daughter like you . . ." Her voice trailed off, but her smile invited me to fill in pieces.

"If I were your daughter, what?"

"I would be scared," she said. To be honest, I was scared. Still, I smiled and leaned my head against the window.

To make the time pass by more quickly, LeEtta told me more stories about her family. LeEtta comes from a line of medicine people. Her grandfather, Sam Osborne, and his mother, as well as LeEtta's father-in-law, were people whom people called upon for guidance in their communities. They would place a black rag over a crystal ball, put that rag over your body, use it to detect what was ailing you, then provide the necessary herbs to ameliorate it.

The land, as in the Lowcountry and Louisiana, was supernaturally powerful for those who remained on their ancestors' soil and knew how to manipulate whatever sprang from it. Chickweed leaves could be made into tea in order to expel parasites. Three green tablets would be put into a gallon jug of water and consumed to quell any kind of pain.

Sam Osborne was the son of Lane Osborne, who had 260 acres of land, including 40 acres of homestead in Hazel County. Lane was born a free man yet was moved from the By Blood to the Freedmen Roll at the turn of the century. Twelve people sued Lane for his 40 acres, and the case was tied up in court for eight years, until his son, Sam, was suddenly murdered. No one was able to figure out who did it, and perhaps the lack of resolution compounded with grief, Lane gave up his 40 acres. Lane had seen such tragedies happen to other families. One freedman in particular disappeared after going to the mailbox. People went out searching for him and followed his tracks on the ground for hundreds of yards, but the tracks eventually disappeared. Decades later, tragedy struck again when the missing man's daughter was found dismembered in her own home.

LeEtta's father was very familiar with hoodoo. He was what she called a showboat. He would throw money on the floor for sport and always paraded around in a brand-new car. His ostentatiousness naturally generated a lot of envy among his neighbors. A root was tied to the gas pedal of one of his cars, and that hex led to his getting into many car accidents. I thought about Griffin Lotson's story of the root in his car in Washington, DC. Maybe that's why he backed away from the car, because the root was placed there to cause him to get into an accident. LeEtta's grandfather Sam was also full of wisdom: Throw red and black pepper on the ground behind a departing visitor if you don't want them to return. To get two people to stop arguing, throw table salt on the ground, but make sure they don't see it. Don't sweep a broom too much around someone's foot unless you want that person to go to jail. If you want retribution of some kind, milk a snake of its venom and place it on a surface that the target will sit on or touch.

He taught LeEtta the lay of the land. If she were to ever get lost, she could find a weeping willow, dig deep into the earth, and find water. She might still be lost by day's end, but at least she would be alive. I became jealous, sad even. For weeks, I traveled across land and water, unable to identify the names of flowers and trees except one or two kinds. I didn't know the difference between high and low tide. I didn't know how to slaughter a hog or skin an animal. I didn't know when harvest was nearing. Those of us whose families moved away from the rural South have lost that familiarity with the land and awareness of the seasons.

LeEtta tells me about her tenure as a council member. "When I sat in that [council] seat, I was like, 'This is not America. This Seminole Nation. There are no civil rights. Martin forgot a few people.'" She laughs. "I can't just walk away. I got too many bones down there."

To prepare for the protest, we pulled into a parking lot adjacent to the Bureau of Indian Affairs (BIA). LeEtta pulled out several posters that she'd made in advance:

CORRUPTION IN THE NATION OF SEMINOLE—
GREED IN THE GOVERNMENT

WE ARE CONNECTED TO OUR ANCESTORS!
WE KNOW WHO WE ARE!

LET'S ROCK THE BOAT

WE ARE ALL ONE

SEMINOLE NATION, STOP DENYING FREEDMEN RIGHTS

IS IT A CRIME TO FIGHT FOR WHAT IS MINE?

DAWES ROLL OR BLOOD DEGREE? WHICH ONE?

STOP BIRTHRIGHT THEFT!

I HAVE A VOICE. I'VE ALWAYS BEEN FREE. I AM STRONG.
I AM A PROUD SEMINOLE FREEDMAN.

Two cars were already parked in the lot with us. Only a handful of freedmen were there. Pickup trucks slowed down as the drivers passed the lot; some with tinted windows rolled them down, but I could never make out the faces. One attendee said, "You're lucky. If this were back in 2015, they would have yelled out 'Nigger!'" I felt I'd stepped back in time. When it was time to cross the street to the parking lot of the BIA, I followed behind the others, who were much more determined and unafraid than I was. We set up camp right on the side. The elders sat in chairs next to the coolers full of water and soda. The youths and a few people around LeEtta's age held up signs, encouraging drivers to honk for support.

LeEtta introduced me to the Seminole freedmen, or *estelusti*, which means "blacks" in the Muskogee Creek language. One of them is named Butch. He is LeEtta's assistant, a relative and fellow council member. Butch and LeEtta have the same great-great-grandmother, Minerva Moppins, whose name is listed on the Freedmen Rolls of Seminole Nation, though Butch claims it's a mistake because of photographic evidence: "She looks straight native," he says. He grew up in Sasakwa, and the vast majority of his classmates were extended-family members, including the current principal chief of Seminole Nation, Leonard Harjo. In the Seminole Nation, there are fourteen bands, or kinship groups, two of which are freedmen bands, and they have been procreating with one another over the course of three to four hundred years. Butch recalls that he and Harjo attended the same church (Seminole Baptist), played at the same camp houses, and participated in Easter egg hunts and home gatherings together.

In 1990, Congress approved a judgment fund ensuring that money would be allotted to the Seminole Nation for essential services, such as burials, elder care, and school clothing assistance, undergraduate scholarships, and household economic assistance. But the Seminole Nation Tribal Council sought a way to exclude freedmen from the money.[7] According to Butch, it was the year before, 1989, when he started to learn how differently he was perceived from family: "I become a black—you know, N word and stuff like that. My citizenship card had my name, social security number, and it had Seminole Nation. It did not have Freedman on there—no blood quantum or 'voting privileges,' all of that. They knew that if they changed the cards, then that would stop us from getting benefits." Once, his late wife, who was part Chickasaw and Seminole and registered By Blood, wondered why Butch was being denied health services. After looking up his name in the system, a representative told Butch's wife that, although Butch was with the Seminole tribe, the Seminoles did not officially recognize him as a full citizen, like LeEtta. They can vote, but that's it. They are not entitled to the other benefits and privileges that Seminoles By Blood have.

LeEtta also introduced me to another one of her associates, a man nicknamed Stopper. He is also kin to LeEtta and Butch through the Osborne name. Sam Osborne was Stopper's great-uncle. Stopper's father, Harper Osborne, like Sam, was a tribal medicine man who later became a preacher at Seminole Baptist Church. When Stopper grew up in Seminole County, the Seminole language was the primary language in his household—not English. Pork, chicken, rabbits, and squirrels were a part of the regular meals, including an indigenous recipe for porridge: hominy, salt and pepper, sugar, and milk. Throughout his life, Stopper has carried an irremovable belief that his life and the history of his people were teetering toward total annihilation.

When Stopper joined the army, he became "an invisible man."

He was a soldier without a paper trail, meaning that there wasn't clear documentation on where he was stationed and what he did there. When he returned to Oklahoma in 1985, he became disenchanted with how his people were being treated, and he migrated to California, where he got married and had a family. In his own words, "If they [the Seminole Nation] can interrupt the bloodline of the Freedman and the next generation, the younger ones, and make them disappear, then there's nobody to step up." And, in a sense, the "disappearance" had already begun in Stopper's family:

"I have one grandson—he embraces here. The rest of them, they don't want nothing to do with here."

"Why is that?" I asked. "Are they ashamed or they just don't want to have to fight?"

"They was raised in San Diego."

Stopper's children did live in Oklahoma City with him until they reached high school age, then returned to San Diego to live with their mother. But, like other black Seminoles who left Oklahoma and got plush jobs in New York during the Great Migration, none of them returned. They "didn't want anything to do with these woods." These woods, though, are home, and like the Lowcountry of South Carolina, that home is decreasing. The stories are horrific. Sam Osborne was found dead in his home. All the doors were locked and every stove in the house was turned up full blast in the summertime. The Osborne family used to be one of the largest landowning freedmen families, and the acres were supposed to be passed down to descendants as heirs property. One relative leased his acres to a property developer, and then that corporation took over everything. No one can say for sure how it happened, but those acres were no longer in the family name anymore.

The protest ran for about three hours before LeEtta mentioned where we would be going next. Stopper and another freedman, nicknamed Happy, followed in their truck behind us. Stopper currently lives in Wichita, 160 miles north of Oklahoma City, but the distance doesn't bother him when LeEtta calls upon him to travel. At first, I didn't understand why they were following behind us to the Burger King and then to the Seminole General Council House, but I didn't mention it. This wasn't about simple hospitality. We were two women traveling with a preadolescent boy in the backseat. The more cornfields we passed, the less reception on my cell phone. Happy and Stopper didn't *want* to follow us; they *needed* to or else they would go their separate ways with guilty consciences about what could have happened to us.

When LeEtta parked the car in the council house lot, she told me that if we're lucky, the council house would be unlocked and I could take as many pictures as I needed. A white-passing woman was fortuitously exiting one of the doors on the other end of the building and kindly said hello before asking us what we were doing. LeEtta cryptically replied that she was just going to show me around, and as she spoke, I hid my phone. The woman turned her back on us and LeEtta twisted the knob. The door was unlocked. Large black-and-white images were behind the black chairs where I assumed that the council members sat. There were two columns framing pews like those of a church. In front of those columns were wooden dividers. Then there were two more columns and more black chairs. I assumed that the black chairs were for those who held more senior roles and the pews were for the constituents.

The first image on the left-hand side of the room was of a lynched black man. His hands and feet were tied together and there was a white cloth over his eyes. The caption reads, "Last Execution Under Seminole Law." This man was whipped by one of the Light Horsemen—the Indian version of police—and his wailing was said to have been heard for many blocks. Butch told me that the lynched man was accused of stealing chickens. LeEtta has tried to get the council to remove the picture but to no avail. Next to the lynching image was one of the Seminole Whipping Tree, which still stands in front of the Seminole County Courthouse. I snapped pictures as fast as I could. If someone came in while I was taking pictures, LeEtta might have gotten into more trouble. She already had her enemies. Besides, I wasn't from here, and a stranger taking pictures would be viewed with suspicion.

Outside, I took pictures of the granite monuments, one dedicated to each band that designates a clan within the Seminole Nation: Ceyvha, Hecete, Osceola, Billy Bowlegs, Ocese, Coacochee (Wildcat), Hvteyievlke, Thomas Palmer, Fushutche (Bird Creek), Tallahassee, Tusekia Harjo, Dosar Barkus, Caesar Bruner, Nurcup Harjo. As we walked toward LeEtta's truck, a car pulled out in front of us and drove off. Once the car pulled back out onto NS Road and sped off, LeEtta grinned and said, "We were being followed."

Although I was exhausted at that point, LeEtta wasn't finished. She drove me down to Wewoka, to the courthouse, so I could see the whipping tree. I tried to quiet the small voice in my head that said, *Do I have to? Do we have to?* I looked behind me at LeEtta's son, who was still preoccupied with his electronics, and I admired his nonchalance in the face of all that we were observing. I wondered how many times he had been to this tree and what other disturbing historical artifacts he now categorized as normal or quotidian.

The city of Wewoka was founded by a Seminole freedman named John Horse in 1849. The name of the town in Seminole means "barking water," from the sound the nearby waterfall makes.[8] In 1923, oil was discovered a mile and a half southeast of Wewoka, and many Seminoles became wealthy from partnership with Magnolia Petroleum Company. By the 1930s, these Seminole oil fields became the largest suppliers of oil in the world. In two years, the population ballooned from 1,527 to 20,000. Once the oil was sapped, jobs decreased, people moved out, and many of those who remained grappled with poverty.[9] That's the official story. LeEtta says that there were billions of dollars' worth of oil in Wewoka. Once the Seminole Indians knew about freedmen sitting on that much wealth, they moved into the territory, ingratiated themselves with the freedmen, married the black women, and before anyone knew it, the whole family would be wiped out. LeEtta and her ilk have chalked up these disappearances as murder but there is no documentation of rampant homicide in this area. In LeEtta's words, "They took the money and ran. They raped the land and killed all the trees, killed the soil. You can't even plant down here. All the granite rock will kill a garden."

LeEtta made her son take pictures of her standing in front of the whipping tree, and I was beside myself that she was smiling in every single snapshot, her own kind of resistance. My eyes started to burn. I was not sure if it was because of the sweltering heat or if I was overwhelmed with emotion, I had to turn my body away from LeEtta and her son to collect myself. When that was insufficient, I took a few steps backward, then walked off to the side, because I could not stare at that tree head-on for more than a few moments.

Stopper and Happy didn't stop following us until we were safely on our way back to Oklahoma City. When LeEtta lost her husband, Stopper made it his responsibility to escort her to and from places as much as he could, coming all the way from Kansas just to accompany her to council meetings. He's been the only one, she says. Sometimes, though, LeEtta would take her chances and go somewhere alone, but the roads have never been safe places. A male relative of hers was coming from Bible study when a drunk driver hit him head-on, killing him instantly. Back near the Bureau of Indian Affairs office, Stopper and Happy said that they had essentially become invisible, and as long as freedmen continued to lose their identities through documentation, their history and line would be lost for good. I thought their complaint was incomplete. What about the women? They're just as vulnerable, if not more so because of their gender. But after hearing about LeEtta's family— her grandfather Sam, who died in an odd manner in his home while the family was fighting over land, and a cousin who died by a drunk driver—I wondered if the deaths of these freedmen were coincidental.

LeEtta admits that she often fears she'll be driven off the road, but just as before, she is not shaken. "People gotta understand that everything that comes in here will die. But sometimes it's at the hand of someone. Envy will kill. I used to be a person that didn't want nobody ever to be angry with me, [would] try to be the good-est person in the world, be there for people, take the second seat, you know. I can't take the second seat down here. I got into this. I said, 'Wait a minute, y'all just taught me something.' The chief said, 'Well, what you learn?' And I said, 'You got me sitting on the other side of God.' They said, 'What does that mean?' I said, 'I am his wrath.'"

I thanked LeEtta for her time and attention and gave her a hug. A part of me wanted to ask if she would be safe returning to her home, but my head was buzzing with everything I'd learned in such a short time that day. She knew what she was doing. She knew the lay of the land. I, on the other hand, was worn-out. I hurried to my hotel room and locked the door behind me. Night had not fallen yet but the darkness didn't matter to me. I was still a bit rattled after all I had seen and heard, afraid that I wouldn't get any sleep that night, afraid that when I returned to the East Coast and slid back into my progressive, liberal New York circles, no one would believe me. Immediately, I uploaded all the pictures, videos, and interview recordings to my Google Drive and sent the audio of everyone's voices to my transcriptionist. But as I sat in silence, I thought, hell, *I* don't even believe me.

Not only was I physically weary, but I was also mentally un-moored and disillusioned. They had documentation of their Sem-inole lineage, yes. And yet still, their identity as black and native people has been either not recognized or recognized but not ac-knowledged with the same rights and privileges as other Seminole people. Then, I wondered, what was the point of documentation?

According to Natasha Hartsfield, vice president of programs at the Tallahassee Museum, "The Dawes Act was an act of colonial economic interest that had a great impact on Native American and African culture and identity. The act . . . [was] used to control people of color with interests other than capital gains." The Dawes Rolls document the American government's white-supremacist intervention in order to divide the Seminole Nation. And if these rolls were tools to dominate and establish racial hegemony, then they cannot be the be-all and end-all of familial relations and land inheritances. The oral histories I gathered undermine the Dawes Rolls. The tribal rolls were rife with flaws. But documentation has always been undermined by African American oral history. According to Jennifer Dos Reis Dos Santos, a PhD candidate at Aberystwyth University, folklore has been our culture's salvation. "Folklore has not just helped African Americans to record and remember large-scale events . . . it has helped with individual family genealogy too. Having an aspect of genealogy in folklore makes African American history not only traceable but more approachable. The stories relate to specific people, their experiences and the places where they lived. . . . They demonstrate and track the fight for freedom and independence."[10]

I was going to take these Seminole freedmen's stories, as well as the stories of everyone else I would interview for this book, as valid and reorient myself to a different kind of truth, one that does not rely solely on documents and textbooks. This different kind of truth is less static and more fluid, persisting throughout generations of marginalized people and outside the traditional framework, which favors the voices of the powerful over the voices of the disempowered. As a Seminole freedman said to me at the protest, "The blood is in the land," and the land was once theirs. But documentation still meant something, or else why would they be fighting?

I called my grandfather and all of his brothers to get a name, any name that I could search for in the Dawes Rolls, but they didn't remember any. I searched for Jerkins in the directory for the Dawes Rolls online. Nothing. I messaged my mother and asked her if she knew of any other names connected to the Jerkins line, and she told me three: Hadley, Wade, and Clarke. There were no freedmen with the last name Hadley. There were some Cherokee freedmen with the last name Wade. But there were both Cherokee and Seminole freedmen named Clarke. Could this be something? The names were there, but were they my people? I shrank in my seat. I'm just a woman from southern New Jersey. I had never heard of any family being in Oklahoma.

Unlike the people I met, all I had were stories. I had stories full of characters with no first names. All details were vague. My mother didn't have any documentation pertaining to indigeneity. My grandfather didn't either. No relative I had interviewed so far made any reference to documentation, not to Cherokees or Seminoles or any other tribe. Besides, after all I'd seen that day, I couldn't imagine that the Seminole Tribe would recognize me, considering what those who looked like me were still fighting for. I mourned, not necessarily for myself but for this story of my great-grandfather and the Seminole woman. If I reimagined that story with what I knew now and thought of them both as black migrants in Indian territory, would she have even helped him? Would she have accepted him? *Who cares*, I thought. It didn't matter. I hadn't even heard of any documentation, so I had no dog in this fight, so to speak.

But I didn't go far enough. There was another family story about our lineage and ethnic identity. There was always one more.

3

WHEN I WAS a preteen, I decided to take an Ancestry DNA test because I thought that scientists from somewhere else in the world would be able to tell me about my heritage with data that none of my family members could provide. The results never indicated that I had indigenous ancestry, but rather pointed me toward the East among the Berber populations of North Africa, the Fula tribe of sub-Saharan Africa, and the Romani people of Europe. I thought this result was conclusive and that blood dictates everything. Now as an adult, I wonder if perhaps my skepticism toward my relatives' oral histories about Native American ancestors was due in part to this DNA test. I can't tell you how many black people I've come across who've told me their family members claim Native American heritage but DNA says otherwise. But after all that I observed so far on my trip, of how families were separated between full-bloods, half-bloods, and those with "no blood" because of their black blood, what if blood could not provide the full truth? Or even more radical—what if blood could not provide any part of the truth whatsoever? If other black families like mine claim Cherokee, where does this persistence come from in spite of the tests? I wanted to know more about how bloodlines in black families may have overlapped with Cherokee families and how DNA tests hinder our ability to continue learning about one another.

The conversation about Indian blood reached a fever pitch in

2018 when Democratic presidential candidate Elizabeth Warren, in response to President Trump's bigoted attacks suggesting that she was a fake "Pocahontas," took a DNA test to prove that she was part Cherokee. The results did in fact show that she had Native American ancestry, but the backlash from Native American people was swift. In a statement to NBC News, Julie Hubbard, the executive director of the Cherokee Nation said, "We are encouraged by this dialogue and understanding that being a Cherokee Nation tribal citizen is rooted in centuries of culture and laws, not through DNA tests."[1] According to Aviva Chomsky, writing in the *Huffington Post*, companies like Ancestry.com and 23andMe construct algorithms that make ethnicity something that can be entirely quantifiable through genes. There are no companies that have databases of ancestral DNA. Instead, these testing companies compare your genes to other people who have already taken the test—and Native Americans are one of the groups that have contributed to these databases the least.[2] Just because Warren may have Native American blood does not mean that she is an enrolled citizen of any tribe; she isn't. And despite the fact that a freedperson's descendant may carry no Native American DNA, that person's ancestors may have been de facto members of the tribe since the nineteenth century.

Hubbard's statement bothered me. If being a Cherokee Nation tribal citizen is rooted in "centuries of culture and laws," then why was it that before 2017 freedmen of African descent were not considered tribal citizens? And what does her statement mean to the countless African Americans who have heard family lore about their native admixture, tales that have been around for centuries?

When black people let DNA tests take precedence over their family stories, as I did, they reinforce narrow, racist misconceptions about blood purity and authenticity. Historian Jean O'Brien says, "New England Indians had intermarried, including with African Americans, for many decades, and their failure to comply with non-Indian ideas about Indian phenotype strained the credence for their Indianness in New England minds. The supposed 'disappearance' of such Indians then justified the elimination of any rights that they might have had to land or sovereignty, the elimination of which, in a form of circular reasoning, only confirmed their nonexistence as a people." Even worse, this assumed nonexistence can change or separate families for generations. The truth is, the relationship between black and indigenous people is both contentious and harmonious, pushed and pulled by racist laws and restrictions.

One woman who showed me how migration, bloodlines, and questions about "authentic" Cherokee heritage upend lives is Darnella Davis, author of *Untangling a Red, White, and Black Heritage: A Personal History of the Allotment Era*. Davis is the daughter of a Creek mother and Cherokee father. When it was time for her to go to grad school, she applied for a scholarship from the Cherokee Nation after learning that cousins of hers had received money for postgraduate study. When she collected her father's relatives' Dawes Roll numbers and submitted them to the board, the Cherokee Nation told Davis that she needed a CDIB, or Certificate of Degree of Indian Blood. Because the people on Davis's father's side were listed as freedmen, officially he had no Indian blood. "I said, 'Well, that's not right.' There's Indian blood on my dad's side, but by the time I figured it out, I'd already finished grad school." This took place thirty years ago. Davis cannot be considered a member of the Cherokee Nation because she's already a Creek citizen, and one cannot be a member of more than one tribe. Despite her Creek citizenship, she still faces challenges: "If I have a health issue and I go down to the complex, if it's a nice day and they remember that my cousin is on the [Creek] Supreme Court, right—he's the chief justice—they might treat me. But otherwise they're not going to give me anything, because I'm only listed as one-sixteenth Creek and that negates all the Cherokee blood that I might or might not have."

This entanglement of Creek and Cherokee blood with the legal

stipulations of racial identity has caused Davis to give up on fighting the powers that be. The process is long, and the affirmation
may never come. She doesn't want to have to prove herself to
anyone, and this has been a fight stretching back decades into her
childhood.

Darnella Davis was born in Oklahoma but as a child moved
with her family to Detroit during the rise of the Black Power movement. Her family migrated after a relative told her father that there
were factory jobs in the North that would offer better pay than
the railroad jobs in Vinita, Oklahoma. To Darnella, Detroit was a
cultural shock. "People ask me, 'How did you call yourself before
Civil Rights?' I tell them that we were the Davis family on my dad's
side and the Adams family on my mom's side. We were a clan
onto ourselves." To her, home in Oklahoma was a "mixed-person
kingdom."

Before Detroit, Davis grew up in a town called Beggs, ten miles
outside of Okmulgee, a city in Creek Nation. In Okmulgee, blacks
were said to live under the bridge and whites lived on the hill.
Beggs was different: "Everybody lived together. I have my great-
grandmother saying blacks, whites, and Indians all ate in the hotel
together. I have my mother remembering a sheriff saying, as to
Jim Crow, 'This is Beggs. We don't do that here. We're not having
separate things.'" Everyone was family, and there was no place that
was unsafe. Growing up in Detroit when Martin Luther King Jr.
came down Woodward Avenue was a triumphant moment for all
black locals, like Davis and her family, but there was no room in
the conversation for both black *and* native identity. Similar to Terry
Ligon's life, the civil rights movement inspired those of African
descent to lean more into black identity than into any other part of
their background.

She didn't know of any other freedmen in Detroit, and there
wasn't much discussion about that status label. Alongside the civil
rights movement, these discussions on black identity have their

origins from the revolution of the American academy. In the 1960s, African American history courses and departments proliferated along with the rise of the civil rights and Black Power movements. Dr. James Leiker, chair of the History and Political Science departments at Johnson Community College, said that this rise inadvertently shed light on the intersections of black identity: "There was a focus to correct earlier narratives, but that focus gets set up through one lens at a time. You have one thread that is African American studies and another thread which is Native American studies, but you're still taking a bigger narrative and breaking it up into categories. In the last ten to twenty years, there are more scholars trying to connect all of these things."

For Darnella Davis, the connection is self-identification. "I am a person of color. I've membership in the Muscogee Creek Nation and a Cherokee freedmen heritage. That's who I am." Part of the pride Davis takes in self-recognition arises from the fact that, once her family moved from Oklahoma to Detroit, her father didn't talk about home or the land that they had owned. She didn't understand. Her father's family was composed of large landowners. They were prosperous, owning a convenience store in their small town for over a hundred years. Davis wanted to know why her relatives fled after World War II. The land allotment rules kept changing, depending on how much Indian blood you had. Originally there were 40 acres for the homestead and 120 for ranching and farming. Her family left because their acreage was shrinking. The land restrictions meant that family members would get taxed more for having less Indian blood than others. These restrictions made it easier for outsiders to come in and buy these land allotments. The encroachment made them realize that their way of life was ending. This proud family was carrying a lot of hurt, hence their migration.

When I asked Davis about DNA tests, she admits that she did take three of them—one of which was the same one I took—but requests that I don't divulge the names so as to not single out any company. I withheld all names so no process of elimination can be done.

Davis took these tests when seeking enrollment in the Cherokee Nation. They showed negligible Native American ancestry. She was found to be 50 percent African, 36 percent European, 8 percent Asian/Pacific Islander, and 5 percent Native American.[3] How can that be if Davis's father was Cherokee? Since we last spoke, Davis reached out to tell me that her profile in two companies had been updated: there was no percentage of Pacific Islander and her Native blood percentage had increased. That still made her less than a quarter native. She tells me these meager amounts are common among her friend group: "For those who find nothing, as has been the case with mixed-race friends who can trace their indigenous connection through family links, it might be premature to question their paternity again and again." Without a sufficiently large database for comparison, one cannot reliably trace indigenous bloodlines. In addition, tribal status is not entirely based off blood, but rather membership and kinship. In other words, for example, no DNA test can accurately determine "Cherokee blood."

Then why do many African Americans claim Cherokee even if they're not enrolled or a DNA test tells them otherwise? According to Davis, there are three reasons: overlapping migration routes, tribal size, and trauma among the descendants of enslaved black people. In her words, "Consider the geographic location and the politics of earlier eras . . . the overlap of indigenous peoples and blacks would have been greatest in the South. Consider size: the Cherokee were the largest tribe and were often seen as the most organized and powerful, both by whites and other tribes. Also consider the nostalgia factor. It's an understatement to say that many blacks lost their history during slavery, in the displacement following the Civil War, or through the silence of shame." She tells me that for those African Americans who heard that they were part Indian, they may have assumed Cherokee or Blackfeet because these two tribes were most prominent in popular culture, especially during the time of the Great Migration. Cindy Walker's "Cherokee Maiden" was a hit in 1941 as recorded by Bob Wills and the Texas Playboys, and Blackfeet Indians were depicted in Western classics like *Broken Arrow* (1950) and *The Big Sky* (1952). The Blackfeet and Cherokee tribes were a part of the American imagination, and arguably, seeing them on-screen inspired black Americans to attempt to re-create the past that they would never know.

If Cherokees occupied North Carolina, Tennessee, and parts of South Carolina and Georgia before and during chattel slavery, how could they *not* have had relations with black people? No matter if these relations were master and slave, man and wife, or parent and children, the bonds are there. It was when these two groups moved out of the South, into Oklahoma and other territories, that their identities came under scrutiny and their kinship ties were contested for generations to come. DNA cannot be the sole arbiter of our truth. But even historians today, though well-intentioned, propagate this belief. Dr. Henry Louis Gates Jr. said in an article for the *Root*, "Those high cheekbones and that straight black hair derive from our high proportion of *white ancestors* and not, for most of us, at least, from our mythical Cherokee great-great-grandmother. Sorry, folks, but DNA don't lie."[4]

In an interview with me, Dr. Arica L. Coleman, an independent scholar and *Time* magazine contributor, criticized both Gates's conclusion and his show, *Finding Your Roots*, "Everybody is looking for a scientific answer, like there needs to be a scientific method of who you are, that it carries more validity than the stories that have been passed down. This is a sticky issue, because everything is not written down. Who can claim Indian is determined by the policies set forth by the federal and state governments." If who can claim Indian is defined by law and DNA cannot yet prove native ancestry, then that means this conflict between African Americans and Native Americans is internecine warfare. We have never been able to have the privilege of defining ourselves for ourselves, and therefore our narratives, despite their endurance, exist outside of the accepted framework.

As Coleman went on to say, "There is this power struggle over memory, what we remember and how we remember it. When I told a man once that I was part Native American, he asked me if it's been authenticated. My blackness has never been authenticated. People assume that because of my hair texture and skin, I'm African American." Dr. Coleman is a brown-skinned woman with locs. People look at her and automatically assume she's black, but they never give her room to comfortably share her other ethnic identity, Rappahannock, an Algonquian-speaking tribe from Virginia. People's assumptions are not only often wrong, but dangerous too. When people assume, they inadvertently erase others' identities. It's the same conundrum I faced in Louisiana: Where is the space to be black *and* not black?

I was trying to figure out my purpose in trying to prove my Cherokee lineage. I am not an enrolled member, and my DNA tells me I have no indigenous blood. People never look at me and assume I have any native ancestry. Shouldn't I chalk up this part of my journey as a failure? I started to lose hope. I wondered how it would feel if African American families were more whole, if there weren't so many gaps in my family's memories. But isn't that indicative of how much we survived in spite of it all? Weren't those gaps the purpose of my trip?

I didn't know how to feel after my conversations with Ms. Davis and Dr. Coleman. On the one hand, I felt affirmed. Dr. Davis knows of her Cherokee lineage, and yet a test indicated that she wasn't even one-sixteenth Indian. If her results were inaccurate, were mine? This trip felt Sisyphean. Each day I felt like I was back at square one. I learned about blood and then found that blood isn't the be-all and end-all. I learned about Dawes Rolls and then found that they're imprecise. I returned home with hundreds of pages of transcriptions, hours upon hours of recordings, yet considered this part of my trip a dead end. I couldn't use my story to show its broader implications about migration and African American families. I was stuck in a rut for a year until, miraculously, my mother sent me some letters written by one of the oldest people on her side of the family, which breathed new life into this work.

4

AT EIGHTY-THREE, Gwen Davis Wiggins is one of the oldest living relatives I have from either side of my family. My paternal grandfather's great-grandad and Gwen's great-grandad were brothers. I don't know what prompted my mom to send me letters that Gwen had written by hand about our family history. In fact, the last conversation we had before I received these letters was about my medical insurance coverage. Why in the hell were we talking about the ancestors when I was trying to figure out my deductible? But my mom sent the letters without any disclaimer or hint of what they contained. Gwen begins with the earliest ancestor that she can trace, Randall Wiggins Sr., who was born somewhere around 1808 or 1809:

It all started (as far back as we can go) with Randall Sr., who was half European, and his wife Winnie, who was of Indian blood. They had thirteen children, though Randall Sr. had to leave them behind to work on another plantation. While he was away, five of his boys were sold to other plantations. One of the daughters looked white and was kept by the slave master and his wife, and that was the end of our family's connection to her. Meanwhile, Randall Sr. fathered two daughters with another woman. When he returned to his wife and children, he lost contact with those other two daughters, and we haven't been able to find them. Therefore, we the family never had any connections. With money Winnie had saved, Randall Sr. was able to find and buy his five boys back.

After a few phone calls to my mother and then to one of my cousins, who is the unofficial historian of the Jerkins family, I was able to find Gwen's number. The letter was dated May 15, 2019, so the chances of her still being of sound mind were very high. Luckily, I was right. Not only was she lively, but she texted—rather quickly, actually—and was so excited to talk to me.

During a phone conversation, Gwen, who lives in Warner Robins, Georgia, told me that she grew up in Andersonville, Georgia, a sister city to Americus in Sumter County. When she was younger, she noted, Andersonville used to be a part of Schley County. During her youth, people assumed that she and her relatives were Indian because of their brown skin and high cheekbones. People still make this assumption. In fact, she told me that just two years ago, at a family reunion in Charleston, a black and native woman asked her about her heritage and then gave her the number of some organization in order to get recognized, or at least search more into her ancestry.

"Was it the Bureau of Indian Affairs, Gwen?"

"I'm not sure what it was. I forget the name. I called the phone number and tried to reach out, but nothing came of it, so I forgot about it." Did she reach out to the Bureau of Indian Affairs and no one picked up, or did someone pick up and give her the cold shoulder? I couldn't be certain, but I was certain that her story aligned with those of Marilyn Vann and other black and native people in Oklahoma, who told me story upon story of the Bureau of Indian Affairs, among other agencies, which rebuffed their requests even with the proper documents in hand.

"Do you remember which tribe Winnie was from, Gwen? Any name would help." I waited with bated breath.

The earliest ancestor that my family can trace on the Wiggins side (my maternal grandfather's mother's side), Randall Wiggins. He was said to be half black and half white. *Gwen Wiggins*

"I don't think I was ever told a name. But I do know that Randall fetched her from the river and she was from the hills of Tennessee."

"Was Randall's wife enslaved too?"

"No, I'm not sure. I was never told that she was enslaved. I was told that she was a black Indian, though."

When I got off the phone with Gwen and did some research, I found out that Schley County, which was carved from portions of Marion and Sumter Counties, was named after William Schley. When William Schley was governor of Georgia beginning in 1835, and he was apprehensive about Cherokees living among whites, so much so that he had informants sent out to spy on the tribe. The informants told Schley that the Cherokees were peaceful and wanted no trouble, but Schley had already made up his mind that they were a threat. State officials and regular civilians alike armed themselves out of fear of an uprising. In 1837, Schley informed President Martin Van Buren that he had two regiments ready to expel "that savage and deluded people." The militia and citizens assisted federal troops in removing Cherokees from their homes. Troops were said to have ". . . cleared woodland, muddied streams, rutted roads, and filled the air with sound and smoke." Sarah Hill writes in *Southern Spaces*, "Georgia led the United States in the expulsion of the Cherokee Nation from its homeland. In the spring of 1838 more than two thousand soldiers arrested some nine thousand Georgia Cherokees, confined them briefly, then marched them to holding camps in east Tennessee to await their miserable trek to Indian Territory eight hundred miles away."[1]

If Winnie came from the hills of Tennessee, I guessed that she was near the border of Tennessee and Georgia. That was also Cherokee territory. *OK*, I thought. *All signs point to Winnie being the Cherokee in the family.* The Oklahoma Historical Society has a website where you can search for a name in the Dawes Final Rolls from 1898–1914. I took a deep breath, typed in the last name Wiggins, and there she was: Peggie Wiggins, thirty-nine years old, roll number 438, search card number 150. Tribe: Cherokee Freedmen. My mother also provided a list of every one of Randall and Winnie's children along with their spouses, which she had received at a family reunion that I was unable to attend. If Peggie was thirty-nine and the Dawes Commission collected names from 1898 to 1914, then she was born between 1859 and 1875. If Randall was born around 1802, then he was, at the earliest, her grandfather.

One of Gwen's nieces reached out to me with a list of all of Randall Sr.'s grandchildren, but there is no Peggie on it. The twelve

Thirty-eight-year-old Peggie Wiggins is certified for tribal enrollment as a Cherokee freedman with an application dated for April 5, 1901. Her owner was George Crapo, her roll number was 459, and her card number was 150. *Oklahoma Historical Society Research Center*

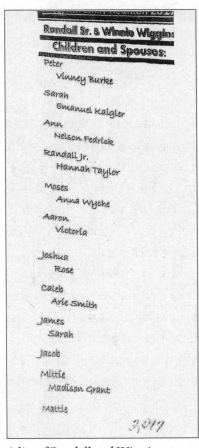

Randall Sr. & Winnie Wiggins
Children and Spouses:

Peter
　Vinney Burke
Sarah
　Emanuel Kaigler
Ann
　Nelson Fedrick
Randall Jr.
　Hannah Taylor
Moses
　Anna Wyche
Aaron
　Victoria
Joshua
　Rose
Caleb
　Arie Smith
James
　Sarah
Jacob
Mittie
　Madison Grant
Mattie

3,017

A list of Randall and Winnie
Wiggins's children and their spouses.
My great-great-great-grandfather is
Moses and he was married to Anna
Wyche. *Gwen Wiggins*

children are listed, but two of them, Jacob and Mattie, are listed as having no children. Were they never parents, or were they separated from their children? If the latter, could it be that their names were never recorded? And what if some of the men, like Randall Sr., had children with other women but because of time and separation, my family lost contact with them, too? What if one of Randall Sr.'s siblings had children with another black Cherokee woman and they were Peggie's parents or grandparents?

I decided to contact the Oklahoma Historical Society and paid them to send whatever information they could find on this Peggie Wiggins. From the Midwest to the East Coast, I gathered stories from relatives about a tribal link, and they always pointed back to the Cherokee. This Peggie Wiggins was listed as a Cherokee freedman, meaning that she was what we may consider today a black Indian. Could this woman be related to my family, perhaps through marriage? The mystery deepened as I kept asking more questions about Peggie Wiggins's family.

In an interview with the Department of Interior Commission to the Five Civilized Tribes, dated April 5, 1901, representatives recorded that she was thirty-eight years old and that her husband's

PETER	SARAH	ANN	RANDALL, JR	MOSES	AARON	JOSHUA	CALEB	JAMES	JACOB	MITTIE	MATTIE
MARY	CHARLIE	ELLEN	AGNES	PEARLIE	HATTIE	MATTIE	COOPER	BESSIE		WILLIE	
RICHARD	TOM	MINNIE	ELIAH	CLIFFORD	COLEY		UTHA	MAXIE		ARTIS	
RUBIE	WINNIE	ALLEN	LEONARD	ROXIE	OLDEN		ANNIE	ALTON		ETHEL	
	GEORGE	SEMMIE	ULYSSES	SONNY LEE	COOPER		WALTER			DUBLIN	
	WILLIAM	NELSON	ZOLA	SHEPHERD	MARY ALICE		C.W.			GEORGE	
		WILLIAM	MINNIE	CLUSTER	ARTHUR						
		RUBE	LUCIOUS	Z.B.	LEONARD						
			VIRGIL	KINNEY	MINNIE						
			ERNEST	WILLIE							
			DALLAS	WALTER							
			ANN MARIE								

The descendants of Randall and Winnie Wiggins. My bloodline is through Randall and Winnie Wiggins's son Moses. *Gwen Wiggins*

name was Mitchell Wiggins, who was not a Cherokee citizen. Peggie Wiggins herself was a slave to George Crapo and was born in Cherokee Nation around 1863. It is not specified where her mother or Mitchell Wiggins was born. He may or may not have been Randall's grandson, but what if Randall had siblings and Mitchell was a direct descendant of that brother or sister? I was told that Randall Sr.'s father had many children. There is no Mitchell Wiggins listed on any Dawes Roll. Was he a black man? If so, what was this African American doing in Indian territory?

Peggie also had a son, Lewis Poole, aged five, whom she tried to get on the rolls—unsuccessfully, as there are no records of him listed. *One more Cherokee freedman erased from history*, I thought. The rest that I could pull up about Peggie's life was about fifty acres that she wanted to relinquish to her brother. In a legal document with regards to her land rights, another party listed was a member of the Vann family, Jesse Vann, who was also Cherokee. Maybe this Jesse Vann was related to Marilyn Vann.

I don't know if I can ever 100 percent prove that I'm related to Peggie. But I do know that she shares the last name of the woman who was said to be a black Indian. Maybe two black Indian women married Wigginses men. I don't know for sure. I do know that Peggie was a Cherokee woman and that Gwen, my mother, her aunt, and many other relatives have been said to have Cherokee ancestry. I began to think about similar stories that I heard from other black people from Georgia and Florida.

I posed a question on Twitter asking black people if they had heard about a possible native link in their family, and I was flooded with responses. One person who responded was Trudy Appling. Trudy has lived in New Jersey and New York for most of her adult life, but her family was a part of the Great Migration, moving to Cleveland from Georgia because of the promise of factory jobs in the North. Her paternal aunt always told her that her mother, Trudy's grandmother, was part Creek. Trudy thought that might be true because her grandmother had high cheekbones and small eyes, and her recipes were unlike those from other African American families that she knew: oyster stew, and hemp, bark, and berries concocted in a pot to remedy an illness. Though Trudy's grandmother died before Trudy got to meet her, her aunt's words made her wonder if she was connected to the tribe, as a slave or a free woman.

"I had suspected that she was a servant or slave connected to the tribe, but at first, when my aunt told me that she was part Creek, I was like, 'No, I don't think so.'" But upon further research, Trudy realized that maybe her aunt was onto something. Trudy's paternal side, the Appling family, is from Appling County of southwestern Georgia. With the exception of the Seminoles, in the 1800s, most white settlers classified the tribes up and around the Chattahoochee River as Creeks. In 1814, during the War of 1812, the Creek people were stripped of their tribal lands, which comprise the present-day counties of Irwin, Early, and Appling.[2]

Another Twitter connection was Sherese Robinson, a woman who lives in New York City like me, but her maternal side is from Lake City, in Columbia County, and from Alachua County, Florida. Both places were Seminole settlements, and the Seminole Nation in Oklahoma is derived from the Seminole Tribe of Florida, which still exists today. Its existence is due in part to the fact that Seminole Indians hid in the Everglades during the Seminole Wars and enforcement of the Indian Removal Act.[3] Sherese's family were farmers; her great-grandfather owned fifty acres of land in the early 1900s, where he raised pigs and cultivated tobacco and corn. When he died, he gave all of his children the land. Sherese made no mention of a will, and I wondered if this was a case of heirs property. Her grandmother eventually returned to the property to care for the land because the rest of her siblings left during the Great Migration and never came back.

Though Sherese regularly visits her family land, the history of their Seminole heritage has been hard to parse. Her great-aunt, who is eighty-seven, has a document that lists family members eligible to receive government assistance. There was an unrecognizable name on that document that no one else in the family paid attention to until Sherese told a relative that that was the name of the Seminole tribe. Before then, Sherese didn't think she had any Seminole ties, because no one in her family spoke of any. Her great-grandfather couldn't read, and whatever was written down on paper was so fragile that people in her family were afraid to touch it. Her great-grandfather's oldest child, Sherese's great-aunt, who passed away at ninety-six, never talked about their lineage, because she was ashamed of having light skin and blue eyes, so unlike the rest of her siblings. Sherese also didn't think she had Seminole ties because her DNA test showed none.

After learning about Sherese's and Trudy's stories, I circled back around to my family, but on my paternal grandmother's side, who comes from the Sandhills region of North Carolina. A man by the name of Floyd T. Jones created a database for the Sandhills Genealogical Society. Jones and his team got the idea for the group after gathering stories from elders and reviewing over a hundred thousand documents. The introductory page regarding the research states:

> Like many families, we got answers to most of our questions and other family information from our parents, grandparents, great-grandparents, and all the local ancestral storytellers in our communities . . . of course, we heard the shocking phrase "things we don't want to talk about." These revelations caused our research efforts to grow well beyond the "so-so-many" people we thought we knew to awaken us to a multicultural and cross-ethnic heritage that includes Native American, European, African, and Asian ancestors.

The parentage of my grandmother Gladys, on my father's side, was questionable. She was a very light-skinned black woman with gray eyes, whose features made her stand out among her siblings. Her "official" name is Gladys Dolores McIver, daughter of Marshall McIver and Mary McIver, née Capel. Family folklore suggests that she was actually the daughter of a Rockefeller who had a playground estate near Sandhills, called Foothills, where my great-grandparents worked and lived. On a census, I saw that her name was Gladys Dolores R. McIver, and this was prior to her being married and becoming a Regis, fueling my suspicion that that R came from someone else.

Because I wasn't too confident about tracking Glady's paternal side, I started with her mother and kept going backward through this website by clicking on the rungs of parents and grandparents before her, until I came upon a woman named Eliza Monroe, who would've been Gladys's great-aunt. She's listed as a sixteen-year-old domestic servant on an 1880 census. While her ethnicity is listed as American, there is an interrogative amendment: "American Indian????"—there really were four question marks. I asked Mr. Jones, the website administrator for the Sandhills Genealogical

Society, about this possible native connection, and he told me that in spite of this open-ended ethnicity label, DNA testing had proven otherwise.

So I kept going back further, until I found Eliza Monroe's grandmother, whose surname was Vann, though her first name is unknown. One of the biggest Cherokee slave owners was James Vann, son of a Scottish father and Cherokee mother. His ownership of enslaved black people and his fluency in English made him "civilized" in the eyes of white settlers, but he still demanded respect whenever whites visited his 137 acres. At the time of his death, at age forty-three, he was said to be one of the richest men in the Cherokee Nation as well as the eastern United States. Eliza's grandmother must have been born about two decades before the passage of the Indian Removal Act in 1830, after which James Vann's son and family and their two thousand slaves marched to Indian Territory.[4] The oldest Vann connected to my family with a disclosed first name was Samuel Vann Sr. Chief James Vann, as he was known in the Cherokee tribe, was Samuel's second cousin. Marilyn Vann, my liaison for my Oklahoma trip, is a distant descendant of James Vann.

I asked myself if I should continue pursuing this Peggie Wiggins or Vann connection. *To what end*, I wondered. I don't want a citizenship card. I'm not attached to Oklahoma in any way. The purpose was not to find an ancestor on the Dawes Roll, carry a membership card with me in my wallet, and receive benefits. I didn't want them. And again, Oklahoma is not my home, though it may have been for some of those who came before me. Out of respect for those who are still in Oklahoma and fighting for their rights, I wouldn't want to go through the process out of mere curiosity. All I wanted was to find a way to shift the narrative to demonstrate that not all of our grandparents were lying.

For years, I had dismissed my relatives' accounts of our Native American ancestry with the Seminole and Cherokee tribes, basically because I thought such accounts were antiblack. Not knowing that we had occupied the same lands as the Cherokees and Seminoles, I thought the claims were a way to exoticize our identities. The ancestors of millions of other black Americans lived in the same areas as the Five Civilized Tribes. Black Americans were enslaved by the Cherokees. We often found refuge with the Seminoles, as my great-grandfather once did. When the Five Civilized Tribes were forced to migrate west of the Mississippi River, black people accompanied them. At one time, in some places, as LeEtta said with regard to the Seminoles, blacks and indigenous tribes were one people. Discussions of American blackness should always include indigeneity, and not as an aside, for both peoples were connected through the plantation economy and the transatlantic slave trade. Actually, it's a wonder that any stories of black-native relationships survived from this horrific system. It was because of this system that a man named Randall Wiggins, a slave, "fetched" a woman of Indian blood named Winnie over two hundred years ago and I, one of their descendants, pushed past my disbelief to find this union. Randall and Winnie are the earliest ancestors my family has been able to find. If I had continued in my disbelief, I would've never found Randall and Winnie, and I would've denied myself knowledge of the intricate layers of my parentage.

There is more potential in these black and native stories than one might think, but because of migration and the arbitrary, racist categorizations of laws and rolls, families have been separated. Our stories have become bifurcated as a result: one side is the official story, and the other is the one we whisper to our relatives for generations. Maybe I didn't seek to prove my Indianness but to prove that the stories we have passed down from both sides of the Mississippi deserve just as much recognition as whatever a history textbook states as fact. These stories about our interrelated cultural identities circulate in our communities, ignore state borders, and mirror one another, proving that we are bound to one another in spite of the displacement. Whatever we've heard should serve as anchors to carry us into the future and ground us in a difficult but insightful semblance of the true past.

I found I couldn't conclude my journey with the Midwest. Geographically, that wouldn't make sense. A whole other region of the United States would've been ignored. There was still the wild, wild West. In 1970, often considered the last year of the Great Migration, California was one of the top three states, along with New York and Illinois, in total black population.[5] But except for my late great-aunt Evelyn Jewell Regis Navarre, I didn't know of any other relatives who had migrated to the West. I got stuck when I tried to think of any other relative who might have gone out west. I searched so far and wide that it took me a while to catch my breath and realize that there was one migrant I hadn't yet considered: me.

PART IV

Los Angeles

AFTER ALL THAT my family had gone through to move to the North, fleeing Americus and settling in an Atlantic City project, you'd have thought they'd have been satisfied with their trajectory. South Jersey should've been the end. After all, my grandparents made a good life there for my mother and my siblings. But no, they were still hungry for more. My grandparents were still dreaming of another place, beyond the boardwalk games and Bible camps and Sunday dinners. In the Atlantic City projects, my family and their black neighbors were always talking about California, namely Los Angeles. It was, in my mother's words, supposed to be "the land of milk and honey." Every black person my mother knew mythologized California to some extent. Friends and strangers alike would exchange stories about such-and-such's cousin who had gone out to Los Angeles, and then their voices would trail off, because every listener's mind would start to imagine all kinds of possibilities. No one needed to explain what happened after so-and-so's cousin went there, because just reaching Los Angeles meant that that person had made it. Television only intensified the California dream. Hollywood made Los Angeles seem a land of make-believe where you could be anyone you wanted to be. For a family like mine, the City of Angels seemed like the perfect goal for a family accustomed to take flight.

California was thought to be a promised land centuries before it became part of the United States. The name California first appeared in a Spanish novel in 1510. California was envisioned as a mythical utopia, "an earthly paradise, with unbounded productiveness without labor" and "handsome black women like Amazons."[1] When Sir Francis Drake became the second European (after Juan Rodríguez Cabrillo) to explore the area that we now know as California, he named it New Albion, which began a linguistic battle between the English and Spanish. The Spanish ultimately won, and Londoners in the 1850s began to use the name California as slang for money. This was during the gold rush, when settlers from many places converged on California after hearing of gold being found there. The Americans' preoccupation with gold intensified the image of the state as paradise. According to Mark Juergensmeyer, the California myth signified freedom from guilt and obligation, as well as transformation from "the purifying powers of change." What could be more enticing than that for a black American of the twentieth century?

A Louisiana Creole family, disillusioned by their loss of status or devastated by the Great Mississippi Flood of 1927, could board the Sunset Limited train from New Orleans to Los Angeles, where memories of Lake Pontchartrain, the red dirt, and the cemeteries where their ancestors slept would be exchanged for visions of manicured green lawns, bougainvillea, and drive-in movie theaters. They would settle in Leimert Park or Jefferson Park, where other Creole families awaited them. There their children and their children's children would leave a cultural imprint on these sections of South Los Angeles with their Catholic churches and Creole restaurants. A Gullah man from Beaufort County, South Carolina, might have worked a number of years at the Philadelphia Transportation Company or as a Pullman porter in Chicago before the desire for warmer weather was too loud a siren call to ignore. He'd read the *Chicago Defender*'s daily train schedules and decide to take the chance. At least the Pacific Ocean wasn't the Atlantic with its odor of slavery.

If that black man had the time and energy from his manufacturing job, he might leave his home near Central Avenue—one of the few places where he was allowed to live—to watch the azure ocean from the docks as it glistened before sunset. A Cherokee freedman from Oklahoma, stripped of his land and public recognition of his multiethnic identity, might leave by a car in the middle of the night. A neighbor up late might see this man from her front porch and, without saying a word, might press a copy of *The Negro Motorist Green Book* to the freedman's chest so he'd know where to stop on Highway 66 if he wanted to stay alive to see the iconic HOLLYWOOD sign. Black people from Alabama, Mississippi, Texas, Northern cities, Midwestern states, and all places in between swarmed into South Los Angeles with nothing else but a dream to be free, or at least freer—to finally be on land that could not be ripped out from underneath their feet, to finally breathe a little easier.

I "migrated" to Los Angeles when I was around six years old. My uncles, Rodney and Freddie, were emerging record producers who got their first big break by collaborating with Brandy (Norwood) on her Grammy Award–winning album, *Never Say Never*. The California dream manifested for them. For the most part, everyone we knew had been born, had lived, and had died in South Jersey. For these Jerkins brothers to go all the way to the other side of the country and end up with more money in their pockets than we had? Well, it would have been unfathomable if it hadn't been the truth.

At the time, I was a budding child actress. Because I was talkative and effervescent, people told my mother to put me in commercials. After doing some research, she took me to my first audition in New York City. I was too young to realize what was going on, but knew I booked the gig. One *Blue's Clues* commercial later, I was off to

Los Angeles with a talent agent and several headshots. My mother and I settled in the Woodland Apartments in Toluca Lake, in the San Fernando Valley of Los Angeles County. There many aspiring child actresses who migrated with their parents from the Midwest and East Coast communed with one another.

But my mom felt out of place. California felt entirely too different from her New Jersey upbringing. For one thing, she couldn't get used to the different territories. "There were just certain places where you weren't supposed to go," she says. One of them was South Central. When my mother told friends that she was taking me out to Los Angeles, they warned her to stay away from South Central because of its extreme violence, because their only knowledge of that area came from John Singleton films, like *Boyz n the Hood*, and late-night crime shows on TV. This fissure, as I'd like to call it, makes all the difference. Yes, television and other media warped our conceptions about black neighborhoods, but were these characterizations of South Central unfair? If so, what could they illuminate about how and where black people could safely settle? What did these territories have to do with our movement? Did we ever get the dream? Could we rest at last?

Since part of my family had migrated westward in the 1990s, well after the official end of the Great Migration, I wanted to speak to some of the people who were a part of the waves of black people who sought the dream in previous decades. I had to use the internet again, and most older folks I knew were on Facebook rather than Twitter. That's how I found Rachelle James. I sent her a message, and she responded within an hour. Before my plane from Oklahoma City took off for Los Angeles, I was on a call with her. It felt as though she'd been waiting for me all along.

Rachelle James was born in Los Angeles, but her mother was a Creek freedwoman from Wewoka, and her father was from Ennis, Texas. One day, Rachelle's father was walking after a long day at work in Dallas, and declined to cross to the opposite side of the street as a white man was walking down the same sidewalk toward him. He confronted Rachelle's father and punched him. Rachelle's father fought back and killed him. The attacker happened to be a KKK member, and soon after, Rachelle's father escaped to Oklahoma City, where he "bottled and bonded." Oklahoma was a dry state until 1959. Rachelle's father and uncle smuggled alcohol into the state by the carload. Though especially dangerous for black bootleggers, the method was extremely lucrative and easier than making bathtub gin. Black Oklahomans loved scotch. The plan was simple: sell bottles of it at after-hours hangouts for fifteen or twenty bucks. Once Rachelle's father had made enough money, he sought to marry a pretty girl and move to California. This pretty girl happened to be Rachelle's mother, a beauty she compared to Lena Horne and Dorothy Dandridge. After they married and moved to Los Angeles in 1945, Rachelle's mother worked as a seamstress under Edith Head, the legendary Hollywood costume designer, and her father worked for a railroad company.

The end of the Great Depression in the 1930s helped enable the westward migration of African Americans in the 1940s. Between 1940 and 1950, the number of black Angelenos increased by a hundred thousand, but many had difficulty finding adequate-paying jobs. Rachelle's family lived in the West Adams district, and the family soon realized that segregation and intimidation were old problems in the new place. When Rachelle was four, her parents wanted to buy a home in the Pico-Fairfax area, but no one would sell to them. This rejection was systemic, not case-specific. West Adams was white, and people were required to sign racially restrictive covenants as part of the deeds to their stately homes. The neighborhood's white upper class readily agreed never to sell to African Americans. Black people were migrating to Los Angeles in overwhelming numbers during the first half of the twentieth century, and their upward mobility needed to be stopped. Because of the Depression, however, white homeowners were desperate, and some reneged on their covenants. Black people moved in, and white people fled to posher neighborhoods, like Beverly Hills and Bel Air.

Rachelle's mother went into the real estate business, working for a prominent developer from Palm Springs who had an office at Wilshire Boulevard and Beverly Drive.

The developer noticed how downtrodden Rachelle's mother was about the rejection, bought the home and drafted the title papers, and the Jameses signed them. As the deal was closing, the Jameses' new neighbors called Rachelle's parents in the middle of the night to tell them that their new home was on fire. They dashed over there, but the house was severely damaged. The neighbors said that the fire chief, who lived down the street, had doused the house with gasoline and lit it. Despite the clear message—You do not belong here—Rachelle's father fought back. "He said to move every gun in the house and move it high—hold it up in the air— let all the neighbors know. And I was taught as a child, it was just instinct, if somebody called me nigger, kick their ass. And if they were your size, fight 'em. If they were bigger than you, take a baseball bat." I recalled my grandparents' move to the suburb of Pomona, outside of Atlantic City, after which the KKK burned crosses in their backyard to try to intimidate them into leaving.

Rachelle and her family soon realized that California was no different from any other part of America. Geography made no difference for black people. For them there were only two regions in America: up south and down south. The hell that they fled was waiting for them in the City of Angels. This duplication of the Deep South in the Far West was by design, from the highest levels of infrastructure down to the bigotry on the streets.

In the 1920s and 1930s, about 10 percent of the police in every California city were Ku Klux Klan members. William Parker, chief of the Los Angeles Police Department (LAPD) from 1950 to 1966, recruited military and police veterans from the South, seeking the most racist cops he could find. While Los Angeles black churches were trying to lure black Southerners to flee to escape the KKK, white supremacists were already in control of the city, now dressed in blue instead of white. The "sundown towns" that black Southerners raced to escape reappeared in Los Angeles County— especially South Pasadena, Culver City, and Glendale. For white readers unfamiliar with the term, a sundown town was an *officially* racist municipality, usually with signs posted at the city limits saying something like NIGGER, DON'T LET THE SUN SET ON YOU HERE, letting everyone know that no one would be punished for murdering a nonwhite person.

Rachelle says, "I can remember when a black person had better not go to Glendale or Culver City and be there after five o'clock. I was in high school from '67 and graduated in June of '70. I was an outstanding journalism student at L.A. High. We were one of the few high schools in the country that produced a six-page-minimum weekly newspaper. The sponsor of the journalism program lived in Glendale, and we had different material that he had to approve that had to be done after school was out but before the next morning. We would sometimes have to drive to his house in Glendale to take it to him. Everyone would joke, because when we went to Glendale, I would say six or seven times out of ten the police would stop us. 'What are you doing here?' That kind of stuff. And same thing in Culver City. In the fifties, when we first lived in Pico-Fairfax, after we had started school, when we would ride our bicycles around the block, white people would turn their sprinklers on to try and wet us up."

Besides the sundown towns and the KKK cops, there were the segregated spaces. While Jim Crow was not sanctioned by law, blacks were routinely kept out of certain neighborhoods like West Adams because whites feared the potential of black people's class mobility and economic growth. In the 1910s, black people began settling in Los Angeles along the lower end of Central Avenue because of the low rents. By 1920, the thirty blocks of Central Avenue, "several blocks east to the railroad tracks," and the neighborhoods around West Jefferson and Temple Street and the area south of Watts was populated mainly by black people. White resentment was already present. A letter to the editor of the *Los Angeles Times* published in 1916 lamented "the insults one has to take from a northern nigger, especially a woman, let alone the property depreciation in the community where they settle." Restrictive covenants were widespread. Sale, lease, or rental of certain lots by a white person to any nonwhite was illegal. Black people were confined to certain blocks and neighborhoods in South Los Angeles. The buildings they inhabited were left to deteriorate. There was inadequate water, poor sanitation, cramped housing, and "high sickness and death rates, high crime rate, police-resident hostility," as Lawrence B. De Graaf, author of "The City of Black Angels: Emergence of the Los Angeles Ghetto, 1890–1930" put it.[2] Educational and recreational services were subpar.

This was all too familiar to me. In South Jersey, there were certain parts of Atlantic County at the Jersey shore where black people were barred from buying and renting. Maybe this is why my family, and many other black families of the sixties and seventies, were confined to the projects. Maybe this was also why my grandparents went through hell to move into a white suburb less than ten miles away. This wasn't state-specific. This was a nationwide effort of white people to impede the movement of black people who were coming in droves to better their lives.

Before my flight took off from Oklahoma City to Los Angeles, I knew what this last, crucial part of my research would entail. This was less of a deep dive into my family history and more of an on-the-ground look at migrants from all of the United States who settled in the last place that they could go. I would study what turned Los Angeles into a powder keg—the result of squeezing black people into restricted territories. Using my family's stories,

I wanted to demonstrate how racist myths formed white beliefs about black people in California, and my relatives' judgments were influenced by them. I wanted to show that, despite black people's distances from one another, we were in perpetual conversation through the mistreatment, displacement, and violence inflicted upon us. And I intended to be the interlocutor.

———————

2

WHEN MY UNCLES were working at the Pacifique Recording Studio in Santa Monica, there was a homeless woman who would always come by, named Geraldine. She was in her fifties and from what my mom could recall, she was clean because she would dig through trash with gloves on. She would always joke to my mother that she wanted me as her child, most likely because we were both light-skinned and she thought I bore more of a resemblance to her than the rest of my family. Geraldine moved to California to become an actress, but her dreams were never realized. Upon learning more about her life, my family realized that she was from South Jersey, like us. Not only was she from South Jersey, but we also knew her family. My uncles tried to coax her into returning home, but she would not budge. She was too embarrassed to go back home and tell the truth about what happened to her. Even if she was homeless, being in California meant that she had made it and there would be no going back, no matter how much she'd been through. My mother and uncles didn't understand her.

When I heard the story, I didn't understand either. Why would she not want to go back to South Jersey, where she could be with her family and have a chance at a home? I didn't know her history.

Geraldine migrated to Los Angeles in the sixties as the city was in sociopolitical turmoil. In 1965, Los Angeles was the scene of the Watts Riots, biggest in our nation's history, a culmination of the rage black migrants felt after they'd settled in the City of Angels and found they couldn't escape racism even there.

On August 11, 1965, twenty-one-year-old Marquette Frye was pulled over on 116th Street and Avalon Boulevard in Watts for reckless driving. A crowd of fifty people watched as Frye failed sobriety tests. As the police were about to tow Marquette's car, his older brother Ronald brought their mother, Rena, to the scene. Like Rachelle James's family, the Fryes had also come from Oklahoma to Los Angeles for more opportunities. According to police reports, Marquette was respectful and compliant at first, but as soon as his mother and brother showed up, he turned spiteful, saying that they had to kill him to take him to jail. When the officers tried to arrest him, he resisted, and Rena jumped onto an officer's back. An officer hit Marquette in the head with his baton, drawing blood. The crowd now swelled to almost a thousand people as Marquette, Ronald, and Rena were hauled off to jail. The chaos that ensued left 34 people dead, including 23 killed by LAPD officers or National Guard troops, as well as 1,032 injured, at least six hundred buildings damaged from fires or looting, another two hundred buildings completely destroyed, and around 3,500 people arrested. The event is now a specter that hovers over black Angelenos, the memory still vivid.

Depending on whom you ask, the Watts Riots may or may not be called an uprising or rebellion. Rachelle told me that black people were just sick and tired of being sick and tired. By the time they reached Los Angeles, they'd just about had it with racism, and the city served as a pressure cooker for black rage. In the 1960s, race riots were happening all over the country, in places like Birmingham and Tampa, but also in Northern cities, like New York (Harlem), Detroit, Chicago, and Newark. After World War II, as millions of black people were migrating north, many white people fled to the suburbs to escape the deterioration of the inner cities as unemployment and poverty due to systemic racism became the norm there. Collectively, the riots were one of the biggest and most destructive uprisings in this country's history.

As in other states I visited, I connected with one black person, who then urged me to talk to another—exactly what Rachelle did. She wanted me to meet the woman who picked up the first call into the police station when Marquette Frye was being arrested; she has been dealing with the fallout ever since. No sooner did I land in Los Angeles and set down my bags in my hotel room than Regina called my cell phone and invited me to come to her home in Country Club Park to talk.

Regina is a first-generation Californian, born in 1942 and raised near Watts. She and Geraldine were close in age. Regina's grandfather, as she succinctly put it, was "an uppity nigga." He owned an insurance company and made so much money that whites considered him a threat. He was a good shooter, who could kill a fish in the water, but like Regina's father, he had to flee a lynch mob. Regina's grandfather gathered his wife and their eight children and moved to California. When Regina's parents married (her father from Texas, her mom from Arkansas), her father, whom she described as "damaged by the war," worked as an elevator starter at the Southern California Edison company, and her mother became a beautician after working as a maid. During Regina's childhood, she tells me, there were some real gangsters there. In the 1940s, white gangs emerged to combat black migrants, and black gangs emerged to resist them and protect the newly formed black neighborhoods. It wasn't so much about territories and knowing one's place, as my mother was told prior to our move to Los Angeles. It wasn't black-on-black crime. No, that shift happened later . . . after an incredible turning point.

By fifteen, Regina was married, and she had four children by the time she was nineteen. She became a police dispatcher because her husband had been employed in the same office previously and because she was not hired at the insurance company that her grandfather had founded. After applying, taking a test, and being hired in 1962, she worked at the Central Division, which is now the Parker Center, LAPD headquarters. During her probational period, she worked three months on the day shift, one month on night shift, and the last month on the graveyard shift. Naturally, with four small children, the hours took a toll on her, but not so much as the work culture. She would be put on disciplinary probation for letting her hair hang over one eye or wearing a sleeveless top, and coworkers would shut the door on her as she came through the entrance right behind them. The episode she recalls most vividly involves a dog. "At a different position, answering phones, this little old white lady . . . was sitting next to me, and she reached in her purse, and she said, 'Have you ever seen my dog?' I said no, and she pulled out a little picture of a little dog and showed it and asked, 'Do you know what his name is?' And I said 'No, Ma'am,' and she said, 'Nigger—he's black.'"

There were only 6 black employees out of 150. Her job was to answer phones for the Seventy-Seventh Street Division, responsible for a predominantly black neighborhood. Unlike the posh communities of Westwood or Beverly Hills, the district required diligent multitasking to alert police of crimes in the area.

"You know, normal nights, come to work at three o'clock in the afternoon. As the evening progresses, it got busier. All of a sudden, I hear that this officer needs help. I'm waiting, and nothing. Then an officer comes in on the radio. I say, 'Please repeat yourself. Who are you? Where are you?' Nothing. All the pains and knots of losing an officer who needs help. Finally I get him to come in, almost whispering, but it wasn't much help because the call was so broken up. I guess he was regretting that he started with 'Officer needs help' versus 'Officer needs assistance.' *Help* means BAM (by any means). *Assistance* means to get another patrol car down there." I figured that BAM was needed rather than waiting for a more orderly approach.

"At that point, I screamed out to the boys in the center, 'I've got an Officer Needs Help such and such.' I finally got his location out of him, and of course they sent another police car, and then they took over from me. But by then every officer in 12 (of the 77th Street division) had heard it and is going completely nuts trying to figure out what it is. So it unfolded in a weird, strange way. I knew though, 'cause, it was 116th and Avalon, and I lived at 118th and Central Avenue, which is not far, OK? So I knew the neighborhood. That's my neighborhood."

Regina tried to tell her superiors not to escalate the situation, but they did so anyway. To this day, she is haunted by a single question: "Why didn't they listen to me?" After work, when Regina ran home, she saw that the grocery store around the corner had been burned down and sparks were still flying from the roof. She made her children stay in the bedroom in the back of the house, thinking it too dangerous for them to be in the front. People were running down the street and looting stores and policemen were shooting. On the second night of the riots, there were military guards right off the Interstate 110 freeway. These white male guards pointed guns in her face and searched her car. Down on Imperial Highway, cars were ablaze and people were screaming.

After the riots were over, Regina's mental health suffered. She obsessed over her children's safety and was often paralyzed by the stress. She would dream of answering phone calls at her job and talk in her sleep, ordering officers to return to the scene to find a missing limb.

When I asked her how she coped with it all, her face took on a solemnity that I have never beheld in any of my other interview subjects. Her eyes were unyielding and unblinking, but I was neither scared nor uncomfortable. I waited patiently for her to continue. Then she replied, "I didn't think about it, and that's a long story that I'm writing about to try and figure out now. I learned very early in life how to compartmentalize, so if something was uncomfortable or painful, I could put it in one section and go on—the point that stuff's even coming up now that I'd forgotten. That's part of the weight on the stomach, and I can feel the pain when it comes up, when I remember and write about it now. They're all shut. All the horrors are shut."

I later ask if microaggressions at the workplace increased after the riots, and she says, "Too numb to know, too numb to know, too numb."

Her "compartments" stored memories well, for she continued in detail: "The hurt and the discouragement and the hopelessness, where we used to feel hope—even in slavery, it was like, if I can just get free. How do you 'get free' now? There's no hope to get free. Where is the hope that you can pull yourself up? Like, I was thirty years old and I was driving down Pico heading to Bullock's department store to take my daughter to what they call White Gloves and Party Banners Class. And we're driving down the street, and I look at the building that's being built down there, and I don't remember if that was the Transamerica Building or what—it's short now by comparison. I started to cry 'cause it was the first time it had ever occurred to me that no matter how hard I worked, what I did, or what I accomplished, I could never own a building like one of those. That my ceiling was way down. No matter what I did—and I remember just sobbing and tried to pull myself together, and I was in a depression hole for a few weeks after that. I was thirty when it hit me. It's kind of bizarre that I was . . . I really believed in the dream. I think they [the rioters] must have had the same realization about whatever they had set for their freedom."

After the Watts riots, the gangs that were around during Regina's childhood were virtually nonexistent. Black migrants began to form solidarity with one another in tandem with the rise of the civil rights movement. Bunchy Carter, the son of Nola Carter, who migrated from Shreveport, Louisiana, to California, became the leader of the Black Panther Party in Los Angeles. Bunchy was a member of the Slauson Street gang, a group of predominately black boys who resisted the white gangs that intimidated them when black families moved into white neighborhoods during the early and mid-twentieth century. After the police and FBI cracked down on the Black Panthers, the Brown Berets, Malcolm X's Organization of Afro-American Unity, and similar groups, the gang violence increased again, but now the gangs' focus was not on protecting neighborhoods but on territory and crime.[1] One had to be mindful of where one was and which gang dominated that area, or else one's life hung in the balance. The solidarity people had with their own block often meant becoming adversaries to another.

Regina told me about a woman she knew whose child was in a gang and was murdered right around the corner from her house. That woman still lives in that house; Regina doesn't know how she does it. Regina suspects that "she's given up." I realized that this is why my mother was hesitant about going to certain areas. It wasn't just a matter of being unfamiliar with Los Angeles; it was also because, depending on which territory you were in, you could be in danger. After the many decades of whites working to confine blacks to impoverished areas of the city, black people created minor communities on their blocks that dictated which interactions with those from adjacent blocks could turn deadly. Gang wars now changed from black versus white to black against black, an effect of the many decades of suppression of their self-actualization. As Regina told me, "The dreams aren't fulfilled here."

I was at a loss for words. Here was a woman who inadvertently found herself in the meat grinder of American history. She was traumatized. You could almost *hear* the stress in her quiet home. There were things that she chose to forget, or that her body made her forget, in order to protect herself and stay alive. I recognized this pattern. This was the impetus of my trip: a recovery from forgetfulness, a pilgrimage from the lands abandoned to the routes traversed. Then a question arose inside of me like a brief glimmer of light. If I knew the pattern from coast to coast, I had to ask this question, and I hoped that she would not be offended.

"When the riots were happening, did you ever feel the impulse to leave?" I asked.

"At some point I had a dream of living in the country and being peaceful and sitting on the front porch making circles in the dirt with my big toe, and then I realized that's too much work."

This exhaustion was of a level that I hadn't confronted till this moment. Regina was well aware of all that her parents had done to get here. She remembered how much she toiled to make a better living for herself, only to find herself swept up in one of the biggest riots the country has ever seen. Even afterward, she realized that she would never get as far as she's dreamed. But it was "too much work" to uproot and replant herself someplace else, no matter if she knew where her family came from or not. There was too much baggage, too much personal history in California.

Like Regina, Geraldine never achieved her dreams. To this day, no one is sure if she's alive or dead. Could Geraldine, like my family, have heard so much about the California dream that no matter what hardships she met when she got here, she had to stay, not just for herself, but for all those who never made it there? Did she, like Regina, believe it was too much work to return home? Did Regina stay because of all this history weighing her down? I was OK with assuming that the answer was yes. After all, she's still affected by the events that happened over a half century ago. But I knew that Regina was just one person. She was also a part of a different generation. Maybe the next generation, those who grew up in the 1970s, '80s, and '90s, had found a better life, with less violence from gangs and police and more economic opportunities. This was what I had to explore next: did those who came after Regina find better in Los Angeles or not?

3

WHEN MY UNCLES Rodney and Freddie were preparing to make their move out to Los Angeles, it was my mother who was most worried for them. She knew that they weren't familiar with the landscape and that there were restricted neighborhoods where they as outsiders shouldn't go. My mother worried that my uncles had to fear violence not only from white people, but also from blacks, if they were not conscious of which territory they entered. Despite both Rodney and Freddie being adults and their living arrangements being in a very affluent part of Los Angeles, she feared for them as black men: "Well, I thought about Rodney King and that video of him getting beat up. If they could do that to one black man, they'd do it to others." I knew the story of Rodney King. His beating happened in 1991, the year before I was born, and it reinforced just how much I, as a black person, should fear the police.

Twenty-five-year-old Rodney King was driving with two friends down the Foothill Highway toward the San Fernando Valley. He was an unemployed construction worker from Altadena who was on parole from a one-year sentence for armed robbery. Knowing that the alcohol on his breath would be a parole violation that would send him back to prison, King tried to outrun the Highway Patrol officers who were pursuing him for speeding. Eventually he stopped, but instead of acting professionally and simply making the arrest, as they almost certainly would have done with a white suspect, four white LAPD officers converged on his car, beat his passengers briefly, shot King with a Taser, and then were filmed beating and clubbing King fifty-six times in revenge for the chase. He sustained many injuries besides eleven broken bones, including a fractured cheekbone and a broken ankle. To add insult to injury, he was held in the Los Angeles County jail for three days before being released. In almost three decades, LAPD's violent racism had not changed at all. The only difference between 1965 and 1991 was the video camera with which witness George Holliday filmed the attack, letting the entire world see the truth despite police lies. This video began the entire genre of videos of police brutality circulating on the internet in the present day. For young black people like me, however, fear of bigot cops had already been instilled in us by our parents and grandparents, who already knew how untrustworthy law enforcement was.

Ironically, in Los Angeles, my uncles weren't targeted, but my aunt Sharene was. She and my mother were in South Central Los Angeles to visit the swap meets, but my aunt was wearing sweatpants and a red bandana. Red is a gang color, signifying affiliation with the Bloods. That day, locals told Sharene to be careful, with good reason. Police were circling the block where my aunt was until she removed the bandana. Before this moment, she had had no idea that simply wearing the color red could make her a target for both gangs and police. My mother, who was in South Central to order soul food, was warned not to sit in her car, because "they" would shoot her. I wanted to know who "they" were and so did my mother, but it didn't matter. Neither my mother nor my aunt knew how to conduct themselves in certain Los Angeles neighborhoods or understood just how deeply the gang lines and racial barriers were embedded there.

Black people who came to California seemed like a problem to law enforcement and white people alike. Whites, schooled in prejudice for centuries, felt threatened by imagined "savages," and redlining and police surveillance were common. But I had not realized how much the gangs and the police brutality were simply an old problem in a new decade. Another riot resulted—the 1992 uprising sparked by the Rodney King beating and the subsequent trial. Although the prosecutor was black, there were no blacks on the jury, which acquitted three of the police officers charged and reached no verdict as to the fourth. The riots began a few hours after the verdict was announced.

Through this fieldwork, I had believed that the gangs and their territories were a response to the racism that curtailed black migration and settlement, and that organizations like the LAPD and the KKK were the root causes of this violence. First, I was going to get into the gangs and their relationship with police. I had preconceived notions about what the gangs were, as many other Americans do, regardless of race and location. They were the scapegoats that white pundits used to avoid discussing white violence against black people. The line was "What about black-on-black crime and gang violence in (insert major city here)?" I thought gangs were filled with members who were often unemployed and shunned from society. I never asked the heavier questions, like how did this unemployment begin and why has society shunned them in the first place? I thought gang members killed recklessly and that anyone who joined them was bloodthirsty. But I wanted to investigate the idea that, if acceptance and community rather than a thirst for blood was what gang members sought, why weren't they getting it elsewhere? Could that speak to the systemic racism that they faced?

At one point, South Los Angeles, particularly Watts and Compton, could not be divorced from their gang culture and vice versa. Snippets from the late Oscar-nominated director John Singleton's oeuvre, especially *Boyz n the Hood* and *Baby Boy*, form a montage in my mind. I can hear Eazy-E and MC Ren, members of the iconic rap group N.W.A. (Niggaz Wit Attitudes), and Bloods & Crips in one ear, and the rapper Warren G, formerly a Crip of a different sort, in the other. Even as a child, I knew that to venture into South LA, one had to proceed with caution. There were certain colors you couldn't wear, depending on which block you walked on, and if you didn't follow the dress code, you were essentially asking for death.

The precursors to well-known gangs like the Crips and Bloods began with whites' anxiety about the influx of black migrants to Los Angeles. It goes without saying that gang culture is not an inherent part of African American culture. Gang culture is a by-product of black migration to Los Angeles, Chicago, New York, and other cities, and the socioeconomic and existential problems they found when they arrived. Los Angeles had been no stranger to gang violence before the arrival of blacks, but the first target for white people was Mexicans.

Young Mexican men loved wearing zoot suits—long suit coats with wide lapels and padded shoulders, paired with baggy trousers secured at the cuffs and pleated from the waist. The "zooters" often wore their hair long and greasy. For white Americans, such flamboyance in the underclass was extremely inappropriate, especially since the country was rationing fabric due to World War II. On June 3, 1943, groups of sailors joined white civilian mobs to roam downtown LA in search of zooters. Any they found were beaten and forced to take off their clothes in front of the crowds. Streetcars and buses were stopped and searched for zooters. The Zoot Suit Riots, as they are now called, lasted for several days. No one knows exactly what the original catalyst was. The high percentage of mothers who worked outside the home at factory jobs led to social anxiety in the community as they wondered who would protect their children. LAPD officers escorted the white mobs, sometimes joined in, and arrested around five hundred of the victims, most of them Mexican Americans but also some Filipinos and blacks.

The secondary target was the black people. White youth gangs were beginning to spread in the 1940s, especially around Huntington Park, Bell, and Southgate. These three neighborhoods weren't far from Compton, a once predominantly white neighborhood that turned black during the Great Migration. One of the most notorious gangs was the Spookhunters, whose logo was a caricature of a black man in a noose. Between Slauson Avenue to the south, Alameda Street to the east, and Main Street to the west, if black people dared to appear, the Spookhunters would attack them. Other whites attacked black-owned properties, bombing, shooting, and setting fires. Black people couldn't leave even if they wanted to. Racially restrictive covenants banned them from living in most Los Angeles neighborhoods. They were allowed to live only where the housing was decrepit and overcrowded and where there were no parks. In self-defense, black youths also formed gangs, like the Slausons, the Gladiators, the Outlaws, and the Rebel Rousers. In *City of Quartz: Excavating the Future in Los Angeles*, Mike Davis, a scholar on power and social class in Southern California, writes of this reaction: "As tens of thousands of 1940s and 1950s Black immigrants crammed into the overcrowded, absentee-landlord-dominated neighborhoods . . . , low-rider gangs offered 'cool worlds' of urban socialization for poor young newcomers from rural Texas, Louisiana, and Mississippi."[1]

The decades that followed were rife with endless cycles of poverty. From 1959 to 1965, black Angelenos were excluded from the good-paying jobs in the construction and aerospace industries. Unemployment rose from 12 to 20 percent in Los Angeles as a whole but was 30 percent in Watts. At the time of the 1965 riots, black migrants were fed up with the violence that could strike them at any moment from white youth and police, but now they felt emboldened by the civil rights and Black Power movements to do something about it. They soon learned that their leaders in the justice movements were being spied on, harassed, framed, and sometimes murdered by the FBI's COINTELPRO operatives, the LAPD's Public Disorder Intelligence Division, and many other city police forces in a concerted effort to halt the march of blacks toward equality under the law. The murder of Black Panther leader Fred Hampton by Chicago police in 1969 was an especially egregious example. During this period, the black youth of Los Angeles were searching for new identities and ways to be empowered, supported, and protected. Enter the Crips and the Bloods.

I met with Cameron Johnson, a former Bloods member, who remembers the family rift over the Black Panthers. "That's one thing I didn't like about my mother and her sisters, is that they were not revolutionary. They were afraid of the Black Panthers. It's definitely because of what they'd seen." I didn't need Johnson to elaborate. If these women were afraid of opposing the system, they obviously had seen with their own eyes what happens when black people protest injustice or seek autonomy. "My mother told me that I had to use the system. She wanted me to work in government or be a police officer. But I can't try to conform to a system that isn't even designed for me." The generational divide is illustrated by how much freedom and expression seemed possible to two members of the same household. Johnson was born in 1963. His mother came to Los Angeles at age five, from Texas, and his father was born in Watts.

Growing up, Johnson had heard of the Slausons and Gladiators, among other black gangs, and he knew that they didn't emerge for no reason: "The system definitely created it. You know the show *Happy Days*, with the sock hops and all that? Well, it didn't include black people. So they had to create their own social groups and their own social settings." When Cameron was around eight or nine years old, he recognized the influence of the local gangs whenever he couldn't watch a movie at a certain theater because the Crips would be there and he didn't want to get them agitated. As the years passed, their influence never waned. Cameron couldn't go to

Inglewood theaters because the Crips would be there. At thirteen, he had had enough. He was tired of not being able to move where he pleased, tired of being jumped and robbed.

Usually, when one wants to join a gang, there is initiation involved. The initiation varies from gang to gang but often the men get "jumped in"—beaten up by the rest of the group. Women usually have to sleep with all the male gang members to establish their subordinate position.

However, there was no initiation to become a Blood in the late seventies. All Cameron had to do was choose not to be a victim by not cowering before other gangs. He told me, "We didn't beat you up . . . no. Just be aggressive—just don't run whenever someone asks you where you from. I began to be a predator and not a victim." As long as Cameron swore that he wouldn't back down, he was in.

Cameron's personal story of frustration is a part of the collective story. The Bloods began in Los Angeles as a defense against the Crips' aggressive expansion. Cameron's grades began to suffer, and most of his previous friendships began to falter as well. Each gang claims certain avenues and street corners as its turf. Cameron had unaffiliated friends who lived in enemy territory. Before he was a Blood, he could sleep over at their houses. Once initiated, these ties had to be severed. By the time he reached high school, these former friends were the ones he fought.

Getting home from school required military strategy. To get to Dorsey High School, he had to walk through Crip territory. He couldn't use the school bus because the vast majority of the riders were Crips too. Cameron never finished high school and went to a juvenile detention center for stealing cars, serving six years in jail and two years in prison.

As far as the relationship with the police went, his neighborhood had a no-snitch code. Law enforcement added nothing of value to the community and therefore was to be ignored at all times, even regarding crimes against innocent people in the neighborhood. Cameron himself was a victim of police violence three or four times. Once he was beaten with a flashlight. On another occasion, after a high-speed chase, he was pulled over and assaulted. If police knew you were in a gang, sometimes they would drop you off in enemy territory, announce your presence over a loudspeaker, and let the gang deal with you. I wondered, if my aunt Sharene hadn't taken off her bandana when she was in South Central, would officers have done that to her, or would they have beaten her themselves?

The Rodney King beating video reaffirmed for Cameron what he and his community, gang and civilian alike, were experiencing. "Society did not have value for us," Cameron says. Cameron tells me that, at the moment the verdict came back from the Rodney King trial declaring the officers not guilty, "Somehow, everybody knew that this is what we was about to do." What they were about to do was riot and loot.

The police preyed on whomever they chose, beating, paralyzing, even killing folks Cameron knew around his neighborhood. As he continued speaking to me about how much profiling the police had done of black Angelenos, I thought about how much police behavior resembled that of the Spookhunters. When I asked him about this, he said, "They're one and the same." If that were true, then in Los Angeles at least, the gangs *were* a reaction to black people's exclusion from mainstream society. The gangs were formed in reaction to white people uprooting black migrants and their children once more. Even when blacks stayed put in their designated areas, the police continued the centuries of systematic brutality whether or not their victims were gang members.

When I ask Cameron more questions about this violence, he admits, like Regina Jones, that he has blocked many instances out of his mind. I realized once again the extent of the collective trauma that black people endured in what was supposed to be the promised land. Through Cameron's story, I learned that gang membership was less a channel for one's aggression than an opportunity for black people to commune with one another while so many mainstream social settings were reserved for whites only. Nevertheless, the gangs made the neighborhoods even worse, causing those like Cameron to fail in school and get caught up in the system that had laid the foundation for gang culture in the first place by redlining, police assaults, civilian white violence, and the biased criminal justice system. Yes, gang life is violent, but it did give those like Cameron a network where they felt accepted and supported. In a city as segregated as Los Angeles, having people who can strengthen one's place, even from the margins, is important.

In response to all the trauma, one man tried to provide a safe haven for black Los Angeles youth before he found himself an eyewitness to the 1992 Rodney King Riots. I met this man through an underground rapper named James "Nocando" McCall, who was showing me around South Central. The man's name was Ben Caldwell, an independent filmmaker and arts educator, who created a studio for video production and experimentation called KAOS Network in Leimert Park. Eazy-E, Lebo M, Ava DuVernay, and many others have passed through his building, which was a neutral zone for all the youth who had to deal with gang culture out on the streets.

In 1990, there were whispers around the neighborhood that the police were going to infiltrate the studio because they believed that Ben was running a drug club. One evening, Ben was working upstairs on a switchboard with a few of his teenage students when someone alerted him to a bunch of cops swarming the studio outside. He peeped through the window and remarked that the scene outside reminded him of SS troops in Nazi Germany. The officers wore black hats and boots and got into position. Ben and everyone else in the studio stepped outside, where they found that cop cars were parked on both sides of the street leading to his building so no one could leave. Arrests were made, but those detained were soon released. Fortunately, no one was murdered. However, Ben says such intimidation tactics catalyzed the riots.

Daryl Gates, former LAPD police chief who began his tenure in 1978, was notorious for his racism. As reporter Joe Domanick put it in the *Los Angeles Times* in 2010, "His troops were arrogant and aggressive in their policing, and the cost was catastrophic." Many unarmed suspects were killed during his reign. In an attempt to control the Bloods and Crips, he sanctioned sweeps throughout Los Angeles County in which many black men were indiscriminately arrested. One of his divisions specialized in framing innocent people for beating and shootings. Ben says of Gates's time, "They were breaking heads and necks just one after another."

When the officers who beat Rodney King were put on trial and the jury found them not guilty, the riots started almost immediately. In six days, there were over fifty deaths and sixteen thousand reported crimes, over 2,300 injuries, seven thousand fires, over twelve thousand arrests, and $1 billion in property damage, surpassing the damage total of the 1965 Watts Riots, which had been the city's biggest uprising by far. Ben told me that all the looting and burning he saw was the closest thing to complete anarchy that he'd seen in his entire life.

James McCall took me over to the intersection of Florence and Normandie Avenues so I could see where the riots started. It was eerie. I stepped outside of the car to take a picture of the street, and there was this thick energy in the air, as if what had happened there was unfinished. Demographically, the neighborhood is different now than it was in the early nineties. This part of town has become more Latinx-heavy, while black people have once again migrated—to the Inland Empire (Southern California east of Los Angeles) or back to the Midwest or East Coast. James made it emphatically clear to me that he is pro-uprising, so I asked him, "Do you think another riot will happen?"

He told me that if people continue to inform themselves about the mistreatment and discrimination still happening in their communities, then it will. "Because of social media, we *see* so many people getting killed by police officers. People who are no threat to the police officers are getting killed. People are told to march, write somebody, make a hashtag, and get that energy out—whatever the fuck it is. It's constructive. But there ain't nothing like a good spanking. Ain't nothing like it. We're wrong because we riot because they beat and kill us and don't get punished? Naw, we're not. You beat and you kill people, and you just walk off free? We commit a crime, with the way that society is structured for us, where we have to deal with your [white people's] violence—crime that's caused by poverty, lack of education, and all that shit—and we get extra penalized, you know what I'm saying? Like fuck that. Burn everything."

Everything from the racial barriers to the police brutality began to connect in a more current and urgent way than before. Black displacement and migration are indelibly a part of our lives. Our presence has always been a "threat" to whites, no matter where we lived or fled. All we wanted was to find safety, and we never gave up in moving to new terrain for that dream. But once there was no place else to go, we got tired of not being treated humanely. Black Angelenos decided that if they couldn't move freely on the land, then the land would have to burn.

I was much more involved in Los Angeles black history than I originally thought, not only because I had once lived in that city, but because everything that the black people in those communities had gone through reverberated throughout the country. I marched to protest the murder of Eric Garner by NYPD officer Joe Pantaleo. I recalled the late nights I spent with my mother watching tear gas being fired at protestors and journalists in Ferguson by the police. I remembered some of the countless names of black people who'd been killed without cause by police officers: Michael Brown, Walter Scott, Eric Garner, Aiyana Jones, Korryn Gaines, Philando Castile, Laquan McDonald, Ezell Ford, Eleanor Bumpurs. . . . The names and bodies kept piling up, and I realized that all these deaths and my understanding of them were connected to the uprisings in Los Angeles, which were caused by the racist systems and institutions used to contain black people and keep us from living freely and autonomously.

When black people first set foot on American soil, their shackles indicated their status as slaves and served as a physical restraint to ensure that we could not move, grow, and achieve as white people could do. When those shackles were removed and we were "free," we were constantly reminded to "know our place," whether through intimidation by the KKK or the police, or by impoverishment and denial of history (the Creole's fate), or by land theft in Oklahoma or corporate land purchase in the Lowcountry. Once we became human in the eyes of the law, we did everything we could to preserve our right to exist and to move. Movement was as much an individual dream as a collective means of survival. We had to move to save our families, move to get better jobs and earn money, or move because we had this unwavering belief, despite endless oppression, that there was a different kind of beauty to be found in another zip code.

On the way back to my hotel, I realized that Los Angeles may have been the end of my trip but that there was no spiritual end to what I'd done. Whatever happened in one place, like the riots or the police beatings, was bound to happen in another. Los Angeles was the emblem of what happens when white people don't leave us alone. Outbursts have proliferated throughout the country. The past and present exist on a continuum, and as I'd learned, there was nothing new under the sun. For black people and their desire for independence, for a true sense of home, everything is cyclical.

Now that I realized that Los Angeles was not the dream for black migrants, what was left to be done? Did everyone, like Regina and Geraldine, choose to stay, or did they, like those before them, move again? This was the last part of my investigation, and as my research pulled me closer to the present, I wanted to pose this question not to the elders but to those as young as me.

LOS ANGELES WASN'T the place for my own dreams. I don't remember ever saying this to my mother, but apparently one of the
reasons we decided to move back to New Jersey is because I told
her that I wanted to go home. I wasn't interested in being a child
actress anymore, though I was getting steady work on commercials and had auditioned to guest-star in a television show. I had
already done read-throughs and everything, but none of that mat-
tered to me. I was tired. California was too far away from New
Jersey, and I wanted to be closer to more of my family. My Uncle
Freddie, who was married and had children, decided to move back
because he wanted to be closer to his own family as well, though
he kept on producing records once he returned home. My Uncle
Rodney still lives in the Los Angeles area with his family. Though
Los Angeles was everything that my mother thought it would be,
the scene was not for her. She wanted to be more connected to
what she knew. And she is not alone. Nowadays, the new migrants
are those around my age group who are ready to take flight for
new opportunities but also wish to connect with their Southern
roots.

One of the youngest people I spoke with was Tyree Boyd-Pates,
who is a history curator at the California African-American Museum (CAAM) in Los Angeles. "You can't have black history without black people," he tells me. In Los Angeles and many Northern

cities, the black population is dwindling quickly in what many commentators have called a reverse migration. Since 1990, the Los Angeles black population has dropped by 150,000. Now black Angelenos only make up 8 percent of the city's population, down from 13 percent.[1] According to a UCLA analysis, during the 2007–09 recession, black workers in Los Angeles county lost jobs at the same rate as white workers but were less likely to find replacement work.

Black people are also getting priced out of their homes and are left with no choice but to move out. As a result, white people are returning to the black neighborhoods that they fled from during the Great Migration. Erin Aubry Kaplan of the *Los Angeles Times* writes, "It's an enduring American truth: Whatever black people have can be taken away. . . . Fifty years ago, Inglewood's white residents saw black newcomers not as neighbors but invaders, existential threats to their property values and to an ironclad social order. . . . The fact that whites are coming back . . . is a warning that my black community is, once again, irretrievably at risk."

Because of these demographic shifts, Tyree finds it important—now more than ever—to document black people's place in Los Angeles history. He said to me, "I think that if you look after '92, there's been a slip in Los Angeles's black population because the promise of opportunity for us was unfulfilled. Black people have been unfulfilled, so we are moving to the Inland Empire, we're moving back down to the South, we're moving to DC, we're moving to all of these areas where we initially fled from." Tyree even admitted that his time in Los Angeles is running out as well.

For others, however, returning home is a family affair full of the renewal and promise that Los Angeles never provided. Misty Broady is the thirty-seven-year-old daughter of a woman from Greenville, Alabama, and a father from New Orleans. Both of her parents came to Los Angeles looking for opportunity and did find work. Her mother worked as a registered nurse, and her stepfather—whom her mother married after her former husband passed away—currently works as an attorney. Unlike many of the other people I interviewed, Misty did not grow up in South Central but rather in the affluent Pacific Palisades neighborhood. During the summers, Misty would travel to Greenville to visit family, and she observed that neighbors were more racist in Los Angeles than they were in the Deep South. The Broady family was one of the few black families in Pacific Palisades, and often their white neighbors would barely speak to her.

As an adult, Misty lived in the San Fernando Valley and worked for the City of Los Angeles in code enforcement. It was in this position where she saw firsthand the displacement problem, and the desire to leave began to take root. Homelessness was rampant. Furthermore, the rising rent prices for Misty's apartment motivated her to seek better stability for her son. Misty's mother was already back in Greenville, and Misty and her son soon followed her to a two-acre property that's been in the family name for decades. Misty says of her place now, "I don't have a lot of anxiety, and my health is in better shape."

Others are moving back to the South, but to cities where they have no family ties, like Atlanta. Thirty-two-year-old Crys Watson has been living in Atlanta for two years as a content writer and founder of a nonprofit organization for women of color. Like Misty, Crys lived in the Valley, but her parents grew up in Compton. Crys's paternal grandmother, a Creole woman, was born in Alexandria, Louisiana, but raised in the Compton/Long Beach area. Crys's maternal grandfather was from Tulsa, and her maternal grandmother, a woman of Cherokee and Chickasaw heritage, was from Clearview, one of Oklahoma's last remaining all-black towns. It was in 2015 when Crys came to Atlanta for a business trip and discovered that, unlike her family members and peers in Los Angeles, black people there were thriving instead of simply surviving. "Black people are coming by the dozens out here from California. There is no glass ceiling, because black people are creating their own way. There are people who are younger than me who have properties—black people who are about ownership so they can retire as early as possible."

That last sentence struck me. Ownership—that's all black people have really wanted since they gained their freedom. That desire is what unites us from region to region and coast to coast. No matter whether we fled or remained in our original lands, all we wanted was to be able to have complete autonomy in our lives and the economic power to have a decent life, and we were willing to risk death to achieve this. Ever since black people were brought to this country, we have been devising, revising, and improvising ways to nestle our families into new spaces. Movement characterizes African American life. Our communities are scattered throughout the country; they are the by-products of movement. But no matter how scattered we are, we are entangled with one another, for we took the same railroads and the same highways, chasing the same dreams. In spite of our different phenotypes, languages and dialects, and lifestyles, we were inadvertently united in our rebellion to strive for better.

I am the physical embodiment of that quest—the daughter of a New Jersey woman and a North Carolina man, whose roots extend to Georgia and Louisiana respectively. My own journey as laid out in this book is an homage to the family members I've never met, a way of saying thanks to their arduous commitment to our survival. In the end, I not only found a fuller version of myself and my family, but also my extensive links to other black families in this beautiful, terrible country that is ours. I followed black people across state lines and rivers throughout the United States with nothing more than a notebook, recorder, and a wild curiosity for the stories that echo and reverberate within our borders.

EPILOGUE

I WROTE THIS epilogue after thirty-one people had been massacred in two separate shootings within twenty-four hours. The second one, on August 4, 2019, happened in Dayton, Ohio; six of the nine victims were black.[1] The previous day, a white man had opened fire in a Walmart in El Paso. Twenty-two people died and twenty-four were injured. John Bash, the US Attorney for the Western District of Texas, announced that his office would be treating this tragedy as a "domestic terrorism case" after the country learned that the shooter posted online that his slaughter was justified as a response to the "Hispanic invasion of Texas."[2]

I am exhausted. I don't know whether to tune in and risk becoming desensitized to the constant racist violence, or tune out for the sake of my mental health. The phrase "Hispanic invasion of Texas" reminds me that this is how history gets distorted in the view of the white man. It reminds me that white people think of those of us who are black and brown as invaders, rather than Americans. I think about the thousands of men, women, and children from Latin American countries who banded together into caravans and made makeshift camps along the way to make it to America, just so they could give their families a better chance in life. I thought about the families who are being separated, the children being abducted from their families by government agents, the random

ICE raids, and constant reports of people dying while under the "care" of the Border Patrol, and I ask myself why people continue to migrate here when they are met with so much hardship, not to mention all the derision from President Trump. But then I remember that they move northward just as black Americans have done: to flee violence, to get better jobs, to finally be at ease—in other words, to escape conditions largely created by the United States by its export of the drug war, its deportation of gang leaders to their home countries in the early 1990s, and its century-long support of corrupt tyrants throughout Latin America to prevent revolutions and enforce neocolonialist economics.

I think about the manifestos, like the one the El Paso shooter wrote. I think about the one by Dylann Roof, who murdered nine black people in a historic black church: "Segregation was not a bad thing. It was a defensive measure. Segregation did not exist to hold back negros. It existed to protect us from them. . . . Not only did it protect us from having to interact with them, and from being physically harmed by them, but it protected us from being brought down to their level."[3]

In a sense, he was right. Jim Crow, the impetus for millions of black Americans to move from the South, *was* a defensive measure— to protect whites from their own irrational fears and from having to acknowledge their own inhumanity. *We* were never protected. We were physically harmed even when we created our own communities and tried our best *not* to interact with whites in any way. White people just could not leave black people alone, and their constant meddling in our lives is one of the biggest reasons why we continue to be displaced, disrespected, disenfranchised, and murdered. We migrate because we want something better. We migrate because we have no other choice. But no matter where we go, we're victims of segregation, redlining, and racial discrimination. We're separated from other family members, separated from our stories, separated from our belief systems, separated from our lineages and our very identity, because if we ever fully understood just how vast and interconnected we are—as most white people do—we would be even more formidable and less exploitable.

As I thought about this and all that I had seen on my journey across America, I saw my identity shift, or enlarge rather, the more I transported my body over states and rivers. When I started this journey, I was just a New Jerseyan–turned–New Yorker who set out to learn more about my roots as a black woman and the migratory roots of black people in general. I wanted to understand my underlying misconceptions about water and rootwork and magic, which drew me to the Gullah Geechee people. I wanted to understand my father's side of the family and what it meant to be Creole. I wanted to understand the connection between blacks and Indians, which led me to Oklahoma. And I wanted to know if there truly was a place in America where black people belonged, which led me to California, once my temporary home. As I came out on the other side of this journey, I realized that I was not just one thing. I was a New Jersey New York Creole African American California migrant with potential Cherokee freedmen ties. I was many things.

Through conversation with all of my interviewees for this book, I realized that my story existed in other stories and that those stories were a call-and-response from my interviewees to me, and now from me to you.

When I finally came back home, I felt . . . changed. My profession is to craft words, but words eluded me. At the time that the seeds of this project began to take root, my birth certificate changed. Now I had both parents listed. But I didn't feel transformed. As a matter of fact, I was nonchalant about the amendment. The real transformation came a year and a half later, after I finished the prologue of this book and decided to show my parents what I had written, something I had never done in the past. I told myself that I shouldn't hide all of the words I had written about my family or hide the inspiration for that work. Wouldn't that be hypocritical of me, to document others' stories without holding a mirror to my own parents and my family's stories? The real reason I wanted to hide that was because I was afraid. My birth was not without controversy, as you might have guessed from reading the prologue. I don't want to cast my parents or any of my interview subjects in some morality play, a strict right-or-wrong binary. They made choices, and I am one of them.

For years, I carried around a feeling of shame that I was not meant to exist, because my family was multilayered, complicated, and often uneven. I thought that I really was the milkman's baby, because as a child of a single mother, it wasn't obvious who my father was. But I knew my father. I always knew my father. Yet this idea of the questionable lineage of a black child always intrigued me. Calling someone the milkman's baby is supposed to be an insult, but I learned—in Toni Morrison's *Song of Solomon*, for example—that the word *milkman* connotes a wanderer who returns to his familial homes to recover his identity. In that sense, I am as much as Jon's daughter as I am the milkman's baby. We all are, in a sense, wandering and searching, covering and recovering pieces of ourselves lost along some journey.

After my travels, I realized that questionable or knotty lineages don't always have to do with fathers. Sometimes they're about land rights, blood politics, or who or what is in control of your story. With this book, I hope to help black people to regain their narratives and recontextualize the shame that has been pressed upon our hearts from time immemorial. We are here because we are in perpetual motion, our migratory patterns rivaling those of birds. I do not believe that there is a promised land for us in America. I am disappointed that I could not find a happier ending for these pages. But you and I know that the promised land does not exist. Racism abides in all zip codes, on every migratory route.

Mason Traveil, a black man whose family has been in California since emancipation, has said, "*We* are the promised land."

The terrains of our bodies, though weary or broken, are not ruined. They are alive and fertile with dreams and possibilities and beauty. If we are the promised land, then that means that you— yes, you—exist on a plane larger than your eyes can see. Home is wherever we decide to settle, but our truest base is one another.

If we are the promised land, then what I want more than anything is for these oral histories to be the rain that awakens other people to bloom, to remember just how far our roots extend.

ACKNOWLEDGMENTS

I WOULD LIKE to thank my editors, Amber Oliver and Emily Griffin, for stretching me further than I ever thought possible. There were so many moments where I thought that I was going to break and that I was ill-equipped to handle a project of this depth but you two never stopped believing in me, and I'm indebted to you for your encouragement and skill.

Thank you to my agent, Monica Odom, for checking in with me not only for my pages but also on the minutiae of my life. I'm so thankful to have a business partner who cares about who I am as both a creative and human being.

Thank you to Leah Sophia Dworkin for her transcriptions. You are a diamond in the rough. Thank you for assisting me with this journey and reaffirming to me that I need to let others help me to do what needs to be done.

Thank you to Kim Racon for all the laughs in the Twitter DMs. Thank you to Hannah Wood, the editor who acquired my debut and brought me into the illustrious Harper family. Thank you to Sofia Groopman for acquiring this book.

Thank you to all my friends who've been there for me throughout the creation of this book: Danny Vasquez, Michelle Pham, Jenn Baker, Brian Taitt, Brandon Zamudio, Angela Chen, Dion Robbins, Aric Jenkins, Maraiya Hakeem, Jade Jones, Liz Cook, Brigitte Malivert, Aditi Juneja, Maria and Juan Robles, Alex Orphanides,

Alana Massey, T. J. Jarrett, Kaitlyn Greenidge, Sire Leo Lamar-Becker . . .

Thank you to all the academics and scholars who both supported and challenged my thinking—Andrew Jolivétte, Antoine Hardy, Monnica Williams, Bridget Goosby, Eric Leiker, Tiya Miles, Arica L. Coleman, Gerald Horne, Angela Walton Raji, Cheylon Woods, Tananarive Due, Simon Gravel, Arlecia Simmons, Brenda Stevenson, Jenny Tung, Barry Jean Ancelet, Edda Fields Black, Kerri Greenidge, and Kendra Field.

Thank you to all those who agreed to be interviewed—even those who couldn't make it in the final draft of this book—Tiffany Young, Amy Roberts, JR Grovner, Griffin Lotson, the Gullah Geechee Shouters, Sallie Ann Robinson, the Jordan family, Ron Daise, Annette Holmes, the Colson family, Kelli, Ron Graham, Eli Grayson, the Harrison family, Marilyn Vann, Stopper, Happy, Butch, Char, LeEtta Osborne-Sampson, Sylvia Davis, Rodslen Brown, Susie Crittenden Chambers, the Riley family, Damario Solomon-Simmons, Hannibal Johnson, Verdie Triplett, Terry Ligon, Darnella Davis, Shonda Buchanan, Rhonda, Gina, Mason Traveil, James "Nocando" McCall, Lisa Pecot-Hébert, Jervey Tervalon, Tim Watkins, Aminah Bakeer Abdul-Jabbaar, Ben Caldwell, Alice Harris, Skipp Townsend, Rachelle James, Regina Jones, Tyree Boyd Pates, Ted Soqui, and Carol Park.

Thank you to all the descendants of migrants, both friends and strangers alike, who shared their family stories with me.

Thank you to the Schomburg Institute for housing the world's best collections on the Diaspora.

Thank you to my mother and father, sisters, aunts and uncles, and other family members who kept me grounded and reminded me that I still have to live life while I'm working. Thank you especially to the elders, my grandparents, Gwen Wiggins, Sasha Lucas, and Colleen Winn for protecting our oral histories with all of your heart. This book would not have been as full if it weren't for your memory and patience.

Thank you to Zora Neale Hurston for showing me that African American life is both mythological and real, unwinding and knotting all at once. I'd never thought I'd do ethnographical work, and you've shown me how scintillating such an endeavor could be.

Thank you to Medium and particularly my *ZORA* colleagues for giving me the space to continue my book as I edited others' stories.

Thank you to the Most High for the strength to see this through. Thank you to the ancestors who I undoubtedly know were watching over me each step of the way.

NOTES

PROLOGUE: THE MILKMAN'S BABY

1. W. Fitzhugh Brundage, "Contentious and Collected: Memory's Future in Southern History," *Journal of Southern History* 75, no. 3 (August 2009): 757, JSTOR, www.jstor.org/stable/27779037.

PART I: LOWCOUNTRY, GEORGIA, AND SOUTH CAROLINA

I

1. Sijie Li, "THE ECONOMIC IMPACT OF THE FIRST MIGRATION," 12, University of Pittsburgh, September, 25, 2019, http://d-scholarship.pitt.edu/37312/7/Li_Dissertation_ETD_Final.pdf.
2. James N. Gregory, "The Second Great Migration: An Historical Overview," *African American Urban History: The Dynamics of Race, Class and Gender since World War II*, ed. Joe W. Trotter Jr. and Kenneth L. Kusmer (Chicago: University of Chicago Press, 2009), 22.
3. Preston Smith, "Exploring the Great Migration," Mount Holyoke College, February 13, 2019, www.mtholyoke.edu/media/exploring-great-migration.
4. Sam Worley, "Where Soul Food Really Comes From," Epicurious, June 29, 2016, www.epicurious.com/expert-advice/real-history-of-soul-food-article.
5. Robert T. Dirks and Nancy Duran, "African American Dietary Patterns at the Beginning of the 20th Century," *Journal of Nutrition* 131, no. 7 (July 2001): 1881–89, https://academic.oup.com/jn/article/131/7/1881/4686889.
6. "History of the Chicago Defender," *Chicago Defender*, http://chicago defender.com/history-of-the-chicago-defender.
7. Tracy N. Poe, "The Origins of Soul Food in Black Urban Identity: Chicago, 1915–1947," *American Studies International* 37, no. 1 (February 1999): 4–33, JSTOR, jstor.org/stable/41279638.
8. Ibid.
9. Suzanne Bopp, "Road Trip: Low Country, South Carolina and Georgia,"

National Geographic, September 14, 2010, www.nationalgeographic.com /travel/road-trips/low-country-south-carolina-georgia-road-trip.

10. Philip D. Morgan, *African American Life in the Georgia Lowcountry: The Atlantic World and the Gullah Geechee* (Athens: University of Georgia Press, 2010).

11. International African American Museum, "Slavery in The Lowcountry," 2017, iaamuseum.org/history/slavery-in-charleston-and-the-lowcountry.

12. William S. Pollitzer, *The Gullah People and Their African Heritage* (Athens: University of Georgia Press, 1999).

13. Peter A. Coclanis, "Business & Economy: Agriculture," *New Georgia Encyclopedia*, https://www.georgiaencyclopedia.org/articles/business-economy /rice.

14. South Carolina Department of Agriculture, "History," SCDA, agriculture .sc.gov/about.

15. Libby Wiersema, "Southern, Lowcountry, Gullah or Soul—What's the Difference Between These SC Cooking Styles?" SC Department of Parks, Recreation and Tourism, discoversouthcarolina.com/articles/southern-low country-gullah-or-soul-whats-the-difference-between-these-sc-cooking -styles.

16. J. Lorand Matory, "The Illusion of Isolation: The Gullah/Geechees and the Political Economy of African Culture in the Americas," *Comparative Studies in Society and History* 50, no. 4 (October 2008): 949–56, JSTOR, jstor.org /stable/27563714.

17. Kim Severson, "Taxes Threaten an Island Culture in Georgia," *New York Times*, September 25, 2012, www.nytimes.com/2012/09/26/us/on-an-island -in-georgia-geechees-fear-losing-land.html.

18. "Darien, Georgia (GA) Poverty Rate Data," City-Data.com, http://www .city-data.com/poverty/poverty-Darien-Georgia.html.

19. William Edward Burghardt Du Bois, *Prayers for Dark People* (Amherst: University of Massachusetts Press, 1980), 7.

2

1. Carson Bear, "Remembering Atlantic City's Black History and Segregated Past," *Atlantic*, CityLab, January 16, 2019, www.citylab.com/equity/2019/01 /african-american-atlantic-city-segregation-northside-tourism/580576.

2. Sitinga (Sitinga Kachipande), "Why Africans Don't Swim," Africa on the blog, March 21, 2013, www.africaontheblog.org/why-africans-dont-swim.

3. Lincoln Anthony Blades, "Trauma from Slavery Can Actually Be Passed Down through Your Genes," *Teen Vogue*, May 31, 2016, www.teenvogue.com /story/slavery-trauma-inherited-genetics.

4. Carl Zimmer, "Tales of African-American History Found in DNA," *New York Times*, May 27, 2016, www.nytimes.com/2016/05/28/science/african -american-dna.html.

5. Anissa Janine Wardi, *Water and African American Memory: An Ecocritical Perspective* (Gainesville: University Press of Florida, 2011), 3–37.

6. Stephen Fastenau, "How the Weather Channel Is Using Beaufort County to Take a Stand on Climate Change," *Beaufort Gazette*, January 26, 2018, www.islandpacket.com/news/local/community/beaufort-news/article196812029.html.

7. Elizabeth Brabec and Sharon Richardson, "A Clash of Cultures: The Landscape of the Sea Island Gullah," *Landscape Journal* 26, no. 1 (2007): 151–67, JSTOR, jstor.org/stable/43323760.

8. Juanita Jackson, Sabra Slaughter, and J. Herman Blake, "The Sea Islands as a Cultural Resource," *Black Scholar* 5, no. 6 (March 1974): 32–39, JSTOR, jstor.org/stable/41065688.

9. Bridget Boakye, "The Tragic Yet Resilient Story of Igbo slaves Who Committed Mass Suicide off U.S. coast in 1803," Face2FaceAfrica, Babu Global, June 12, 2018, face2faceafrica.com/article/the-tragic-yet-resilient-story-of-igbo-slaves-who-committed-mass-suicide-off-u-s-coast-in-1803.

10. Public Broadcasting Service (PBS), "The Weeping Time," *Africans in America*, Part 1, 1450–1750, "The Terrible Transformation: From Indentured Servitude to Racial Slavery," 1998, PBS Online, www.pbs.org/wgbh/aia/part4/4p2918.html.

11. Marquetta L. Goodwine, *The Legacy of Ibo Landing: Gullah Roots of African American Culture* (Atlanta: Clarity Press, 1998).

12. Gay Wilentz, "If You Surrender to the Air: Folk Legends of Flight and Resistance in African American Literature," *MELUS* (Multi-Ethnic Literature of the United States) 16, no. 1 (Spring 1989–Spring 1990): 21–32, JSTOR, jstor.org/stable/467579.

13. Jeff Wiltse, *Contested Waters: A Social History of Swimming Pools in America* (Chapel Hill: University of North Carolina Press, 2007): 106–7.

14. Rachel Martin, "Racial History of American Swimming Pools," National Public Radio, May 6, 2008, https://www.npr.org/templates/story/story.php?storyId=90213675.

15. Horace Cort (photographer), "Motel Manager Pouring Acid in the Water When Black People Swam in His Pool, 1964," Rare Historical Photos, rarehistoricalphotos.com/motel-manager-pouring-acid-water-black-people-swam-pool-1964.

16. Lindsay Mondick, "Why Are Black Youth at Highest Risk for Drowning?" YMCA, www.ymca.net/summer-buzz/highest-risk-for-drowning.

17. James Hamblin, "A Racial History of Drowning," *Atlantic*, June 11, 2013, www.theatlantic.com/health/archive/2013/06/a-racial-history-of-drowning/276748.

18. Thomas Brendler, "A Part of This Earth: The Story of the Sapelo Foundation," Sapelo Island Foundation, 2015, sapelofoundation.org/wp-content/uploads/2014/01/A-Part-of-This-Earth-2015.pdf.

19. Chris Dixon, "The Heart of Sapelo," *Garden & Gun*, June–July 2015, garden andgun.com/feature/the-heart-of-sapelo.

20. Alexis Diao, "Remembering Cornelia Walker Bailey, a Giant of Gullah Geechee Culture," National Public Radio, October 25, 2017, www.npr.org /sections/thesalt/2017/10/25/560093667/remembering-cornelia-walker-bailey -a-giant-of-gullah-geechee-culture.

21. United States District Court, Northern District of Georgia, Atlanta Division, *Drayton v. McIntosh County, Georgia*, Second Amended Complaint, Relman, Dane & Colfax PLLC, December 9, 2015, https://www.relmanlaw.com /cases-sapelo.

22. Henry Leifermann, "Sanctuaries In the Sea Off Georgia," *New York Times*, September 6, 1987, https://www.nytimes.com/1987/09/06/travel/sanctuaries -in-the-sea-off-georgia.html.

23. Karen Rubin, "Discovering Sapelo Island, Georgia and the Gullah-Geechees of Hog Hammock," Going Places, Far and Near, goingplacesfarandnear .com/discovering-sapelo-island-georgia-and-the-gullah-geechees-of-hog -hammock.

24. Scott Bryant, "A Hidden Gem: Sapelo Island, Hog Hammock," *Savannah Morning News*, Savannah Now, February 18, 2007, www.savannahnow.com /2007-02-18/hidden-gem-sapelo-island-hog-hammock.

25. Mary Ann Anderson, "On Georgia's Sapelo Island, Change Comes Slowly, If at All," *Washington Post*, September 5, 2013, www.washingtonpost.com /lifestyle/travel/on-georgias-sapelo-island-change-comes-slowly-if-at-all /2013/09/05/a145ee72-10f4-11e3-b4cb-fd7ce041d814_story.html.

26. "Butler Island Plantation—Darien, Georgia," ExploreSouthernHistory.com, www.exploresouthernhistory.com/butlerisland.html.

27. National Park Service, Park Ethnography Program, "Africans in the Low Country," National Park Service, www.nps.gov/ethnography/aah/aaheri tage/lowCountryA.htm.

28. Mildred Europa Taylor, "Black Babies Were Once Used as Alligator and Crocodile Bait in America in the 1900s," Face2Face Africa, August 19, 2018, face2faceafrica.com/article/black-babies-were-once-used-as-alligator-and -crocodile-bait-in-america-in-the-1900s.

29. N-Georgia, "Visit Butler Island Plantation in Darien Georgia," N-georgia .com, August 17, 2019, www.n-georgia.com/darien-butler-island.html.

30. Georgia Historical Society, "Applying for a New Historical Marker," georgia history.com/education-outreach/historical-markers/new-historical -markers.

31. Kwesi Degraft-Hanson, "Unearthing the Weeping Time: Savannah's Ten Broeck Race Course and 1859 Slave Sale," Southern Spaces, southern spaces.org/2010/unearthing-weeping-time-savannahs-ten-broeck-race -course-and-1859-slave-sale.

32. Barbara J. Little, *Text-Aided Archaeology* (CRC Press, 1991), 60–63.

33. Frances Kemble, *Journal of a Residence on a Georgian Plantation 1838–1839* (New York: Harper & Bros., 1863), Project Gutenberg, www.gutenberg.org /files/12422/12422-h/12422-h.htm.

34. Frances Kemble, *The Views of Judge Woodward and Bishop Hopkins on Negro Slavery at the South: Illustrated from the Journal of a Residence on a Georgian Plantation* (Philadelphia, c. 1863; Sacramento: Creative Media Partners, 2018).

3

1. Lisa Irizarry, "Hidden Treasures: Traces of the Past Brought to Light in a Little-Known Museum," Black History Month: A Search for Identity, ed. Beverly M. Reid, NJ.com, January 31, 2008, updated April 2, 2019, blog .nj.com/ledgerarchives/2008/01/black_history_month_a_search_f.html.

2. Yvonne Chireau, *Black Magic: Religion and the African American Conjuring Tradition* (Berkeley: University of California Press, 2003).

3. Vinson Synan, "Notable History: The Quiet Rise of Black Pentecostals," *Charisma*, February 26, 2016, www.charismamag.com/life/culture/24137 -notable-history-the-quiet-rise-of-black-pentecostals.

4. Richard W. Thomas, "Social Consciousness and Self-Help: The Heart and Soul of Community Building," chapter 6 of *Life for Us Is What We Make It: Building Black Community in Detroit, 1915–1945* (Bloomington: Indiana University Press, 1992).

5. John Eligon, "About That Song You've Heard, Kumbaya," *New York Times*, February 9, 2018, www.nytimes.com/2018/02/09/us/kumbaya-gullah-geechee .html.

6. Cornelia Walker Bailey, *God, Dr. Buzzard, and the Bolito Man* (New York: Anchor, 2000), 7–8.

7. Alex Starace, "Tales of Daufuskie Island," International Opulence, www .internationalopulence.com/intriguing-tales-roger-pinckney-life-historic -daufuskie-island.

8. *Newsweek* staff, "An Island's Vanishing Culture," *Newsweek*, January 13, 1991, www.newsweek.com/islands-vanishing-culture-202734.

9. Ron Harris, "Plantations Again: The Gullahs: An Upside-Down World," *Los Angeles Times*, August 28, 1988, www.latimes.com/archives/la-xpm-1988 -08-28-mn-1718-story.html.

10. Roger Pinckney, "Blue Root Real Estate," *Orion*, orionmagazine.org/article /blue-root-real-estate.

11. Peter Hull, "Daufuskie Island Club & Resort Looking for Investors to Step up Development," Hotel Online, March 1, 2006, www.hotel-online.com /News/PR2006_1st/Mar06_Daufuskie.html.

12. United States Securities and Exchange Commission, Form 10-K, 1999, https://www.sec.gov/Archives/edgar/data/929455/000092945500000002 /0000929455-00-000002-d11.pdf

13. Nancy Keates, "Daufuskie Island: An Idyllic Spot with a Stormy History," *Wall Street Journal*, July 13, 2017, www.wsj.com/articles/daufuskie-island-an -idyllic-spot-with-a-stormy-history-1499954865?ns=prod/accounts-wsj.

14. Alex Kincaid, "This Daufuskie Island Resort Is out of Bankruptcy. But what's next?" *Island Packet*, April 10, 2018, www.islandpacket.com/news /business/real-estate-news/article208437254.html.

15. Catherine Yronwode, "How to Use Sachet Powders in the Hoodoo Root-work Tradition," Lucky Mojo Curio Co., www.luckymojo.com/powders .html.

16. Stephanie Rose Bird, *Sticks, Stones, Roots & Bones: Hoodoo, Mojo & Conjuring with Herbs* (Saint Paul, MN: Llewellyn Publications, 2004).

17. International African American Museum, "Victoria A. Smalls," iaamuseum .org/about/staff/victoria-a-smalls.

18. "Dr. Buzzard," *South Carolina Encyclopedia*, www.scencyclopedia.org/sce /entries/%C2%93dr-buzzard%C2%94.

19. Terrance Zepke, *Coastal South Carolina: Welcome to the Lowcountry* (Sarasota, FL: Pineapple Press, 2006).

20. Beverly Willett, "LowCountry Root Doctors," *South*, December 2016– January 2017, www.southmag.com/Dec-Jan-2017/LowCountry-Root-Doctors.

21. Yvonne Chireau, *Black Magic: Religion and the African American Conjuring Tradition* (Berkeley: University of California Press, 2003).

22. John Roberts, "African American Belief Narratives and the African Cultural Tradition," *Research in African Literatures* 40, no. 1 (Spring 2009): 112–26, JSTOR, jstor.org/stable/30131190.

4

1. AJC staff, "Hundreds More Were Lynched in the South Than Previously Known: Report," *Atlanta-Journal Constitution*, June 14, 2017, www.ajc.com /news/local/hundreds-more-were-lynched-the-south-than-previously -known-report/gOEGtsSud4utD6Uiqkx1LN.

2. Leah Douglas, "African Americans Have Lost Untold Acres of Land over the Last Century," *Nation*, August 26, 2017, https://www.thenation.com /article/african-americans-have-lost-acres.

3. Dahleen Glanton, "Ex-Slaves' Land Heirs Feel Island Shift," *Chicago Tribune*, July 11, 2006, www.chicagotribune.com/news/ct-xpm-2006-07-11-0607 110145-story.html.

4. Mandy Matney, "Wahoo! Hilton Head Named Best Island in the U.S. for the Second Time This Year," *Island Packet*, October 9, 2018, www.island packet.com/news/local/article219732455.html.

5. "Hilton Head Island History & Heritage: Rich in Culture, Rich in Spirit," Hilton Head Island–Bluffton Chamber of Commerce & Visitor and Convention Bureau, 2018, www.hiltonheadisland.org/our-island/history.

6. Douglas, "African Americans Have Lost Untold Acres."

7. "Hilton Head Island, South Carolina," City-Data.com, www.city-data.com /city/Hilton-Head-Island-South-Carolina.html.

8. Art Benoit, "Security," Hilton Head Plantation Property Owners' Association, www.hiltonheadplantation.com/security/tabid/67/default.aspx.

9. "Hilton Head Island History & Heritage."

10. Rich Benjamin, "The Gated Community Mentality," *New York Times*, March 29, 2012, www.nytimes.com/2012/03/30/opinion/the-gated-community-mentality.html.

11. Melissa Denise Hargrove, "Reinventing the Plantation: Gated Communities as Spatial Segregation in the Gullah Sea Islands," PhD dissertation, University of Tennessee, 2005, Tennessee Research and Creative Exchange (TRACE), University of Tennessee–Knoxville, http://trace.tennessee.edu /utk_graddiss/4304.

12. Kelly Meyerhofer, "Protests During the Heritage Tournament: A Long History with Few Immediate Successes," *Island Packet*, March 2017, www .islandpacket.com/sports/golf/rbc-heritage-tournament/article137181488 .html.

13. South Carolina Department of Archives and History, "Preservation Laws," scdah.sc.gov/historic-preservation/resources/preservation-laws.

14. Dominique T. Hazzard, "The Gullah People, Justice, and the Land on Hilton Head Island: A Historical Perspective," Wellesley College honors thesis, https://repository.wellesley.edu/thesiscollection/60.

15. David Lauderdale, "Businesses Have Shaped Our Community, Even Our Lives," *Island Packet*, December 25, 2012, www.islandpacket.com/opinion /opn-columns-blogs/david-lauderdale/article33492636.html.

16. Luana M. Graves Sellers and Lloyd Wainscott, "First Families of Hilton Head: The Aikens," *Hilton Head Monthly*, May 26, 2017, www.hiltonhead monthly.com/people/4367-first-families-of-hilton-head-the-aikens.

17. Katherine Kokal, "Hilton Head Officials Walked Out on This Restaurant Owner, but He Got a Win in Court," *Island Packet*, March 14, 2019, www .islandpacket.com/news/business/article227590044.html.

PART II: LOUISIANA CREOLE

I

1. Diana J. Kleiner and Ron Bass, "Frenchtown, Houston," Texas State Historical Association, tshaonline.org/handbook/online/articles/hrfvg.

2. Public Broadcasting Service (PBS), *Africans in America*, Part 1, 1450–1750, "The Terrible Transformation: From Indentured Servitude to Racial Slavery," PBS Online, www.pbs.org/wgbh/aia/part1/1narr3.html.

3. James Hardy, "The Black Mark: America's History of Slavery," History Cooperative, historycooperative.org/black-mark-americas-history-slavery.

4. "Inventing Black and White," Facing History and Ourselves, https://www
.facinghistory.org/holocaust-and-human-behavior/chapter-2/inventing
-black-and-white.

5. John C. Hill, "For Free People of Color, a Precarious Niche in Society,"
New Orleans Times-Picayune, June 14, 1993, www.nola.com/politics/1993/06
/for_free_people_of_color_a_pre.html.

6. Matthew Wills, "The Free People of Color of Pre-Civil War New Orleans,"
JSTOR Daily, February 20, 2019, daily.jstor.org/the-free-people-of-color-of
-pre-civil-war-new-orleans.

7. Sylvie Dubois and Megan Melançon, "Creole Is, Creole Ain't: Diachronic
and Synchronic Attitudes toward Creole Identity in Southern Louisiana,"
Language in Society 29, no. 2 (June 2000) 237–58, JSTOR, jstor.org/stable
/4169003.

8. Gwendolyn Midlo Hall, *Africans in Colonial Louisiana* (Baton Rouge: LSU
Press, 1995), 157–60.

9. Thomas A. Klingler and Ingrid Neumann-Holzschuh, "Louisiana Creole," in
The Survey of Pidgin and Creole Languages, vol. 2, *Portuguese-Based, Spanish-Based,
and French-Based*, ed. Susanne Michaelis, Philippe Maurer, Martin Haspelmath,
and Magnus Huber (Oxford, UK: Oxford University Press, 2013), 229–40.

10. Jay B. Haviser and Kevin C. MacDonald, eds., *African Re-Genesis: Confronting Social Issues in the Diaspora* (London: UCL Press, 2006).

11. Ken Ringle, "Up through Slavery," *Washington Post*, May 12, 2002, www
.washingtonpost.com/archive/lifestyle/2002/05/12/up-through-slavery
/9b489aa3-fefa-4695-9544-34ab58f1fe87.

2

1. David DeWitt Turpeau Sr., *Up from the Cane-Brakes: An Autobiography*, 1942,
www.yumpu.com/en/document/read/16062581/up-from-the-cane-brakes
-turpeau-family, p 8.

2. Maggie Martin, "*Steel Magnolias* Still Impacts Town after 25 Years," *Shreveport Times*, July 10, 2016, www.shreveporttimes.com/story/news/local
/louisiana/2014/10/02/steel-magnolias-still-impacts-town-years/16604503.

3. Sarah Glaser, "From a Few Humble Acres: The Many Incarnations of Melrose Plantation," PorterBriggs.com, porterbriggs.com/from-a-few-humble
-acres-the-many-incarnations-of-melrose-plantation.

4. National Trust for Historic Preservation, "African House at Melrose Plantation," savingplaces.org/places/african-house-at-melrose-plantation#.WzIc
GxJKj3Q.

5. Elizabeth Shown Mills and Gary B. Mills, *The Forgotten People: Cane River
Creoles of Color* (Baton Rouge: LSU Press, 2013), 218–22.

6. Ibid., 218–30.

7. Cane River Colony, "The Story of the Melrose Plantation," Cane River Colony, www.canerivercolony.com/History/story of melrose.htm.

8. David W. Morgan, Kevin C. MacDonald, and Fiona J. L. Handley, "Economics and Authenticity: A Collision of Interpretations in Cane River National Heritage Area, Louisiana," *George Wright Forum* 23, no. 1 (June 2005): 45–62, www.georgewright.org/231morgan.pdf.

9. Elizabeth Shown Mills and Gary B. Mills, "Slaves and Masters: The Louisiana Metoyers," *National Genealogical Society Quarterly* 70, no. 1 (March 1982): 163–89, www.historicpathways.com/download/slavnmast.pdf, 175.

10. R. Halliburton Jr., "Free Black Owners of Slaves: A Reappraisal of the Woodson Thesis," *South Carolina Historical Magazine* 76, no. 3 (July 1975): 129–42, JSTOR, jstor.org/stable/27567319.

11. Melrose Plantation, "History," www.melroseplantation.org/history.

12. Allison Bazzle, "Meet Natchitoches' Very Own Filé Man," KALB, Alexandria, LA, August 11, 2017, www.kalb.com/content/news/Meet-Natchitoches-very-own-File-Man--439946713.html.

13. Philip Gould, *Natchitoches and Louisiana's Timeless Cane River* (Baton Rouge: LSU Press, 2002), 54.

3

1. Jamelle Bouie, "anyway, to borrow from dubois a bit . . ." Twitter, March 22, 2019, twitter.com/jbouie/status/1109055469400793095.

4

1. Palmer, "St. Martinville, LA," Born and Raised in the South, February 1, 2009, ltc4940.blogspot.com/2009/02/st-martinville-la.html.

2. Louisiana Office of Tourism, "History & Heritage in St. Martinville Louisiana," www.louisianatravel.com/st-martinville/history-heritage.

3. Shane K. Bernard, *Teche: A History of Louisiana's Most Famous Bayou* (Jackson: University Press of Mississippi, 2016).

4. Elizabeth Shown Mills and Gary B. Mills, *The Forgotten People: Cane River Creoles of Color* (Baton Rouge: LSU Press, 2013), 53–54.

5. Beyoncé Knowles, "Beyoncé in Her Own Words: Her Life, Her Body, Her Heritage," *Vogue*, August 6, 2018, www.vogue.com/article/beyonce-september-issue-2018.

6. Treva B. Lindsey and Jessica Marie Johnson, "Searching for Climax: Black Erotic Lives in Slavery and Freedom," *Meridians* 12, no. 2 (2014): 169–95, JSTOR, jstor.org/stable/10.2979/meridians.12.2.169.

7. Penny Kilbane, *The Melting Pot* (self-published, 2004), www.angelfire.com/folk/the_melting_pot/Documents/The%20Melting%20Pot.pdf, 55.

PART III: OKLAHOMA

I

1. Terry Bouton, "Slave, Free Black, and White Population, 1780–1830," Uintah Basin Medical Center, User Pages, https://userpages.umbc.edu/~bouton /History407/SlaveStats.htm.
2. William J. Collins and Marianne H. Wanamaker, "Selection and Economic Gains in the Great Migration of African Americans: New Evidence from Linked Census Data," *American Economic Journal: Applied Economics* 6, no. 1 (January 2014): 220–52, JSTOR, jstor.org/stable/43189471.
3. Desalyn Stevenson, "Court Cases," 2014, Our Shared Family History: Freedmen of the Five Civilized Tribes, African-American, Native American, and the Southern States, http://www.oursharedfamilyhistory.com /resources/cases/allcases/casespg.html.
4. Earchiel Johnson, "Slaves of the Tribe: The Hidden History of the Freedmen," *People's World*, November 29, 2017, www.peoplesworld.org/article /slaves-of-the-tribe-the-hidden-history-of-the-freedmen.
5. History channel, "Trail of Tears," History, A&E network, March 5, 2019, www.history.com/topics/native-american-history/trail-of-tears.
6. Henry Louis Gates Jr., "What Was the 2nd Middle Passage?" *Root*, January 28, 2013, www.theroot.com/what-was-the-2nd-middle-passage-1790895016.
7. Tiya Miles, "Pain of 'Trail of Tears' Shared by Blacks as Well as Native Americans," Cable News Network (CNN), In America blog, February 25, 2012, inamerica.blogs.cnn.com/2012/02/25/pain-of-trail-of-tears-shared-by -blacks-as-well-as-native-americans.
8. Natasha Hartsfield, "Racial Hegemony in America: The Struggle for Identity among the Black Indians of the Five Civilized Tribes of the Southern United States," *PSU McNair Scholars Online Journal* 1, no. 1, https:// pdxscholar.library.pdx.edu/cgi/viewcontent.cgi?article=1010&context =mcnair.
9. Arrell Morgan Gibson, *Oklahoma: A History of Five Centuries*, 2nd ed. (Norman: University of Oklahoma Press, 1965), 195.
10. Brendan I. Koerner, "Blood Feud," *Wired*, September 5, 2005, www.wired .com/2005/09/seminoles.
11. Alysa Landry, "Paying to Play Indian: The Dawes Rolls and the Legacy of $5 Indians," *Indian Country Today*, March 21, 2017, newsmaven.io/indian countrytoday/archive/paying-to-play-indian-the-dawes-rolls-and-the-legacy -of-5-indians-3yhaoLldYUaH7smRsrks8A.
12. Molly Osberg, "The Long, Thorny History of the Cherokee Who Owned African Slaves," *Splinter*, October 18, 2017, splinternews.com/the-long -thorny-history-of-the-cherokee-who-owned-afri-1819655748.
13. Karen Kaplan, "From the Archives: DNA Testing Raises a Delicate Question: What Does It Mean to Be Native American?" *Los Angeles Times*, Octo-

ber 16, 2018, www.latimes.com/science/la-sci-dna-testing-native-americans
-archive-20181016-story.html.

14. Kat Chow, "Judge Rules That Cherokee Freedmen Have Right to Tribal
Citizenship," *The Two-Way*, National Public Radio, August 13, 2017, www
.npr.org/sections/thetwo-way/2017/08/31/547705829/judge-rules-that-cher
okee-freedmen-have-right-to-tribal-citizenship.

15. Henry Louis Gates Jr., "The African American Migration Story," *The African Americans: Many Rivers to Cross*," Public Broadcasting Service (PBS),
https://www.pbs.org/wnet/african-americans-many-rivers-to-cross/history
/on-african-american-migrations.

16. Stacie Boston, "Walkingstick Wants Freedmen Ruling Appealed," *Cherokee
Phoenix*, November 7, 2017, www.cherokeephoenix.org/Article/index/11769.
Accessed 30 June 2018.

17. Tony Russell, "Muskogee Parents, Freedmen Descendants Call for MPS Director of Indian Ed to Step Down," KJRH (Tulsa), December 7, 2017, www
.kjrh.com/news/local-news/muskogee-parents-freedmen-descendants-call
-for-mps-director-of-indian-ed-to-step-down. Accessed 30 June 2018.

18. Cathy Spaulding, "MPS Seeks New Indian Education Director," *Muskogee Phoenix*, January 28, 2018, www.muskogeephoenix.com/news/mps
-seeks-new-indian-education-director/article_06cd79ec-512b-551e-8154
-ff0a90d5cbdc.html.

2

1. Hope Babowice, "How Many Native American Tribes Are in the US?"
Chicago Daily Herald, August 7, 2011, https://www.dailyherald.com/article
/20110607/news/706079944.

2. Gregory D. Smithers, "Why Do So Many Americans Think They Have
Cherokee Blood?" *Slate*, October 1, 2015, slate.com/news-and-politics/2015
/10/cherokee-blood-why-do-so-many-americans-believe-they-have-cher
okee-ancestry.html.

3. John D. Schroer, "Forest Habitat Management Plan For Okefenokee National Wildlife Refuge," U.S. Fish & Wildlife Service, January 23, 1987, 6,
https://ecos.fws.gov/ServCat/DownloadFile/26395?Reference=27593.

4. Kathleen Kuiper, "Black Seminoles," *Encyclopædia Britannica*, www.britan
nica.com/topic/Black-Seminoles.

5. Joseph A. Opala, "The Gullah: Rice, Slavery, and the Sierra Leone–American
Connection," glc.yale.edu/sites/default/files/files/Black%20Seminoles%20.pdf.

6. Allison Herrera, "Part of the Tribe, but Shut Out," KOSU (Tulsa), August 30,
2016, www.kosu.org/post/part-tribe-shut-out.

7. Lydia Edwards, Protecting Black Tribal Members: Is the Thirteenth Amendment the Linchpin to Securing Equal Rights within Indian Country, *Berkeley Journal of African-American Policy* 8, no. 1 (2006): 122–54.

8. Kendra Fox, "History of Seminole Nation Revealed through Song, Story," *Oklahoman*, June 12, 1998, newsok.com/article/2619167/history-of-seminole-nation-revealed-through-song-story.

9. Triposo, "Wewoka, Oklahoma History," Triposo.com, www.triposo.com/loc/Wewoka2C_Oklahoma/history/background.

10. Jennifer Dos Reis Dos Santos, "How African American Folklore Saved the Cultural Memory and History of Slaves," The Conversation, October 8, 2018, theconversation.com/how-african-american-folklore-saved-the-cultural-memory-and-history-of-slaves-98427.

3

1. Alex Seitz-Wald, "Cherokee Nation Says Elizabeth Warren Apologizes for DNA Test Flap," NBC News, February 1, 2019, https://www.nbcnews.com/politics/2020-election/elizabeth-warren-apologizes-cherokee-nation-over-dna-test-flap-n965921.

2. Aviva Chomsky, "How DNA Tests Make Native Americans Strangers in Their Own Land," *Huffington Post*, November 2018, www.huffpost.com/entry/making-native-americans-strangers-in-their-own-land_b_5c00601ce4b0ee1b06c83176.

3. Neely Tucker, "A Mixed-Race Woman's Long Quest to Prove Her Native American Ancestry," *Washington Post*, January 4, 2019, https://www.washingtonpost.com/outlook/a-mixed-race-womans-long-quest-to-prove-her-native-american-ancestry/2019/01/04/4f2ada42-0c6d-11e9-831f-3aa2c2be4cbd_story.html.

4. Henry Louis Gates Jr., "High Cheekbones and Straight Black Hair?" *Root*, December 29, 2014, www.theroot.com/high-cheekbones-and-straight-black-hair-1790878167.

4

1. Sarah Hill, "All Roads Led from Rome: Facing the History of Cherokee Expulsion," *Southern Spaces*, February 20, 2017, southernspaces.org/2017/all-roads-led-rome-facing-history-cherokee-expulsion.

2. Carol Ebel, "Appling County," New Georgia Encyclopedia, December 17, 2003, https://www.georgiaencyclopedia.org/articles/counties-cities-neighborhoods/appling-county.

3. Dru J. Murray, "The Unconquered Seminoles," http://funandsun.com/1tocf/seminole/semhistory.html.

4. Molly Osberg, "The Long, Thorny History of the Cherokee Who Owned African Slaves," *Splinter*, October 18, 2017, splinternews.com/the-long-thorny-history-of-the-cherokee-who-owned-afri-1819655748.

5. Jacob Lawrence, "African American Migration Patterns," *The Migration*

Series, Phillips Collection, https://lawrencemigration.phillipscollection.org
/culture/migration-map.

PART IV: LOS ANGELES

1

1. Erwin Gustav Goode, *California Place Names: The Origin and Etymology of
   Current Geographical Names* (Berkeley: University of California Press, 1969),
   48, via Google Books.
2. Lawrence B. De Graaf, "The City of Black Angels: Emergence of the Los
   Angeles Ghetto, 1890-1930," *Pacific Historical Review* 39, no. 3 (1970), https://
   www.jstor.org/stable/3637655.

2

1. "Gang History," South Central History, http://www.southcentralhistory
   .com/gang-history.php.

3

1. Mike Davis, *City of Quartz: Excavating the Future in Los Angeles* (New York:
   Verso Books, 2006), 293–94.

4

1. Jacob Woocher, "Los Angeles Is Quickly Becoming a Place Exclusively
   for the White and Rich," *Medium,* November 7, 2017, https://knock-la.com
   /los-angeles-is-quickly-becoming-a-place-exclusively-for-the-white-and
   -rich-c585953e0614.

EPILOGUE

1. Timothy Williams and Farah Stockman, "Dayton Shooting Live Updates:
   Gunman Killed 9, Including His Sister," *New York Times,* August 4, 2019,
   www.nytimes.com/2019/08/04/us/dayton-ohio-shooting.html.
2. BBC News, "Texas Walmart Shooting: El Paso Attack 'Domestic Terrorism'," BBC News, 4 Aug. 2019, www.bbc.com/news/world-us-canada
   -49226573.
3. Andrew Buncombe, "Dylan Roof: Experts Believe Charleston Shooting
   Suspect Was Author of Racist Manifesto and 'Self-Radicalised' Online,"
   Independent (London), https://www.independent.co.uk/news/world/amer
   icas/dylan-roof-experts-believe-charleston-shooting-suspect-was-author-of
   -racist-manifesto-and-self-10353971.html.

BIBLIOGRAPHY

AJC staff. "Hundreds More Were Lynched in the South Than Previously Known: Report." *Atlanta-Journal Constitution*, June 14, 2017, www.ajc.com /news/local/hundreds-more-were-lynched-the-south-than-previously -known-report/gOEGtsSud4utD6UiqkxiLN.

Anderson, Mary Ann. "On Georgia's Sapelo Island, Change Comes Slowly, If at All." *Washington Post*, September 5, 2013, https://www.washingtonpost .com/lifestyle/travel/on-georgias-sapelo-island-change-comes-slowly-if-at -all/2013/09/05/a145ee72–10f4–11e3-b4cb-fd7ce041d814_story.html.

Babowice, Hope. "How Many Native American Tribes Are in the US?" *Chicago Daily Herald*, August 7, 2011, www.dailyherald.com/article/20110607 /news/706079944.

Bazzle, Allison. "Meet Natchitoches' Very Own Filé Man." KALB, Alexandria, LA, August 11, 2017, https://www.kalb.com/content/news/Meet-Natchitoches-very-own-File-Man—439946713.html.

BBC News, "Texas Walmart Shooting: El Paso Attack 'Domestic Terrorism.'" BBC News, August 4, 2019. www.bbc.com/news/world-us-canada-49226573.

Bear, Carson. "Remembering Atlantic City's Black History and Segregated Past." *Atlantic*, CityLab, January 16, 2019, www.citylab.com/equity/2019/01 /african-american-atlantic-city-segregation-northside-tourism/580576.

Benjamin, Rich. "The Gated Community Mentality." *New York Times*, March 29, 2012, www.nytimes.com/2012/03/30/opinion/the-gated-community-mental ity.html.

Benoit, Art. "Security." Hilton Head Plantation Property Owners' Association, www.hiltonheadplantation.com/security/tabid/67/default.aspx.

Bernard, Shane K. *Teche: A History of Louisiana's Most Famous Bayou*. Jackson: University Press of Mississippi, 2016.

Bird, Stephanie Rose. *Sticks, Stones, Roots & Bones: Hoodoo, Mojo & Conjuring with Herbs*. Saint Paul, MN: Llewellyn Publications, 2004.

Blades, Lincoln Anthony. "Trauma from Slavery Can Actually Be Passed Down through Your Genes." *Teen Vogue*, May 31, 2016, www.teenvogue.com/story /slavery-trauma-inherited-genetics.

Boakye, Bridget. "The Tragic Yet Resilient Story of Igbo Slaves Who Committed Mass Suicide off U.S. Coast in 1803." Face2FaceAfrica, June 12, 2018, face2faceafrica.com/article/the-tragic-yet-resilient-story-of-igbo-slaves-who-committed-mass-suicide-off-u-s-coast-in-1803.

Bopp, Suzanne. "Road Trip: Low Country, South Carolina and Georgia." *National Geographic*, September 14, 2010, www.nationalgeographic.com/travel/road-trips/low-country-south-carolina-georgia-road-trip.

Boston, Stacie. "Walkingstick Wants Freedmen Ruling Appealed." *Cherokee Phoenix*, November 7, 2017, www.cherokeephoenix.org/Article/index/11769.

Bouie, Jamelle. "anyway, to borrow from dubois a bit . . ." Twitter, March 22, 2019, twitter.com/jbouie/status/1109055469400793095.

Bouton, Terry. "Slave, Free Black, and White Population, 1780–1830." Uintah Basin Medical Center, User Pages, userpages.umbc.edu/~bouton/History 407/SlaveStats.htm.

Brabec, Elizabeth, and Sharon Richardson. "A Clash of Cultures: The Landscape of the Sea Island Gullah." *Landscape Journal* 26, no. 1 (2007): 151–67. JSTOR, jstor.org/stable/43323760.

Brendler, Thomas. "A Part of This Earth: The Story of the Sapelo Foundation." Sapelo Island Foundation, 2015, sapelofoundation.org/wp-content/uploads/2014/01/A-Part-of-This-Earth-2015.pdf.

Brown, Gregory Christopher, et al. "The Ghettoization of Blacks in Los Angeles: The Emergence of Street Gangs." *Journal of African American Studies* 16, no. 2 (June 2012): 209–25. JSTOR, www.jstor.org/stable/43526688.

Brundage, W. Fitzhugh. "Contentious and Collected: Memory's Future in Southern History." *Journal of Southern History* 75, no. 3 (August 2009): 757. JSTOR, jstor.org/stable/27779037.

Bryant, Scott. "A Hidden Gem: Sapelo Island, Hog Hammock." *Savannah Morning News*, Savannah Now, February 18, 2007, www.savannahnow.com/2007-02-18/hidden-gem-sapelo-island-hog-hammock.

Buncombe, Andrew. "Dylan Roof: Experts Believe Charleston Shooting Suspect Was Author of Racist Manifesto and 'Self-Radicalised' Online." *Independent* (London), https://www.independent.co.uk/news/world/americas/dylan-roof-experts-believe-charleston-shooting-suspect-was-author-of-racist-manifesto-and-self-10353971.html.

Burghardt Du Bois, William Edward. *Prayers for Dark People*. Amherst: University of Massachusetts Press, 1980.

"Butler Island Plantation—Darien, Georgia." ExploreSouthernHistory.com, www.exploresouthernhistory.com/butlerisland.html.

Cane River Colony, "The Story of the Melrose Plantation." Cane River Colony, www.canerivercolony.com/History/story_of_melrose.htm.

Chireau, Yvonne. *Black Magic: Religion and the African American Conjuring Tradition*. Berkeley: University of California Press, 2003.

Chomsky, Aviva. "How DNA Tests Make Native Americans Strangers in Their

Own Land." *Huffington Post,* November 2018, www.huffpost.com/entry/making-native-americans-strangers-in-their-own-land_b_5c00601ce4b0ee 1b06c83176.

Chow, Kat. "Judge Rules That Cherokee Freedmen Have Right to Tribal Citizenship." *The Two-Way,* National Public Radio, August 13, 2017, www.npr.org/sections/thetwo-way/2017/08/31/547705829/judge-rules-that-cherokee-freedmen-have-right-to-tribal-citizenship.

Coclanis, Peter A. "Business & Economy: Agriculture." *New Georgia Encyclopedia,* www.georgiaencyclopedia.org/articles/business-economy/rice.

Collins, William J., and Marianne H. Wanamaker. "Selection and Economic Gains in the Great Migration of African Americans: New Evidence from Linked Census Data." *American Economic Journal* 6, no. 1 (January 2014): 220–52. JSTOR, jstor.org/stable/43189471.

Cort, Horace (photographer). "Motel Manager Pouring Acid in the Water When Black People Swam in his Pool, 1964." Rare Historical Photos, rarehistorical photos.com/motel-manager-pouring-acid-water-black-people-swam-pool-1964.

Cortés, Carloes E., ed. *Multicultural America: A Multimedia Encyclopedia.* Thousand Oaks, CA: SAGE Publications, 2013.

"Darien, Georgia (GA) Poverty Rate Data." City-Data.com, www.city-data.com/poverty/poverty-Darien-Georgia.html.

Davis, Mike. *City of Quartz: Excavating the Future in Los Angeles.* New York: Verso Books, 2006.

De Graaf, Lawrence B. "The City of Black Angels: Emergence of the Los Angeles Ghetto, 1890–1930." *Pacific Historical Review* 39, no. 3 (August 1970): 323–52. JSTOR, jstor.org/stable/3637655.

Degraft-Hanson, Kwesi. "Unearthing the Weeping Time: Savannah's Ten Broeck Race Course and 1859 Slave Sale." Southern Spaces, February 18, 2010, southernspaces.org/2010/unearthing-weeping-time-savannahs-ten-broeck-race-course-and-1859-slave-sale.

DeWitt Turpeau Sr., David. *Up from the Cane-Brakes: An Autobiography,* 1942, www.yumpu.com/en/document/read/16062581/up-from-the-cane-brakes-turpeau-family.

Diao, Alexis. "Remembering Cornelia Walker Bailey, a Giant of Gullah Geechee Culture." National Public Radio, October 25, 2017, www.npr.org/sections/thesalt/2017/10/25/560093667/remembering-cornelia-walker-bailey-a-giant-of-gullah-geechee-culture.

Dirks, Robert T., and Nancy Duran. "African American Dietary Patterns at the Beginning of the 20th Century." *Journal of Nutrition* 131, no. 7 (July 2001): 1881–89, https://academic.oup.com/jn/article/131/7/1881/4686889.

Dixon, Chris. "The Heart of Sapelo." *Garden & Gun,* June–July 2015, gardenand gun.com/feature/the-heart-of-sapelo.

Domanick, Joe. "Daryl Gates' Downfall." *Los Angeles Times,* April 18, 2010, https://

www.latimes.com/archives/la-xpm-2010-apr-18-la-oe-domanick18–2010apr18
-story.html.

Dos Reis Dos Santos, Jennifer. "How African American Folklore Saved the Cultural Memory and History of Slaves." The Conversation, October 8, 2018, theconversation.com/how-african-american-folklore-saved-the-cultural -memory-and-history-of-slaves-98427.

Douglas, Leah. "African Americans Have Lost Untold Acres of Land over the Last Century." Nation, August 26, 2017, www.thenation.com/article/african -americans-have-lost-acres.

"Dr. Buzzard." South Carolina Encyclopedia, www.scencyclopedia.org/sce/entries /%C2%93dr-buzzard%C2%94.

Dubois, Sylvie, and Megan Melançon. "Creole Is, Creole Ain't: Diachronic and Synchronic Attitudes toward Creole Identity in Southern Louisiana." Language in Society 29, no. 2 (June 2000): 237–58. JSTOR, jstor.org/stable/4169003.

Ebel, Carol. "Appling County." New Georgia Encyclopedia, December 17, 2003, https://www.georgiaencyclopedia.org/articles/counties-cities-neighbor hoods/appling-county.

Edwards, Lydia. "Protecting Black Tribal Members: Is the Thirteenth Amendment the Linchpin to Securing Equal Rights within Indian Country?" Berkeley Journal of African-American Policy 8, no. 1 (2006): 122–54. https://scholar ship.law.berkeley.edu/cgi/viewcontent.cgi?article=1070&context=bjalp.

Eligon, John. "About That Song You've Heard, Kumbaya." New York Times, February 9, 2018, www.nytimes.com/2018/02/09/us/kumbaya-gullah-geechee .html.

Fastenau, Stephen. "How the Weather Channel Is Using Beaufort County to Take a Stand on Climate Change." Beaufort Gazette, January 26, 2018, www .islandpacket.com/news/local/community/beaufort-news/article1968 12029.html.

Fox, Kendra. "History of Seminole Nation Revealed through Song, Story." Oklahoman, June 12, 1998, newsok.com/article/2619167/history-of-seminole -nation-revealed-through-song-story.

"Gang History." South Central History, www.southcentralhistory.com/gang -history.php.

Gates Jr., Henry Louis. "The African American Migration Story." The African Americans: Many Rivers to Cross. Public Broadcasting Service (PBS), www .pbs.org/wnet/african-americans-many-rivers-to-cross/history/on-african -american-migrations.

———. "High Cheekbones and Straight Black Hair?" Root, December 29, 2014, www.theroot.com/high-cheekbones-and-straight-black-hair-1790878167.

———. "What Was the 2nd Middle Passage?" Root, January 28, 2013, www.the root.com/what-was-the-2nd-middle-passage-1790895016.

———. "White Like Me." New Yorker, Life and Letters, June 17, 1996, 66–67, ar chives.newyorker.com/?i=1996–06–17#folio=066.

Georgia Historical Society. "Applying for a New Historical Marker." georgia
history.com/education-outreach/historical-markers/new-historical-markers.

Glanton, Dahleen. "Ex-Slaves' Land Heirs Feel Island Shift." *Chicago Tribune*,
July 11, 2006, https://www.chicagotribune.com/news/ct-xpm-2006–07–11
–0607110145-story.html.

Glaser, Sarah. "From a Few Humble Acres: The Many Incarnations of Melrose Plantation." PorterBriggs.com, porterbriggs.com/from-a-few-humble
-acres-the-many-incarnations-of-melrose-plantation.

Goodwine, Marquetta L. *The Legacy of Ibo Landing: Gullah Roots of African American Culture*. Atlanta: Clarity Press, 1998.

Gould, Philip. *Natchitoches and Louisiana's Timeless Cane River*. Baton Rouge:
LSU Press, 2002.

Graves Sellers, Luana M., and Lloyd Wainscott. "First Families of Hilton Head:
The Aikens." *Hilton Head Monthly*, May 26, 2017, www.hiltonheadmonthly
.com/people/4367-first-families-of-hilton-head-the-aikens.

Gregory, James N. "The Second Great Migration: An Historical Overview," in
*African American Urban History: The Dynamics of Race, Class and Gender since
World War II*, ed. Joe W. Trotter Jr. and Kenneth L. Kusmer. Chicago: Uni-
versity of Chicago Press, 2009.

Halliburton Jr., R. "Free Black Owners of Slaves: A Reappraisal of the Woodson Thesis." *South Carolina Historical Magazine* 76, no. 3 (July 1975): 129–42.
JSTOR, jstor.org/stable/27567319.

Hamblin, James. "A Racial History of Drowning." *Atlantic*, June 11, 2013, www
.theatlantic.com/health/archive/2013/06/a-racial-history-of-drowning
/276748.

Hardy, James. "The Black Mark: America's History of Slavery." History Cooperative, March 21, 2017, historycooperative.org/black-mark-americas-history
-slavery.

Hargrove, Melissa Denise. "Reinventing the Plantation: Gated Communities as
Spatial Segregation in the Gullah Sea Islands." PhD dissertation, University
of Tennessee, 2005, Tennessee Research and Creative Exchange (TRACE),
University of Tennessee–Knoxville, http://trace.tennessee.edu/utk_graddiss
/4304.

Harris, Ron. "Plantations Again: The Gullahs: An Upside-Down World." *Los
Angeles Times*, August 28, 1988, www.latimes.com/archives/la-xpm-1988–08
–28-mn-1718-story.html.

Hartsfield, Natasha. "Racial Hegemony in America: The Struggle for Identity
among the Black Indians of the Five Civilized Tribes of the Southern United
States." *PSU McNair Scholars Online Journal* 1, no. 1 (2004–5): 150–64, https://
pdxscholar.library.pdx.edu/cgi/viewcontent.cgi?article=1010&context
=mcnair.

Haviser, Jay B., and Kevin C. MacDonald, eds., *African Re-Genesis: Confronting
Social Issues in the Diaspora* (London: UCL Press, 2006).

Hazzard, Dominique T. "The Gullah People, Justice, and the Land on Hilton Head Island: A Historical Perspective." Wellesley College honors thesis, 2012, https://repository.wellesley.edu/thesiscollection/60.

Herrera, Allison. "Part of the Tribe, but Shut Out." KOSU, Tulsa, August 30, 2016, www.kosu.org/post/part-tribe-shut-out.

Hill, John C. "For Free People of Color, a Precarious Niche in Society." *New Orleans Times-Picayune*, June 14, 1993, www.nola.com/politics/1993/06/for_free_people_of_color_a_pre.html.

Hill, Sarah. "All Roads Led from Rome: Facing the History of Cherokee Expulsion." *Southern Spaces*, February 20, 2017, southernspaces.org/2017/all-roads-led-rome-facing-history-cherokee-expulsion.

"Hilton Head Island History & Heritage: Rich in Culture, Rich in Spirit." Hilton Head Island–Bluffton Chamber of Commerce & Visitor and Convention Bureau, 2018, www.hiltonheadisland.org/our-island/history.

"Hilton Head Island, South Carolina." City-Data.com, www.city-data.com/city/Hilton-Head-Island-South-Carolina.html.

History channel. "Trail of Tears," History, A&E network, March 5, 2019, www.history.com/topics/native-american-history/trail-of-tears.

———. "Zoot Suit Riots." History, A&E network, September 27, 2017, www.history.com/topics/world-war-ii/zoot-suit-riots.

"History of the Chicago Defender." *Chicago Defender*, chicagodefender.com/history-of-the-chicago-defender.

Hull, Peter. "Daufuskie Island Club & Resort Looking for Investors to Step Up Development." Hotel Online, March 1, 2006. www.hotel-online.com/News/PR2006_1st/Mar06_Daufuskie.html.

International African American Museum. "Slavery in the Lowcountry," 2017, iaamuseum.org/history/slavery-in-charleston-and-the-lowcountry.

———. "Victoria A. Smalls," iaamuseum.org/about/staff/victoria-a-smalls.

"Inventing Black and White." Facing History And Ourselves, https://www.facinghistory.org/holocaust-and-human-behavior/chapter-2/inventing-black-and-white.

Irizarry, Lisa. "Hidden Treasures: Traces of the Past Brought to Light in a Little-Known Museum." Black History Month: A Search for Identity, ed. Beverly M. Reid. NJ.com, January 31, 2008, updated April 2, 2019, blog.nj.com/ledgerarchives/2008/01/black_history_month_a_search_f.html.

Jackson, Juanita, Sabra Slaughter, and J. Herman Blake. "The Sea Islands as a Cultural Resource." *Black Scholar* 5, no. 6 (March 1974): 32–39. JSTOR, jstor.org/stable/41065688.

Johnson, Earchiel. "Slaves of the Tribe: The Hidden History of the Freedmen." *People's World*, November 29, 2017, www.peoplesworld.org/article/slaves-of-the-tribe-the-hidden-history-of-the-freedmen.

Kaplan, Erin Aubry. "Op-Ed: Whites Are Moving back to Inglewood. There Goes Our Neighborhood." *Los Angeles Times*, November 26, 2017, https://

www.latimes.com/opinion/op-ed/la-oe-kaplan-inglewood-gentrification
-20171126-story.html.

Kaplan, Karen. "From the Archives: DNA Testing Raises a Delicate Question: What Does It Mean to Be Native American?" *Los Angeles Times*, October 16, 2018, www.latimes.com/science/la-sci-dna-testing-native-americans-archive -20181016-story.html.

Keates, Nancy. "Daufuskie Island: An Idyllic Spot with a Stormy History." *Wall Street Journal*, July 13, 2017, www.wsj.com/articles/daufuskie-island-an-idyllic -spot-with-a-stormy-history-1499954865?ns=prod/accounts-wsj.

Kemble, Frances. *Journal of a Residence on a Georgian Plantation 1838–1839. An account of life on the plantation owed by her first husband, Pierce Mease Butler, and circulated among abolitionists for years, published to help turn the tide of the Civil War*. New York: Harper & Bros., 1863. Project Gutenberg, www.gutenberg .org/files/12422/12422-h/12422-h.htm.

Kemble, Frances, George Washington Woodward, and John Henry Hopkins. *The Views of Judge Woodward and Bishop Hopkins on Negro Slavery at the South: Illustrated from the Journal of a Residence on a Georgian Plantation*. Philadelphia, c. 1863; Sacramento: Creative Media Partners, 2018.

Kilbane, Penny. *The Melting Pot*. Self-published, 2004, http://www.angelfire.com /folk/the_melting_pot/Documents/The%20Melting%20Pot.pdf.

Kincaid, Alex. "This Daufuskie Island Resort Is out of Bankruptcy. But What's Next?" *Island Packet*, April 10, 2018, www.islandpacket.com/news/business /real-estate-news/article208437254.html.

Kleiner, Diana J., and Ron Bass. "Frenchtown, Houston." Texas State Historical Association, tshaonline.org/handbook/online/articles/hrfvg.

Klingler, Thomas A., and Ingrid Neumann-Holzschuh. "Louisiana Creole," in *The Survey of Pidgin and Creole Languages*, vol. 2, *Portuguese-Based, Spanish-Based, and French-Based*, ed. Susanne Michaelis, Philippe Maurer, Martin Haspelmath, and Magnus Huber, 229–40. Oxford, UK: Oxford University Press, 2013.

Knowles, Beyoncé. "Beyoncé in Her Own Words: Her Life, Her Body, Her Heritage." *Vogue*, August 6, 2018, www.vogue.com/article/beyonce-september -issue-2018.

Koerner, Brendan I. "Blood Feud." *Wired*, September 5, 2005, www.wired.com /2005/09/seminoles.

Kokal, Katherine. "Hilton Head Officials Walked Out on This Restaurant Owner, but He Got a Win in Court." *Island Packet*, March 14, 2019, www .islandpacket.com/news/business/article227590044.html.

Kramer, Alisa Sarah. "William H. Parker and the Thin Blue Line: Politics, Public Relations and Policing in Postwar Los Angeles." PhD dissertation, American University, 2007, dra.american.edu/islandora/object/thesesdisser tations%3A3293/datastream/PDF/view.

Kuiper, Kathleen. "Black Seminoles." *Encyclopædia Britannica*, www.britannica .com/topic/Black-Seminoles.

Landry, Alysa. "Paying to Play Indian: The Dawes Rolls and the Legacy of $5 Indians." *Indian Country Today*, March 21, 2017, newsmaven.io/indiancoun trytoday/archive/paying-to-play-indian-the-dawes-rolls-and-the-legacy-of -5-indians-3yhaoLldYUaH7smRsrks8A.

Lauderdale, David. "Businesses Have Shaped Our Community, Even Our Lives." *Island Packet*, December 25, 2012, www.islandpacket.com/opinion /opn-columns-blogs/david-lauderdale/article33492636.html.

Lawrence, Jacob. "African American Migration Patterns." *The Migration Series*. Phillips Collection, lawrencemigration.phillipscollection.org/culture /migration-map.

Leifermann, Henry. "Sanctuaries in the Sea Off Georgia," *New York Times*, September 6, 1987, https://www.nytimes.com/1987/09/06/travel/sanctuaries -in-the-sea-off-georgia.html.

Li, Sijie. "THE ECONOMIC IMPACT OF THE FIRST MIGRATION,"12, University of Pittsburgh, September 25, 2019, http://d-scholarship.pitt.edu /37312/7/Li_Dissertation_ETD_Final.pdf.

Lindsey, Treva B., and Jessica Marie Johnson. "Searching for Climax: Black Erotic Lives in Slavery and Freedom." *Meridians* 12, no. 2 (2014): 169–95. JSTOR, jstor.org/stable/10.2979/meridians.12.2.169.

Little, Barbara J. *Text-Aided Archaeology*. Boca Raton: CRC Press, 1991.

Lorand Matory, J. "The Illusion of Isolation: The Gullah/Geechees and the Political Economy of African Culture in the Americas." *Comparative Studies in Society and History* 50, no. 4 (October 2008): 949–80. JSTOR, jstor.org/stable /27563714.

Louisiana Office of Tourism. "History & Heritage in St. Martinville Louisiana," www.louisianatravel.com/st-martinville/history-heritage.

Martin, Maggie. "*Steel Magnolias* Still Impacts Town after 25 Years." *Shreveport Times*, July 10, 2016, www.shreveporttimes.com/story/news/local/louisiana /2014/10/02/steel-magnolias-still-impacts-town-years/16604503.

Martin, Rachel. "Racial History of American Swimming Pools." National Public Radio, May 6, 2008, https://www.npr.org/templates/story/story.php?story Id=90213675.

Matiash, Chelsea, and Lily Rothman. "The Beating That Changed America: What Happened to Rodney King 25 Years Ago." *Time*, March 3, 2016, time .com/4245175/rodney.

Matney, Mandy. "Wahoo! Hilton Head Named Best Island in the U.S. for the Second Time This Year." *Island Packet*, October 9, 2018, www.islandpacket .com/news/local/article219732455.html.

Meares, Hadley. "The Thrill of Sugar Hill." *Curbed Los Angeles*, February 22, 2018, la.curbed.com/2018/2/22/16979700/west-adams-history-segregation -housing-covenants.

Melrose Plantation. "History." Melrose Plantation.org, www.melroseplantation .org/history.

Meyerhofer, Kelly. "Protests During the Heritage Tournament: A Long History with Few Immediate Successes." *Island Packet*, March 2017, www.island packet.com/sports/golf/rbc-heritage-tournament/article137181488.html.

Midlo Hall, Gwendolyn. *Africans in Colonial Louisiana.* Baton Rouge: LSU Press, 1995.

Miles, Tiya. "Pain of 'Trail of Tears' Shared by Blacks as Well as Native Americans." Cable News Network (CNN), In America blog, February 25, 2012, inamerica.blogs.cnn.com/2012/02/25/pain-of-trail-of-tears-shared-by-blacks-as-well-as-native-americans.

Mills, Elizabeth Shown, and Gary B. Mills. *The Forgotten People: Cane River's Creoles of Color.* Baton Rouge: LSU Press, 2013.

———. "Slaves and Masters: The Louisiana Metoyers." *National Genealogical Society Quarterly* 70, no. 1 (September 1982): 163–89, at 175, www.historicpath ways.com/download/slavnmast.pdf.

Mondick, Lindsay. "Why Are Black Youth at Highest Risk for Drowning?" YMCA, www.ymca.net/summer-buzz/highest-risk-for-drowning.

Morgan, David W., Kevin C. MacDonald, and Fiona J. L. Handley. "Economics and Authenticity: A Collision of Interpretations in Cane River National Heritage Area, Louisiana." *George Wright Forum* 23, no. 1 (June 2005): 45–62, www.georgewright.org/231morgan.pdf.

Morgan, Philip D., ed. *African American Life in the Georgia Lowcountry: The Atlantic World and the Gullah Geechee.* Athens: University of Georgia Press, 2010.

Morgan Gibson, Arrell. *Oklahoma: A History of Five Centuries,* 2nd ed. Norman: University of Oklahoma Press, 1965.

Murray, Dru J., "The Unconquered Seminoles," http://funandsun.com/1tocf/seminole/semhistory.html.

National Park Service, Park Ethnography Program. "Africans in the Low Country," www.nps.gov/ethnography/aah/aaheritage/lowCountryA.htm.

National Trust for Historic Preservation. "African House at Melrose Plantation," savingplaces.org/places/african-house-at-melrose-plantation#.WzIc GxJKj3Q.

Newsweek staff. "An Island's Vanishing Culture." *Newsweek,* January 13, 1991, www.newsweek.com/islands-vanishing-culture-202734.

N-Georgia. "Visit Butler Island Plantation in Darien Georgia." N-georgia.com, August 17, 2019, www.n-georgia.com/darien-butler-island.html.

Opala, Joseph A. "The Gullah: Rice, Slavery, and the Sierra Leone–American Connection," glc.yale.edu/sites/default/files/files/Black%20Seminoles%20.pdf.

Osberg, Molly. "The Long, Thorny History of the Cherokee Who Owned African Slaves." *Splinter,* October 18, 2017, splinternews.com/the-long-thorny-history-of-the-cherokee-who-owned-afri-1819655748.

Osofsky, Gilbert. *Harlem: The Making of a Ghetto—Negro New York 1890–1930,* 2nd ed. New York: Harper & Row, 1971.

Palmer. "Saint Martinville, LA." Born and Raised in the South, February 1, 2009, ltc4940.blogspot.com/2009/02/st-martinville-la.html.

Pinckney, Roger. "Blue Root Real Estate." *Orion*, orionmagazine.org/article /blue-root-real-estate.

Poe, Tracy N. "The Origins of Soul Food in Black Urban Identity: Chicago, 1915–1947." *American Studies International* 37, no. 1 (February 1999): 4–33. JSTOR, https://www.jstor.org/stable/pdf/41279638.

Pollitzer, William S. *The Gullah People and Their African Heritage*. Athens: University of Georgia Press, 1999.

Public Broadcasting Service (PBS). *Africans in America*, Part 1, 1450–1750, "The Terrible Transformation: From Indentured Servitude to Racial Slavery," 1998. PBS Online, www.pbs.org/wgbh/aia/part1/1narr3.html.

———. "The Weeping Time." PBS, 1998, www.pbs.org/wgbh/aia/part4/4p2918 .html.

Queally, James. "Watts Riots: Traffic Stop Was the Spark That Ignited Days of Destruction in L.A." *Los Angeles Times*, July 29, 2015, www.latimes.com /local/lanow/la-me-ln-watts-riots-explainer-20150715-htmlstory.html.

Ringle, Ken. "Up through Slavery." *Washington Post*, May 12, 2002, www.washing tonpost.com/archive/lifestyle/2002/05/12/up-through-slavery/9b489aa3 -fefa-4695–9544–34ab58f1fe87.

Roberts, John. "African American Belief Narratives and the African Cultural Tradition." *Research in African Literatures* 40, no. 1 (Spring 2009): 112–26. JSTOR, jstor.org/stable/30131190.

"The Rodney King Affair." *Los Angeles Times*, March 24, 1991, www.latimes .com/archives/la-xpm-1991–03–24-me-1422-story.html.

Rubin, Karen. "Discovering Sapelo Island, Georgia, and the Gullah-Geechees of Hog Hammock." Going Places, Far & Near, March 7, 2015, goingplaces farandnear.com/discovering-sapelo-island-georgia-and-the-gullah-geechees -of-hog-hammock.

Russell, Tony. "Muskogee Parents, Freedmen Descendants Call for MPS Director of Indian Ed to Step Down." KJRH (Tulsa), December 7, 2017, www.kjrh .com/news/local-news/muskogee-parents-freedmen-descendants-call-for -mps-director-of-indian-ed-to-step-down.

Seitz-Wald, Alex. "Cherokee Nation Says Elizabeth Warren Apologizes for DNA Test Flap." NBC News, February 1, 2019, www.nbcnews.com/politics /2020-election/elizabeth-warren-apologizes-cherokee-nation-over-dna -test-flap-n965921.

Severson, Kim. "Taxes Threaten an Island Culture in Georgia." *New York Times*, September 25, 2012, www.nytimes.com/2012/09/26/us/on-an-island-in -georgia-geechees-fear-losing-land.html.

Sitinga (Sitinga Katchipande). "Why Africans Don't Swim." Africa on the blog, March 21, 2013, www.africaontheblog.org/why-africans-dont-swim.

Smelser, Neil J. "Collective Myths and Fantasies." *Humboldt Journal of Social*

Relations 11, no. 1 (Fall–Winter 1983–84): 1–15. JSTOR, jstor.org/stable/2326 1554.

Smith, Preston. "Exploring the Great Migration." Mount Holyoke College, February 13, 2019, www.mtholyoke.edu/media/exploring-great-migration.

Smithers, Gregory D. "Why Do So Many Americans Think They Have Cherokee Blood? The History of a Myth" *Slate*, October 1, 2015, slate.com/news-and-politics/2015/10/cherokee-blood-why-do-so-many-americans-believe-they-have-cherokee-ancestry.html.

South Carolina Department of Agriculture. "History." SCDA, agriculture.sc.gov/about.

South Carolina Department of Archives and History. "Preservation Laws," scdah.sc.gov/historic-preservation/resources/preservation-laws.

Spaulding, Cathy. "MPS Seeks New Indian Education Director." *Muskogee Phoenix*, January 28, 2018, www.muskogeephoenix.com/news/mps-seeks-new-indian-education-director/article_06cd79ec-512b-551e-8154-ff0a90d5cbdc.html.

Spear, Allan H. *Black Chicago: The Making of a Negro Ghetto, 1890–1920*. University of Chicago Press, 1967.

Starace, Alex. "Tales of Daufuskie Island." International Opulence, www.internationalopulence.com/intriguing-tales-roger-pinckney-life-historic-daufuskie-island.

Stevenson, Desalyn. "Court Cases," 2014. Our Shared Family History: Freedmen of the Five Civilized Tribes, African-American, Native American, and the Southern States, www.oursharedfamilyhistory.com/resources/cases/allcases/casespg.html.

Synan, Vinson. "Notable History: The Quiet Rise of Black Pentecostals." *Charisma*, February 26, 2016, www.charismamag.com/life/culture/24137-notable-history-the-quiet-rise-of-black-pentecostals.

Taylor, Mildred Europa. "Black Babies Were Once Used as Alligator and Crocodile Bait in America in the 1900s." Face2Face Africa, August 19, 2018. face2faceafrica.com/article/black-babies-were-once-used-as-alligator-and-crocodile-bait-in-america-in-the-1900s.

Triposo. "Wewoka, Oklahoma: History." Triposo.com, www.triposo.com/loc/Wewoka2C_Oklahoma/history/background.

Trowell, C. T. "Human History of the Okefenokee Swamp." *New Georgia Encyclopedia*, June 2017, www.georgiaencyclopedia.org/articles/geography-environment/human-history-okefenokee-swamp.

Tucker, Neely. "A Mixed-Race Woman's Long Quest to Prove Her Native American Ancestry." *Washington Post*, January 4, 2019, www.washingtonpost.com/outlook/a-mixed-race-womans-long-quest-to-prove-her-native-american-ancestry/2019/01/04/4f2ada42-0c6d-11e9-831f-3aa2c2be4cbd_story.html.

United States District Court, Southern District of Georgia, Brunswick Division, Case 2:16-cv-00053-RSB-BWC, filed March 7, 2019, https://www.relmanlaw

.com/media/cases/40_199%20-%20Pls_%20Second%20Amended%20 Complaint.pdf.

United States Securities and Exchange Commission. Form 10-K, 1999, https:// www.sec.gov/Archives/edgar/data/929455/000092945500000002/000092 9455-00-000002-d11.pdf.

Walker Bailey, Cornelia. *God, Dr. Buzzard, and the Bolito Man.* New York: Anchor, 2000.

Wardi, Anissa Janine. *Water and African American Memory: An Ecocritical Perspective.* Gainesville: University Press of Florida, 2011.

Wiersema, Libby. "Southern, Lowcountry, Gullah, or Soul—What's the Difference Between These SC Cooking Styles?" SC Department of Parks, Recreation and Tourism, discoversouthcarolina.com/articles/southern-low country-gullah-or-soul-whats-the-difference-between-these-sc-cooking -styles.

Wilentz, Gay. "If You Surrender to the Air: Folk Legends of Flight and Resistance in African American Literature." *MELUS* (Multi-Ethnic Literature of the United States) 16, no. 1 (Spring 1989–Spring 1990): 21–32. JSTOR, jstor.org /stable/467579.

Willett, Beverly. "LowCountry Root Doctors." *South*, December 2016–January 2017, www.southmag.com/Dec-Jan-2017/LowCountry-Root-Doctors.

Williams, Timothy, and Farah Stockman. "Dayton Shooting Live Updates: Gunman Killed 9, Including His Sister." *New York Times*, August 4, 2019, www.nytimes.com/2019/08/04/us/dayton-ohio-shooting.html.

Wills, Matthew. "The Free People of Color of Pre-Civil War New Orleans." JSTOR Daily, February 20, 2019, daily.jstor.org/the-free-people-of-color-of -pre-civil-war-new-orleans.

Wiltse, Jeff. *Contested Waters: A Social History of Swimming Pools in America.* Chapel Hill: University of North Carolina Press, 2007.

Worley, Sam. "Where Soul Food Really Comes From." Epicurious, June 29, 2016, www.epicurious.com/expert-advice/real-history-of-soul-food-article.

Yronwode, Catherine. "How to Use Sachet Powders in the Hoodoo Rootwork Tradition." Lucky Mojo Curio Co., www.luckymojo.com/powders.html.

Zepke, Terrance. *Coastal South Carolina: Welcome to the Lowcountry.* Sarasota, FL: Pineapple Press, 2006.

Zimmer, Carl. "Tales of African-American History Found in DNA." *New York Times*, May 27, 2016, www.nytimes.com/2016/05/28/science/african-american -dna.html.

INDEX

ABOUT THE AUTHOR

MORGAN JERKINS is a senior editor at Medium's *ZORA* magazine. Her work has been featured in the *New Yorker*, *Vogue*, the *New York Times*, the *Atlantic*, *Elle*, *Rolling Stone*, *Lenny Letter*, and *BuzzFeed*, among many other outlets. She lives in New York.